Philosophical Problems of Psychology

Philosophical Problems *of* Psychology

EDWARD H. MADDEN, *San Jose State College*

GREENWOOD PRESS, PUBLISHERS
WESTPORT, CONNECTICUT

The Library of Congress has catalogued this publication as follows:

Library of Congress Cataloging in Publication Data

Madden, Edward H
    Philosophical problems of psychology.

    Reprint of the 1962 ed.
    1. Psychology. 2. Philosophy. I. Title.
[BF41.M18 1973]   150'.19   72-11481
ISBN 0-8371-6668-3

150.19

M26p

103462

Jan. 1978

Originally published in 1962 by The Odyssey Press, Inc.,
New York

Reprinted with the permission of The Bobbs-Merrill
Company, Inc.

Reprinted by Greenwood Press, Inc.

First Greenwood reprinting 1973
Second Greenwood reprinting 1977

Library of Congress catalog card number 72-11481

ISBN 0-8371-6668-3

Printed in the United States of America

Preface

IN THE following chapters I am mainly concerned with philosophical problems that arise in Gestalt theory, learning theory, *verstehende* psychology, psychoanalysis, and certain aspects of classical nineteenth-century psychology. Throughout I have the dual aim of clarifying the logical structure of explanation in psychology and of separating scientific and philosophical discourse where they have been inadvisably joined.

In this book I follow a convention in the use of quotation marks adopted by many logicians. I use single quotes around a word or sentence whenever I am saying something about the word itself, or the concept it represents—for example, 'finger' has six letters, or 'sister' and 'female sibling' have the same meaning. I use double quotes in the usual ways, as in direct quotations, in calling special attention to a word, and in "setting off" a word that is used uncritically or in an unusual sense.

I am indebted to many teachers and colleagues for the clarification of puzzles in the philosophy of psychology and for the encouragement so necessary to put together a book—even a small one. In the present work I have been aided particularly by Professors Gustav Bergmann, Curt J. Ducasse, John W. Lenz, and Ernest Nagel. I am also indebted to the editors of several journals for their permission to use material of mine which first appeared in their pages: "The Philosophy of Science in Gestalt Theory," *Philosophy of Science,* Vol. 19 (1952); "A Logical Analysis of 'Psychological Isomorphism'," *The British Journal for the Philosophy of Science,* Vol. 8 (1957); "The Nature of Psychological Explanation," *Methodos,* Vol. 9 (1957); "Psychoanalysis and Moral Judgeability," *Philosophy and Phenomenological Research,* Vol. 18 (1957). Even in these cases, however, I have revised the original articles. I owe most thanks, as always, to Marian Madden for discussing carefully with me all the problems in the following pages and for critically reading the whole of the manuscript.

E. H. M.

San Jose State College
San Jose, California

Contents

Philosophical Problems of Psychology

ONE

Wholes and Parts

GESTALT THEORY includes a philosophy of science, and positions in epistemology, metaphysics, and value theory, as well as psychological notions. According to Wertheimer, Gestalt theory is "a palpable convergence of problems ranging throughout the sciences and the various philosophic standpoints of modern times."[1]* He also asserts that Gestalt theory was the result of concrete work done in psychology, logic, and epistemology.[2] In this chapter I will be concerned only with Gestalt interpretations of, and claims for, the method and structure of science in general.

Wertheimer and Köhler both regard the Gestalt view as a new interpretation of the structure and method of science insofar as it offers an alternative to the Newtonian or "analytical" interpretation of science. Wertheimer and

* For the notes to Chapter One see pages 125-29.

Köhler both reject the universality of "analytical" method, their thesis being that this traditional approach cannot account for some aspects of science which can be done justice only in Gestalt terms. Wertheimer's most formal condemnation of the analytical view of science and his thesis that there are areas to which it does not apply is to be found in his address of 1924 to the *Kantgesellschaft*.

> It has long seemed obvious—and is, in fact, the characteristic tone of European science—that "science" means breaking up complexes into their component elements. Isolate the elements, discover their laws, then reassemble them, and the problem is solved. All wholes are reduced to pieces and piecewise relations between pieces.[3]

> The word science often suggested a certain outlook, certain fundamental assumptions, certain procedures and attitudes—but do these imply that this is the only possibility of scientific method? Perhaps science already embodies methods leading in an entirely different direction, methods which have been continually stifled by the seemingly necessary, dominant ones. . . . Even though the traditional methods of science are undoubtedly adequate in many cases, there may be others where they lead us astray.[4]

Köhler takes the same position in saying that if problems of self-distribution in macroscopic physics were more familiar "the belief would not be so general that physics is under all circumstances an 'analytical' science in which the properties of more complex extended facts are deduced from the properties of independent local elements."[5]

In this examination of Gestalt philosophy of science I will first try to make clear the Gestalt views and then go on to construct an analytical terminology by means of which I try to show (a) that all legitimate distinctions of the Gestalters can be rendered in this language and (b) that Gestalters use such terms as "additive," "bundle," "interaction," and "field" both ambiguously and misleadingly.

A. EXPOSITION OF GESTALT THEORY

Following the example of K. Grelling and P. Oppenheim we begin by distinguishing between W-Gestalts and K-Gestalts, the former term referring to a pattern or configuration which determines the nature of its parts and the latter term to systems of functional interdependence.[6]

Concerning what we have called "W-Gestalts" Wertheimer writes,

There are wholes, the behaviour of which is not determined by that of their individual elements, but where the part-processes are themselves determined by the intrinsic nature of the whole. It is the hope of Gestalt theory to determine the nature of such wholes.[7]

A whole the behavior of which determines the natures of its individual elements is formally the negation of complexes the behavior of which is determined in the piecewise fashion. Wertheimer's schema for the latter kind of complexes follows:

> If I have a_1 b_1 c_1 and b_2 c_2 are substituted for b_1 c_1, I then have a_1 b_2 c_2. We are dealing essentially with a summative multiplicity of variously constituted components (a "bundle") and all else is erected somehow upon this and-summation.[8]

Any complex which transcends the nature of a summation or a "bundle" is a W-Gestalt. Examples are simple and numerous. The effect of transposing a melody is a familiar classic illustration. A melody made up of one series of notes is heard as the same as a melody composed of another series of different notes. In other words, a melody persists and is recognized even when played in different keys. According to the Gestalters it is this identification of melodies when the individual elements (notes) are different that supports the interpretation that the melody is not merely a sum of its parts but that as the whole it determines how the parts shall be heard. In addition Wertheimer discusses many factors, largely relational, which are intended to demonstrate the inadequacy of part-summation and the priority of wholes in determining perception. Such factors are likeness, nearness, common fate, objective set, closure, position and so forth.[9]

Wholes and Parts

Turning to the K-Gestalt, a system of functional inter-dependence, we find that Köhler makes a basic distinction between microscopically and macroscopically organized physical states.[10] As a help in establishing the difference, Köhler refers to a network of pipes—three sections connected to the same inlet and outlet—through which water flows. He points out that the behavior of the water in each branch is not a local affair independent of any condition outside the particular pipe. If a valve in one pipe is closed the current will flow faster in those pipes remaining open, and if other pipes are added to the original three the current in the original ones will be slower. Knowledge of these interdependencies is contingent, of course, on one's observing the activity in a larger part of the network than one branch. If one considers activity within a branch pipe as well as what goes on in the rest of the network then the activity in the branch is seen to be relatively microscopic because it is not independent of outside occurrences and interferences. The entire network or, for that matter, any part larger than a branch is, relative to that branch, a macroscopic entity. According to Köhler, a certain kind of analysis of macroscopic entities is possible, a kind of analysis which tells us how events act within a macroscopic context. However, he points out, "More often . . . analysis is expected to give us *independent* elementary facts, the mere synthesis of which would yield the complex entities found in primary observation."[11] Analysis in this sense, Köhler concludes, is incompatible with the nature of macroscopic states.

The example of the pipes is a special case of "dynamic interaction" because the rigid channels permit interaction only at specific points. Köhler also considers the case of a single vessel with one opening for the incoming water and another for the outgoing water. How will the current be distributed in this continuous volume and how will alteration in the position of the openings affect the distribution? The important point in this case is that the current at each point depends more directly on the current at all points because the system is no longer restricted in its points of interaction. In these situations an equation for the steady distribution as a whole must be found if the equation for the steady flow at a point is to be found. Köhler contends that if such problems as these were more familiar "the belief would not be so general that physics is under all circumstances an 'analytical' science in which the properties of more complex extended facts are deduced from the properties of independent local elements."

B. ANALYTICAL SCIENCE AND THE W-GESTALT

What one must do to refute the Gestalter's claim that certain aspects of science cannot be described adequately in analytical terms but must be described in Gestalt terms is to show that what the Gestalters say about relations, wholes, interaction, and fields—or better, everything they say legitimately about them—can also be stated in analytical terms. This reformulation in analytical terms of those features of science which the Gestalters emphasize and think that only they adequately describe might be called "methodological refutation." Semantically such a procedure amounts to a clarification of such terms as 'additive,' 'interaction,' and 'field.' More particularly, my methodological refutation must show that the features which Köhler thinks are unique to macroscopic situations are present already in what he calls the analytical parts of physics—i.e., where "the properties of more complex extended facts are deduced from the properties of independent local elements." I begin the refutation by describing in analytical terms the classical Newtonian problem of n bodies.

I will assume that the classical Newtonian problem of n bodies is known and will simply stress those features which are important for my purposes. We must distinguish two things at the outset, namely, description and explanation. First, there is the *configuration* of n bodies and its initial and subsequent *conditions* at any given moment of time; second, there is the *law* which yields the values of the variables characteristic of one condition from those of an earlier or later condition (prediction or postdiction). All that pertains to the former—the masses and the position and momentum coordinates—constitutes a scientific *description;* all that pertains to the latter constitutes a scientific *explanation.* A W-Gestalt, which we have defined as a pattern or configuration, is a concept primarily relevant to scientific description; a K-Gestalt, which we have defined as a system of functional interdependence, is a concept primarily relevant to scientific explanation. Let us turn our attention first to scientific *description*.

Given a configuration of n objects (mass points), O_1, O_2, . . ., O_n, the physicist knows from previous observations that each O is characterized by a number which is the value of an empirical construct called mass, which remains constant in time $\left(\frac{dm_i}{dt}\right)=O$. The mass of a physical object is thus an "index," a constant characterizer which is the non-configurational element entering into gravitational behavior. At least it is non-configurational (non-relational) as long as we do not push our analysis into a definition of mass itself. However it is not necessary to do this for our purposes because all we would gain would be a repetition of the situation we wish to discuss, repetition on a level more elementary in the sense of ultimate epistemological reduction but less suitable for our expository purposes.

At a particular time ($t=O$) the physicist can obtain measurements which, as a class, determine the *condition* of the configuration at that moment. (The configuration itself is determined by the values of the masses.) The constructs measured are the positions and momenta of the n bodies. These, we notice, are *relational* concepts; for the rest we assume that the distances and the time intervals out of which they are defined can be measured in some meaningful fashion without further analyzing these ideas.

The statement of these data at $t=0$ as a *logical con-junction* ("and" connection) of, say, k sentences consti-tutes a "description" of the initial configuration. E.g., " (The mass of O_1 is m_1) & (The mass of O_2 is m_2) & ... (The distance between O_1 and O_2 is $r_{1,2}$) & ... & S_k." In stating this conjunction of k sentences $S_1, S_2, ..., S_k$, one is asserting the truth of all the sentences so conjoined; if at least one of the member sentences is false, then the whole conjunction is false. Such a logical product will con-stitute a description of the system and its condition at any time t.

In the light of this illustration let us now examine Wertheimer's thesis that "the whole is more than the sum of its parts," interpreting it at the moment as an emphasis on configuration or pattern, and let us see what are the possible meanings of it in analytical terms. In the analyt-ical terminology of initial condition (description of the configuration at time t_0) and prediction of the condition at time t (description of the configuration at time t_1), Wertheimer's thesis simply means that a description con-sists of several statements about physical objects, non-relational properties of such objects, and also statements of relations obtaining among them. Insofar as Wertheimer is emphasizing that statements of relations such as "*a* is to the left of *b*" are fundamental and not defined in terms of statements about objects or their properties, he is making an important point. In this case, however, his meaning is formulable in ordinary analytical terms. In fact we just did so formulate it. Only the classical materialists have tended to neglect the fundamental role undefined relation terms play in the description of nature.

In analytical terms another just and perfectly correct meaning can be given in the area of description to the classical adage that the whole is more than the sum of its parts. Consider a Newtonian system consisting of, say, six mass points. We can *conceptually* decompose this system into two sub-systems of three bodies each. One sub-system (P_1) of the whole system can be described as consisting of the masses of three bodies (m_1, m_2, m_3), their momenta, and their three distances. The remaining sub-system (P_2) likewise can be described in the same manner. With descriptions P_1 and P_2 conceived as constituting the meaning of the term 'parts', the term 'whole' may be applied to a system P composed of P_1 and P_2. Then it will be found that the description of P is not simply the conjunction of the descriptions of P_1 and P_2 but contains *as further conjunctive terms at least some of the mutual distances between the bodies of the two parts of sub-systems.* In this sense it may be said that even in the realm of description the whole is more than the sum of its parts. This meaning of part and whole may of course be generalized. A "part," then, is a description of a sub-system of any group of entities. The description of the "whole" consists of the descriptions of all sub-systems *plus* the descriptive characters which indicate the relations between the sub-systems of the "whole" (in our example, mutual distances).

However, because Wertheimer's rejection of the "and" or "bundle" hypothesis indiscriminately includes both the "and" of description and the "and" of explanation and because he maintains that the latter—which would hold that the behavior of two systems S_1 and S_2 in spatial juxtaposition or partial overlap is the sum of the behavior of the two systems in isolation—is untenable, he consequently is insisting that the former—which is a logical "and" and simply means that the statements about objects, properties of objects, and relations between them are asserted together—is also untenable. The "and" of explanation does not in fact even have a clear meaning and should be rejected, but this does not impair the legitimacy of the logical "and" in description. To think that it does rests on a confusion between description and explanation.

That Wertheimer does consider the "and" of description untenable is implicit in his further consideration of the melody illustration. He considers the following explanation of this transposition phenomenon: one recognizes the melody in different keys because he responds not to notes but to intervals—relations—and *these* are what remain constant. Wertheimer, however, rejects this view because, he says, there are some cases in which the relations too are varied and the melody is still recognized.[12]

Wertheimer in this situation apparently is trying to discredit the elementaristic or summative view by showing the empirical inadequacy of adding new elements, relational ones, to the individual notes in an effort to account for the recognition of a melody despite a transposition. But even if it is true that a melody may be recognized even when the relations are not all maintained in transposition, it is not evidence detrimental to the legitimacy of the logical "and." In analytical terms I would simply say that the description of initial conditions, which are conjoined by the logical "and," is not complete. Let us amplify the notion of complete description in connection with the classical Newtonian n-body problem.

In the classical Newtonian n-body problem one says that a *complete description* embraces only mass points, distances, and speeds. But how does one know that the initial description is complete when only these constituents are listed? How does one know, for example, that the color of the bodies is not also a determining factor? Completeness simply means finding the empirical law; no *a priori* criterion for the completeness of a description exists. One must continue to add constituents to the initial description until he can state a law enabling him to predict subsequent conditions. The experimental check on this procedure is obvious. One observes several systems equated in all respects mentioned in the description. If the same results do not occur, then there is an "uncontrolled variable" that needs to be added. When it is discovered and added (by the logical "and") the description is complete.

Let us apply this analytical insight to Wertheimer's discussion of the melody. If indeed the relations between notes can be changed without altering the perceived melody, then we would say that adding relations to the notes still does not complete the description. If the constancy of response to groups of different elements (notes) cannot be attributed to something already contained in the description of the initial conditions we should (1) recognize the description as incomplete and (2) try to supplement it in one of the two possible ways: either add new basic data or derive new relations (e.g., ratios of ratios) from data already present. However there is nothing in this situation that justifies the belief that our account of description is in principle inadequate because it is too elementaristic.

The Gestalters would probably object at this point because we are consistently dealing with physical stimuli rather than with how the subject "sees" the stimuli. In our descriptions the statements refer to frequencies, to the ratio of frequencies, and to other matters of the "geographical environment." All we shall say now is that how a subject "sees" the stimuli is a matter of a lawful relationship between the subject's behavior and a complex stimulus situation rather than of the behavior *of* the elementary components *in* the complex. We shall return to this point in Chapter 3.

C. ANALYTICAL SCIENCE AND THE K-GESTALT

We turn now to an analysis of the K-Gestalt and a formulation of its characteristic features in analytical terms. Given the values of mass, position, and momentum at time

T_0 the physicist can substitute these values in a formula—
let us call it the computation rule—which will yield the
values of these same variables at any time t (that is, the
computation rule yields the values of the variables as functions of the initial conditions and a continuous time pa-
rameter). The computation rule, of course, will be
different when different numbers of objects exist simultaneously. The curve (law) for two bodies is different
from the curve for three bodies and so forth. In the case
of two bodies we have the law of a conic orbit; in the case
of three or more bodies more complicated curves occur.
In analytical terms any such empirical curve will constitute
an "explanation." An explanation, then, is any function
connecting subsequent descriptions of a system. When
properties occur in any curve which do not occur in the
curves of any lesser number of bodies, we will speak of this
situation as *novelty* in respect to laws.

Let us assume that we have a computation rule for two
bodies, so that a physicist could predict the future conditions for any given configuration of two bodies. Now this
computation rule tells us nothing about the behavior of
three or four . . . or n bodies together. However, we can
take the combination of three bodies, for example, and
conceptually decompose it into sub-complexes or elements.
The "elements" involved in the three-body configuration
would be three configurations of two bodies each. Now we
can apply our two-body computation rule to each of the
elements separately. Next we discover inductively a rule

which will produce the law for the three-body complex by combining in some definite manner the computation rules for the elements (in this example the rule is the so-called vector addition of forces). We will call this rule, which we discovered for predicting the behavior of a complex configuration out of the re-application of the computation rule to the "elements" of the complex, a *composition rule.* The general idea of the composition rule is to discover a single rule which will enable one to derive the computation rule for any given number of bodies. It must be emphasized that such a composition rule is just as much an empirical law, albeit independent of the empirical laws that obtain for the elementary configurations, as these laws themselves.

The success of this technique in wide areas of science is a fact. If one wishes to describe it by saying that science is "elementaristic," "mechanistic," or "additive," one is free to do so. Regardless of how one chooses his terms, though, it is important to note that 'additive' in this sense has a different meaning from the 'additive' whose meaningful and nonsensical connotations we tried to distinguish in the area of description. In particular, a composition rule is not a logical summation or "and" connection. (The terms "vector addition" and "vector sum" are rather unfortunate in this context and probably are among the causes of the confusion.) Nor does a composition rule, if it holds, imply that the parts of a whole independently go through the processes they would go through if they existed in isolation. Thus this "additive," "analytical," or "mechanistic" feature of science does not deny dynamic interaction of the parts of a whole. This point is sufficiently important to bear further elaboration and repetition.

As we have seen, Köhler stresses interaction in the sense that a change in one element causes alteration in all areas of a system. This is essentially what is meant by saying that a K-Gestalt is a system of functional interdependence. In analytical language, a prediction which holds for one set of initial conditions will in general not hold in *any* of its particulars if even *one* of the variables in the initial conditions is changed. The interrelations that actually obtain find their complete and exhaustive expression in the mathematical structure of the process law. Likewise, interaction is accounted for in the correct statement of the composition rule. In the case of planetary laws, if we know the Newtonian law for two bodies and for three bodies we still do not know *a priori* what the law for five bodies will be. This must be determined as a matter of fact. The deduction of the law of a complex from the laws of the elements is not a matter of linking together two laws by a logical "and." It is patently false to say that the composition rule is additive in the descriptive sense because in the case of planetary systems we would have planets with more than one orbit; planets in two places at once! A composition rule is *another* law, not a pre-existing rule for getting a logical product; this shows that Köhler is confused when he complains that in "analytical" science "the properties of more complex extended facts are deduced from the properties of independent local elements."

In summary, we see that both scientific description and explanation have several features which are rightly stressed by the Gestalters but which may be rendered in analytical terms. Moreover, by thus rendering them in analytical terms I have shown that some of these features are not quite what the Gestalters think they are and do not carry the implications which they think they do. The usual answer to this kind of claim is that the entire Gestalt thesis is not captured in these reformulation tactics, that the essence of the whole escapes the analytical net. We now turn to these "something more" aspects of the Gestalters' position.

D. INTRINSIC WHOLES AND EXPLANATORY EMERGENCE

Wertheimer says that "there are wholes, the behaviour of which is not determined by that of their individual elements, but where the part-processes are themselves determined by the intrinsic nature of the whole."[13] If Wertheimer meant by this statement that sometimes the behavior of a subject toward a stimulus is (in part) determined by the whole or complex of which it is an element, then he is certainly correct. No psychologist, whether or not he is a Gestalter, would hold that a response to a stimulus S_1 is the same as the response to a stimulus P of which S_1 is a constituent even if the subject has been given the "analytical" set of responding to S_1, which is thus once the whole and once a part of the presented stimulus configuration. In the analytical schema

(1) $S_1 \rightarrow R_1$
(2) $\underbrace{S_1 \text{ and } \ldots \rightarrow R_2}_{P}$ (organism "constant" in both situations)

The "and" in (2) is of course the logical "and" of description, so the total stimulus is different and there is therefore no reason why the response should not be different. Whether or not it actually is different is a matter of the law that happens to govern this particular situation. But when Wertheimer claims that the intrinsic nature of the parts is determined by their being in a whole, I must confess that I do not know what he means. Is not S_1, as an event, S_1 whether or not it appears alone or in conjunction with something else? The thing which may or may not change, according to conditions, is the *response* to S_1. This response is determined both by the elementary stimulus event and its context. But this event is the same in isolation or in context.

This discussion has concerned the "something more" aspect of the Gestalt doctrine in the area of description. In the area of explanation this "something more" aspect can be considered as a belief in *explanatory emergence*. Like other historical formulations of emergence the Gestalt formulation is not particularly clear. It usually takes the form of denying the possibility of predicting one set of characteristics from another. Koffka writes,

> Moreover, hydrogen occurs in nature in a form in which it is not composed of hydrogen atoms but of hydrogen molecules, each composed of two hydrogen atoms. Thus we have H, H_2, H_2O. This sounds like a straight molecular theory, but it is not anything of the kind. For H, H_2, H_2O have all different properties which cannot be derived by *adding* properties of H's and O's.[14]

This assertion is misleading because scientifically no matter of fact by itself forms the basis for predicting the occurrence of another fact. *Predictability is always a matter of a set of conditions and a law or a theory in terms of which a future set of conditions can be predicted.* But let me characterize the matter in greater detail. First, Koffka is not contending in his chemical example simply that new laws arise with novel characteristics. Rather he is making the stronger claim (translated into my terminology) that *composition rules* or theories using them break down not only in the organic realm, as the vitalist contends, but already in the physical realm. This claim which I like to call *explanatory emergence* is not, however, a metaphysical assertion; rather it is the empirical meaning of the doctrine of emergence. Nor is the adequacy or breakdown of a composition rule an *a priori* matter. Whether or not a composition rule is adequate and to what extent it is adequate is a matter of scientific ascertainment. The allegedly "novel" and super-additive characters of the classical chemical illustrations, already favored by J. S. Mill, are by now in fact "mechanistically" explained in terms of quantum chemistry. That the Gestalters do not seem to realize the logic of this situation is borne out in Köhler's *Mentality of Apes* and other Gestalt literature in which the main contention is, in my terms, that empirical laws of insight are not only novel but also *must be* theoretical or explanatory emergents with respect to trial and error learning.

Any breakdown of a theory with composition rules at a certain level of complexity would be a case of explanatory emergence. The Gestalters, misled by their conceptions of "additive" and "analysis," as we have seen, claim that this level is already to be found in physics itself as well as in organic behavior. In spite of what I said above about explanatory emergence being an empirical matter, I do believe, given the complexity of organisms, that it seems at least *prima facie* more plausible that they are the kinds of wholes that resist explanation by means of composition rules. But even here, no doubt, the ultimate decision rests on scientific achievement or lack of it. (And certainly we do not seem on the brink of any notable composition law achievement in this area!) At any rate, it is plausible to conjecture that the Gestalt claim of explanatory emergence occurring already in physics has something to do with the halo with which the Gestalters have surrounded the notion of "field," since, as they say, Einsteinian mechanics is a field theory while Newtonian mechanics is "analytical," "mechanistic," and "additive." It is in order, then, that I say a few words about fields and the role this notion plays in Gestalt thinking.

E. FIELD THEORY

Köhler always speaks of the necessity of *field theory* in psychology. Concerning field theory in perception and in its physiological correlates, he writes,

> By this (field theory) we mean that the neural functions and processes with which the perceptual facts are associated in each case are located in a continuous medium; and that the events in one part of this medium influence the events in other regions in a way that depends directly on the properties of both in their relation to each other. This is the conception with which all physicists work.[15]

Whether in physics or elsewhere, we can and must distinguish two meanings of the terms 'field' and 'field theory.' In its more general meaning 'field' simply designates a system of interaction; in its special meaning it refers to theories that work with a continuously spread medium and, accordingly, use the mathematical technique of partial differential equations. The planetary system, e.g., treated in the Newtonian manner, *like all scientific theories,* is a field theory in the first sense; but all scientific theories are not field theories in the second sense.

In order to understand better the second notion of field theory we will return to the n-body paradigm. Even though the concrete terms 'configuration,' 'conditions,' and 'objects' were used, we must not lose sight of the formal arithmetical schema—which we can call a calculus and which is coordinated with the empirical data. The system is in this case the finite and discrete ordered set of positive real numbers "corresponding" to the masses; a state is the finite and discrete ordered set of real numbers "corresponding" to the positions and momenta that determine a temporal cross section of the process; a process is always a continuous series of the states of the system as a function of time. So in the Newtonian case of n bodies a process is an ordered set of $6n$ functions of time. This discreteness and finiteness are characteristic of systems of interaction which are not fields in the second sense. A process schema is called a field schema in this second, narrower sense when either states or systems or both are not defined as finite ordered sets of numbers but as functions or ordered sets of functions spread out continuously through space like, e.g., temperature or electric field strength. That psychology has no field theory in this second sense is obvious when one examines the present state of this science. That it must be a field theory in the general sense is an analytical truth which results from its being a science; for every science is a field theory in the sense of interaction because, as we have seen, a change in one variable at time t_0 may alter all conditions at time t_1, and if L_1 and L_2 are laws of the parts of the whole in isolation it does not follow that 'L_1 and L_2' is the law of the whole. The Gestalters have consistently blurred the distinction between the general and specific meanings of 'field.'

The reasons for this blurring may be found on at least two levels. Everybody familiar with the history of Western thought during the last century knows that certain specious semantic dichotomies have been erected upon the slender foundation of science half understood. Newtonian *mechanics* is not a field theory in the second sense; Maxwell's contribution to electro*dynamics* is a field theory in the second sense. And so, of course, is Einstein's general theory of relativity. Field theories, therefore, have prestige and supersede mechanics. "Mechanics," furthermore, is in our cultural tradition associated with "mechanistic," "elementaristic," and "analytical." And Wundt is "elementaristic" and "analytical" and, of course, the Gestalters are always in revolt against him.

On a different level, we can say that the Gestalters seize upon fields in the second sense because they feel, rightly or wrongly, that such systems share an intuitively clear "structural" characteristic with perceptual phenomena. In other words, this reason for their preference for fields in the narrower sense, like the distribution of charges on a conductor or in an electrolyte, is grounded in their principle of isomorphism. This kind of interaction that can be observed in such physical systems is peculiarly attractive to them simply because they believe its nature to be immediately translatable into terms of perception. As an example of this intuitivity one may cite the concept of a "good Gestalt." The left and right halves of a face, for example, are perceived as symmetrical although physically the face is more often than not only approximately symmetrical. As Köhler says, if a face is sufficiently near a standard condition of simple regularity, it will be perceived in a way which will eliminate its minor irregularities. "With regard to symmetry it will have 'too good' an appearance."[16] Then Köhler goes on, characteristically, to point out that macroscopic physical states like electric currents in electrolytes show exactly the same tendency. Such systems tend to develop in the direction of maximum "regularity" and "simplicity."

I hope by now to have carried out what I proposed as the task of this chapter.[17] What the Gestalters wish to say in their characteristic way about science can be said more clearly in the ordinary, analytical way which they reject as in principle inadequate. Some of what they actually do say in their own characteristic way turns out to be misleading. Thus, I believe, their claim that Gestalt theory is, among other things, a new philosophy of science is ill-founded.

T W O

Isomorphism

THE CONCEPT of isomorphism plays a prominent role in logic and mathematics and accordingly it has received a good deal of historical and systematic analysis. The concept also plays a prominent role in some empirical sciences, most notably in the psychology of sensation and perception, where, however, it has received neither an adequate historical nor systematic analysis. Historically, analysis is confined to one or another type of isomorphism or is interwoven with other material so it does not form a unit. Systematically, analysis often is preoccupied with doubtful *a priori* judgments, pro and con.[1]*

After making preliminary statements about mathematical isomorphism, for the sake of subsequent comparison and contrast, I will provide what I take to be the elements

* For the notes to Chapter Two see pages 129-31.

of a historical and logical analysis of the concept of psycho-logical isomorphism. The Gestalt variety of isomorphism, and its *a priori* epistemological justification, will figure prominently in this analysis.

A. DIFFERENT TYPES OF ISOMORPHISM

The mathematical idea of isomorphism has two compo-nents. First, there must be a one-to-one correspondence be-tween the elements of the two interpretations—or, as I shall also say, domains—which satisfy a set of axioms. Two sets of objects are in a one-to-one correspondence if they are paired off with each other so that to each element of the first set corresponds one and only one element of the second, and conversely. So one can say that the set of all mothers is in one-to-one correspondence with the set of all eldest children, whereas the correspondence between the set of all mothers and the set of all children is one-many. The second feature of isomorphism is that the different interpretations of an axiom set exhibit the struc-ture specified by the axioms, although the interpretations may be very different in all other respects. Cohen and Nagel, for example, in their discussion of isomorphism give one arithmetical and one geometrical interpretation of a few axioms of projective geometry. Then they pro-ceed to give the following general definition of isomor-phism:

Isomorphism

Given two classes *S*, with elements *a, b, c, . . .* and *S'*, with elements *a', b', c', . . .*; suppose the elements of *S* can be placed in one-one correspondence with those of *S'*, so that, say, *a* corresponds to *a', b* to *b',* and so on. Then, if for every relation *R* [that is, in the axiomatic system] between elements of *S* (so that, for example, *a R b*) there is a relation *R'* between the corresponding elements of *S' (a' R' b')*, the two classes are *isomorphic.*[2]

What Cohen and Nagel call the two relations *R* and *R'* are, of course, in my way of speaking, two interpretations in different domains of one relational predicate of the axiom system. But the question now arises, what has become of this notion of isomorphism in psychology?

There are several domains believed or claimed to be in some sense isomorphic, in which there has been great interest shown in the history of psychology. The first pair consists of the domain of stimulus events, on the one hand, and the domain of sensory events, on the other. The study of the relation between these two classes of events was referred to by Fechner as outer psychophysics as distinguished from inner psychophysics which concerns the relation of sensations to neural excitations.[3] However, the relation between the events of the two domains of outer psychophysics, as the classical psychologists conceived it, is not isomorphic in the full sense; at best it could be said that some classical psychologists proceeded on the assumption of a one-to-one relationship between stimulus and sensory events. But it will have to be shown that according to more recent results even *this* frame of reference is over-simplified and is not borne out by the facts.

In the area which Fechner called outer psychophysics variations in the physical dimensions were found to be correlated with variations in sensory dimensions. As Boring has pointed out, the procedure of Fechner, Hering, G. E. Mueller, and others was to vary only *one* stimulus dimension at a time and to observe concomitant changes in a *single* sensory dimension. "Out of such analysis grew the false belief that every simple dimension of sensation is correlated to a simple dimension of the stimulus—brightness or loudness to energy, quality to wave length or frequency."[4] If it were true that each sensory attribute were determined by, or dependent on, a single stimulus dimension the sensory attributes and stimulus dimensions would be characterized as being in a one-to-one relationship. There is in this, besides the idea of one-to-one correspondence, also, of course, the idea of a causal dependency in that the physical event determines the phenomenal event. Such a one-to-one relationship could be asserted if hue were in fact dependent solely on wave length, brightness solely upon energy of light, and saturation upon mixture of wave lengths. However it has been established that some such correlations are not one-to-one. The basic fact is that some sensory attributes are dependent on more than one stimulus dimension, e.g., hue varies with wave length and energy as well. It is possible, then, to produce the same sensory character by different combinations of physical stimuli. The situation is further complicated where not only is there not a one-to-one causal relationship between physical and phenomenal events but there is not even the *same number* of stimulus dimensions as there are sensory attributes determined by them. Boring cites, for example, the study of S. S. Stevens on the attributes of tone. Stevens found that for a bi-dimensional stimulus (a tone having the two dimensions of frequency and energy) there are *four* sensory attributes—pitch, loudness, density, and volume.[5] (The Gestalters emphasize such cases of lack of one-to-one correspondence between stimulus and sensory response and conclude that something must be "added" in the organism in order to account for the response. This is their point of departure for speculation about what must "happen" in the organism.)

There are, however, other domains in psychology which are, or were, believed to be isomorphic in a *full sense;* that is, domains which, in addition to one-to-one correspondence, allegedly shared certain "structural" characteristics. The first pair consists of the domain of receptor events, on the one hand, and the domain of afferent neural processes entering the brain, on the other; the second pair consists of the domain of neural events and of phenomenal events. The first type of full isomorphism found its most important exemplification in certain nineteenth-century "nativistic" (i.e., non-learning) theories of space perception;[6]

the second type, usually called psychophysical isomorphism, found important exemplifications, in the nineteenth century, in the color theory of E. Hering and, in the present century, in the numerous theories of Gestalt psychology and epistemology.[7]

(i) The domains which supposedly are isomorphic in nativistic theories of space perception are retinal or skin stimulation and the excitations in the afferent endings in the brain (leaving out the complication of depth perception). Such "projection" theories generally held that there is a one-to-one correspondence between the two sets of excited points and that the spatial relations of the retinal image are preserved in some topological fashion in the afferent fibres entering the brain. Also J. Bernstein proposed that the processes in the sensory surfaces of the skin were projected by nerve fibres upon the brain in a similar manner. These are cases of real isomorphism because they include in addition to a simple one-to-one correspondence between points on the receptors and points in the brain certain topological relations exhibited in both sets of events. Such projection theories were physiological models, speculatively formulated, designed to account for the perception of space. I am not here concerned with the question whether such theories are, in fact, right or wrong. They have been held by respectable scientists and there is no logical or methodological objection to them. On the other hand, it *is* important to point out that projection theories alone would not constitute a "nativistic" account

of, say, space perception. In order for the spatially isomorphic domains in the first pair to account for space perception there must also be structural relations in common
between the domain of brain events and the domain of
phenomenal events. What I have in mind is this: the nativistic solution to the problem of how space is perceived
depends upon projecting the spatial relations of receptor
stimulation on to the brain, but in order for these patterns
of stimulation of nerve endings entering the brain to be
efficacious in giving rise to *perceived* space, an isomorphic
relation between the domains of central nervous events
and phenomenal events—psychophysical isomorphism—
must also be assumed.

(ii) Psychophysical isomorphism, both historically and
systematically, plays a most prominent role in the use of
the isomorphism concept in psychology. As I have indicated, Hering, and others, and also the Gestalters, pro-
pounded their various theories within the framework of
this sort of isomorphism. Their procedure, because of a
paucity of pertinent physiological knowledge, was to infer
from phenomenal experiences the nature of the correlative
physiological process. That is, *first* one assumes an isomorphic relation to exist between these two sets of events;
then he uses features of the phenomenal world to characterize certain physiological events—isomorphic with phenomenal experiences—which will explain these features.

According to Köhler,[8] the isomorphism to which Hering
and G. E. Mueller referred obtains between the "logical

abstracted" orders of experiences on the one hand and physiological events on the other. This "logical" aspect of Hering's and Mueller's isomorphism consists in this: if a sound of a given pitch is presented a number of times at different intensities, and the various presentations are ordered on the basis of loudness, their logical order may be likened to a straight line. That is, the loudnesses proceed from softest to loudest without reversal. On the other hand, if colors are arranged on the basis of hue, the dimension is "circular" in form—as in the color cone. The principle of isomorphism states, then, for Hering and Mueller, that if the underlying physiological events were examined for the properties corresponding to these attributes, these properties would be found to exhibit the same order, linear in the one case, circular in the other. These ideas on isomorphism were explicitly formulated by Mueller in several very general psychophysical axioms which were, as Boring says,[9] accepted universally if implicitly. They state, among other things, (*a*) that underlying each state of consciousness there is a concomitant material (psychophysical) process; (*b*) that for similar or different sensations there are similar or different psychophysical processes, respectively; and (*c*) that for changes of sensation in a certain direction there are corresponding changes in psychophysical processes in the same direction.

The "abstract" or "abstracted" aspect of the Hering-Mueller isomorphism on which Köhler insists refers to the ordering of events within a particular sensory dimension on the basis of certain relations (louder, brighter, etc.). In such a situation the observer has a set to attend to a particular sensory attribute, say saturation, while the other attributes—hue and brightness—are disregarded. Since each stimulus gives rise to a sensation having potentially all three attributes, the experience of saturation under the conditions of the particular set is an "abstract" one and the ordering of the stimuli on the basis of the one attribute is in this sense an "abstract" ordering.

The principle of psychophysical isomorphism espoused by the Gestalters is, according to Köhler, "more general and more concretely applicable" than that of Hering and Mueller.[10] To explain his meaning he considers the example of three white dots on a black surface. "This," he says, "is also an order; but, instead of being of the merely logical kind, it is concrete and belongs to the very facts of experience."[11] The claim then is that *there is also an isomorphism between phenomenally given relations, on the one hand, and certain relational features of their physiological correlates, on the other.* If the point is made in this way one avoids at least the misleading suggestion that the "logical" order with which Hering and Mueller are concerned is not based on experience whereas the Gestalt isomorphism is. The simple point must be made that the sensory experience resulting from an analytical set is just as much a fact of experience as an experience without an analytical set. The "logical" or "abstract" aspect of Hering's and Mueller's isomorphism is the subject's concentration on the topological relations of non-relational characters—e.g., the series of directional gradations. Köhler need not quarrel with this. All he needs to do is *add* that experienced relations have their isomorphic physiological counterparts. Accordingly, Gestalt isomorphism claims in the case of Köhler's dot paradigm that the underlying physiological processes "are distributed in a certain order . . . and . . . this distribution is just as symmetrical in functional terms as the group of dots is in visual terms."[12] In other words, in the physiological processes there must be something corresponding to the perceived betweenness of the middle dot. Köhler formulates this characteristic emphasis in three principles.[13]

I Experienced order in space is always structurally identical with a functional order in the distribution of underlying brain processes.

II Experienced order in time is always structurally identical with a functional order in the sequence of correlated brain processes.

III Units in experience go with functional units in the underlying physiological processes.

The terms 'experienced order' in principles I and II and 'units in experience' in principle III unfortunately do not capture all that is involved in Gestalt isomorphism. That is, if one interprets, as is natural, the terms 'experienced order' and 'units in experience' so that they apply to *experienced* relations or *experienced* units within a perceptual field, then it would not refer to and would not include cases of a relational but nonexperienced character such as the field character and the character of a system altering its own medium. Since it seems that these principles are intended to cover these cases, the situation is worth exploring in some detail.

To give an example of Gestalt procedures: they take perceptual phenomena such as stroboscopic movement, perceptual grouping of *stationary* objects, and reversible figure-ground phenomena as requiring the concept of *phenomenal field,* by which is meant that events or objects located in one area of the visual field influence events in other areas "in a way that depends directly on the properties of both in their relation to each other."[14] Now this field character of visual experience, by means of the isomorphic principle, sets a requirement for the brain processes: the brain processes must have a physical nature which meets this requirement. Consequently Gestalt psychologists say that we must assume that physiological processes have the nature of a macroscopic physical system capable of dynamic interaction of the kind they hold is characteristic of fields—and electrolytic processes, they believe, best fill this bill. It is clear in the case of the perceptual grouping of stationary objects that we can say that a subject has one perceptual experience when stimulus entities bear certain relations to each other (similarity, proximity, and so forth), whereas the subject will see a different grouping when one or more of the relations among the stimulus elements are changed. But it is also clear that immediate experience does not include the observation of the elements in one part of a group *as depending* upon the other elements in the group in the way, say, that the spatial relations of before and between are a matter of immediate experience. In other words, the field character is not itself either a qualitative visual datum or a relational datum *within* the visual field like 'between' and 'to the right of'—characters exemplified by particulars within the visual field. Rather it is from *two* perceptual responses to two different stimulus situations that one *infers* that all parts of a system or group are interdependent in the sense that alterations of any one stimulus element or relation will affect how all the other stimulus elements are seen.

Let us recall Köhler's dot paradigm in which a matter of immediate observation, the experience of *a* being *between b* and *c,* sets the requirement which is to be met by the physiological processes. One dot is seen between the other two and this relation is part of immediate observation in the same way that the whiteness of the dots is a matter of immediate observation. Köhler says that there must therefore be something in the physiological events to correspond to this visual experience of betweenness. He writes, ". . . our principle refers to the relation between concrete experienced order and the underlying physiological processes."[15] However, we can see in the case of the field character that it is not always (and in fact it is not usually) a concrete experienced order which sets the requirements for physiological processes. Consequently the dot paradigm is not universal in the sense that it does not cover all the kinds of relations which are supposedly shared by the two domains of phenomenal and physiological events. If its natural interpretation is given to the term 'experienced order'—that is, if it is interpreted to refer to experienced relations in the various perceptual fields—then it would not refer to a relational but non-experienced character such as the field character. In another place, Köhler himself indicates that the phenomena which set the field requirements are not matters of immediate experience. He writes that "We seldom experience much of the actual genesis of visual percepts, but we can observe what things or figures appear under different conditions of stimulation. . . ."[16] We could say, then, that the conditions which cause certain perceptual phenomena are located in the brain field but unlike the physiological correlates of these phenomena the physiological conditions themselves do not have a phenomenal counterpart.

As a result of our analysis it would seem that one must interpret Köhler's term 'experienced order' to refer simply to the fact that he uses unanalyzed experience rather than analyzed experience as his point of departure for isomorphic speculation. It is in this sense that Gestalters are correctly said to have a "phenomenological" approach to introspection in contrast to the analytical set required in the classical introspectionism of Wilhelm Wundt and in the isomorphic speculation of Hering and Mueller.

B. A PRIORI JUSTIFICATIONS OF PSYCHOPHYSICAL
ISOMORPHISM

The interesting question remains, of course, why anyone should accept the hypothesis of psychophysical isomorphism, whether it be the Hering-Mueller type or the Gestalt variation. One might, of course, argue that the assumption is justified because it is scientifically fruitful. Suppose, Köhler says,[17] that an empirical law in psychology [designated $R(A, B)$] is discovered. The psychological terms will have their counterparts in brain processes (a, b) and the functional relationship R will be interpreted as r, in some form of physiological or physical interaction between a and b [$r (a, b)$]. The problem at this point is some specific determination of the nature of a, b, and r, in lieu of adequate physiological detail. Specific assumptions about a, b, and r will give these processes a position within the "system of concepts with which the natural sciences deal." These assumptions will not only have the characteristics of A, B, and R which the theorist had in mind when he selected the assumptions about a, b, and r but also will yield "implications" as a result of their position in a larger structure of physical knowledge. *With deductive elaboration of these assumptions we find that we get further assumptions about the physiological processes, say a', b', and r'.* With isomorphism functioning as a return bridge, there should then be in the phenomenal realm R' (A',

B'). If such a law already has been found independently in psychology, then (i) its theoretical connection with *R (A, B)* becomes apparent and (ii) it acts as a "partial verification of our physiological theory." If no such law exists as yet in psychology, then an experimental situation must be contrived to test its existence.

I do not wish to guess how good or how poor the isomorphism hypothesis is from this viewpoint of scientific fruitfulness; but I do wish to urge, since the concepts of this hypothesis are not inherently unclear, that it will be uselessness, and not *a priori* argument about the philosophical untenability of isomorphism,[18] that will remove this concept from serious consideration, if it is to be removed at all.

Conversely, the isomorphic assumption cannot be established by *a priori* or logical arguments either. This conclusion follows from the fact that there are significant empirical alternatives, in specific explanatory contexts, which do not involve the isomorphic assumption. To see this point, let us compare, e.g., the two classical color theories of Hering and Young-Helmholtz. One of the points of departure for Hering's color theory is the existence of four phenomenally fundamental or irreducible colors, the so-called primaries—blue, yellow, red, green— in addition to achromatic black and white. This suggested to him that there are three visual substances in the retina —yellow-blue, red-green, and black-white—which can undergo chemical changes in two antagonistic directions from an equilibrium point. All hues other than the six phenomenally fundamental ones were assumed to result from various combinations of these processes, that is, the excitation of more than one process. One principle of the psychophysical isomorphism on which Hering is operating is thus that to the four phenomenal "primaries" correspond four physiological "primaries." As is well known, Hering's hypothesis can be fitted to a large number of data including of course the arrangement of hues in a topological circle. *However it is also possible to account for (approximately) the same range of facts by the speculative model of Helmholtz which does not involve isomorphism with respect to primaries.* For Helmholtz, unlike Hering, took as his main point of departure the physical facts of color mixture discovered by Newton. And since three properly chosen colors mixed in various proportions match all other colors, Helmholtz assumed that not more than three primary processes, in the physiological sense of 'primary,' are operative in the visual apparatus. (It is only fair to point out, however, that Helmholtz's model leads to a question which finds an immediate answer in Hering's, while this is not so in Helmholtz's model. This question is of course: which are the features that characterize the processes corresponding to the four phenomenal primaries? I do not know what answer, if any, the Helmholtzians have given to this question, nor is this important. For the logical multiplicity of possible answers, e.g., certain maximal-minimal properties in the distribution of the three Helmholtz primaries, is very great. But again in this answer there is no trace of isomorphism.)

Nevertheless, *a priori* arguments *have* been offered which allegedly establish the isomorphic assumption independently of the question of its scientific usefulness. Köhler, for example, offers the following argument.[19] The phenomenal field, he says, consists of two different sorts of percepts—percepts of things like tables, chairs, and instruments, on the one hand, and percepts of the self, on the other. The concept of objective experience refers to the whole set of thing percepts within the phenomenal field. Now the physicist using this objective experience has successfully inferred the nature of the physical events which caused it. If there were no basic similarity, no isomorphism, between objective experience and physical events, then, of course, one could not "infer" or "draw a picture of" the nature of physical events. However, the phenomenal world is more "closely related," both causally and existentially, to the physiological realm than the physical, so *a fortiori* these two realms must be isomorphic and one is able to infer from the nature of the phenomenal the nature of the physiological.

This *a priori* argument for isomorphic speculation is open to criticism because, in fact, no isomorphic relation obtains between the phenomenal and physical realms, or, more precisely, between the givennesses of perception on the one hand and the theoretical concepts of physics on the other. For example, where is the isomorphism in any precise sense of the term between the movements of molecules and the immediately experienced character 'warm' which one naïvely ascribes to physical objects? All one can say is: first, in theoretical physics the concept 'temperature' is co-ordinated to some function of the average velocity of the particles. Second, after the co-ordination of all thermodynamic concepts to various features of the particle model is completed one expects to derive the thermodynamic laws as special instances of the laws of mechanics by applying the latter to the model. Third, the only necessary requirement is therefore that the functional relations among the concepts of the model be mathematically the same as the ones between the corresponding concepts of what physicists call phenomenological thermodynamics. Fourth, it is not clear why or how an isomorphism in any precise sense need or does obtain even between the concepts of phenomenological thermodynamics and the elements of untutored perception. As to the two domains of physical objects and phenomenal experience, then, it is not only not necessary but in fact false that the former mirrors the latter in the way Gestalt epistemologists call isomorphic.

To elaborate further this important point, consider the phenomenal experience of color, on the one hand, and the physical events which give rise to it, on the other. On the basis of phenomenal experience the hues form a topological circle, represented in the color cone, in which there are gradual transitions from one hue to a neighboring hue and a doubling back of hues towards the one with which one starts. But what about the physical events which give rise to these experiences? Of course, no such "topological circularity" is to be found in the physical basis of light and color.

These arguments, it should be noticed, eliminate the basis of the whole *a priori* argument; and so it is unnecessary to explore the hazy notion of the phenomenal field being "closer" to the physiological than to the physical field.

C. THE NATURE OF GESTALT EPISTEMOLOGY

Gestalt psychologists invariably formulate and defend their isomorphic assumption within the framework of an epistemological dualism, namely, representative realism.[20] Thing percepts belong to the phenomenal world; the theoretical concepts of physics and physiology refer to transphenomenal real entities which cause the percepts. As effects the percepts "represent" their causes in the transphenomenal realm. And, of course, the phenomenal and physical-physiological realms are isomorphic. I think the isomorphic assumption can be stated within the framework of any epistemological system and that it would be wise to state it in common-sense terms since this epistemological framework, unexamined to be sure, is the one in which scientists ordinarily operate. However, since the Gestalters believe that representative realism is the only correct way to formulate the isomorphism hypothesis, it is necessary, finally, to examine the nature of the grounds of their philosophical predilection.

Koffka says[21] that the difference between the phenomenal and physical realms is equivalent to the philosopher's distinction between appearance and reality. And indeed the subtance of Koffka's argument for the existence of the phenomenal—or behavioral—realm or "appearance" emerges clearly as the traditional philosophical argument from illusion, the function of which is to establish the existence of sense data or percepts as distinct from physical objects. According to the philosophical dialectic, in cases of illusion *something* is being experienced and inasmuch as it is not the object it must be a percept or, in other formulations, sense data. In terms of a classic example, I see a straight stick partly submerged in water as bent. My experience of "bent stick" may not have a physical counterpart but nevertheless I am perceiving something—sense data or percepts. In Koffka's terminology, my "behavioral" environment is "bent stick" while the physical stick is not bent. The next step in the dialectic is to extend the claim that we apprehend percepts, and not objects, to all experiences. And Koffka appropriately universalizes his concept of behavioral environment: "But every *datum* is a behavioral datum; physical reality is not a datum but a constructum."[22] And in cases of illusion he tells us that the organism is not acting in a behavioral environment only at the moment of illusion but that it has been acting in the behavioral environment all along.[23]

Isomorphism

Koffka thus asserts that the particulars of awareness are always percepts and never physical objects, but how does he establish the 'always' and 'never' in his claim? In characterizing certain experience as illusory he is assuming the validity of some other experience by which the illusion is discovered. In order to universalize his behavioral environment, then, he would have to supply, as he does not, in this context, some second reason why the apprehensions in these cases of valid perception are still percepts.

Koffka and Köhler in other contexts, however, do try to justify the universalization of their sense-data or percept claims. The dualist, Köhler says,[24] is able to tell "an impressive story" in which a representative element is present not as a philosophical theory but as a matter of physiological fact: stimulus energy impinges on nerve endings; nerve energy is transmitted into the central nervous system; phenomenal experience results. In one place Köhler *appears* to realize that this does not establish his representative realism. He admits that one might easily object that the use of words like "objects" already presupposes the existence of a world which is independent of and represented by experience and that consequently his procedure is circular. This criticism is too hasty, however, Köhler continues, because the phenomenalist for example does not contend that such things as brains, nerves, and sense organs are "unreal" but rather insists that what is ordinarily known as a physical object must be *interpreted* as a phenomenal entity. He concludes, "They cannot, for such reasons, refuse to listen to the Dualist's report. As a report, then, . . . [physiology] is common ground for both the Dualist and the Phenomenalist."[25]

If we are permitted to put Köhler's argument in our own terminology then we could say he holds that "the impressive story" is something every philosophical position has to take into account but that this story does not establish epistemological dualism. In spite of occasional passages that seem to acknowledge this familiar philosophical dialectic, however, Köhler does not seem to appreciate what seems to me an obvious truth, namely, that no amount of empirical data, as collected and interpreted by science, can establish an epistemological position directly. For example, he writes,

> Epistemological Dualism holds that percepts cannot be identified with physical objects, because percepts emerge only after many events have happened between the objects and the organism, in peripheral parts of the organism and eventually in the brain.[26]

However, that "objective experience," or the world of thing percepts, depends upon such things as physical energy impinging on receptors and transmission of neural impulses is a matter of scientific fact, and in this sense having percepts is a matter of physiology and psychology. It is clear that a percept in this scientific sense is not what it is the percept of and that when you and I look at the same galvanometer we yet do not have the same percept. This argument, however, is irrelevant to an epistemological discussion. When a person points out that objective experience depends upon certain complicated processes in the organism he is asserting laws which belong to the body of scientific knowledge. In such assertions obviously one has already accepted what constitutes a valid basis of knowledge and consequently such assertions have no epistemological significance. Epistemologically the question is what constitutes the valid basis of knowledge irrespective of the causal genesis of that basis.

One might try, of course, to establish as a philosopher and by philosophical argument a representative realism and, within its framework, what has sometimes been called a causal theory of perception. However this sort of argument is much different from Köhler's point. What we have called the causal theory of perception would hold that 'This is x' is equivalent to 'This is caused by x' where 'this' refers to a sense datum or percept and 'x' to a physical object. The essential point in such a contention is that the physical object that is singled out as the cause of what is immediately observed is not itself a matter of observation. In Köhler's discussion of the galvanometer illustration, however, the physical object and sense data are both aspects within experience and between which scientific correlations are discovered.

I conclude then that the Gestalt variety of representa-

47

tive realism, in which Gestalt psychologists present and defend their isomorphism hypothesis, not only does not bolster their hypothesis, but is itself philosophically dubious. The Gestalters at this point might well deny themselves the luxury of a philosophical position on the problem of perception and let their isomorphism hypothesis stand on its own merit.

THREE

Lawfulness

IS IT POSSIBLE to predict a person's response knowing only some physical or social stimulus or is it necessary to know how the person "sees" or "understands" this objective stimulus before predicting his response? This question has plagued psychologists, social scientists, historians, and biographers from the very beginning of their enterprises and radically different answers have been given to it. The Gestalt theorist says no and the learning theorist yes, and each supports his view with reasons of varying degrees of merit. I want to examine these different views of lawfulness and prediction and will suggest each is legitimate within limits and each goes astray when it lays claim to exclusive excellence. Finally, I shall be highly critical of the *verstehende* psychologists who, while they share the Gestalt view, introduce 'empathy' as an explanatory concept.

A. THE GESTALT AND LEARNING VIEWS

On the Gestalt view, external physical and social concepts are useless in the explanation of human behavior. One cannot use them to help explain behavior because he does not know how they are "internalized"—that is, how the subject "sees" or apprehends them. On the other hand, if one does know how the subject apprehends them, then he is in a position to explain or predict behavior. According to Koffka, one explains behavior by referring to the "psychological" or "behavioral" environment, never by the "physical" or "geographical" environment.[1]* Koffka uses many examples, both anecdotal and experimental, to justify his point. Through a snow storm a man walks over what he thought was a snow-covered plain only to learn later that the plain was actually the frozen surface of Lake Constance.[2] Knowing the frozen lake fact would not make it possible either to predict or explain the traveller's response; knowing his behavioral environment is necessary for that. He cites also the case of Revesz' chicks which were trained to peck at the smaller of two objects.[3] When two physically equal segments of circles were presented to the chicks they pecked most consistently at the one which, to us, *looks* smaller. Koffka says we must assume that the behavior of the chicks was determined by a relation and, since this relation has no geographical isomorph, it must

* For the notes to Chapter Three see pages 131-36.

be present in the behavioral environment. Other evidence which, he believes, compels him to assume a behavioral environment are the so-called constancy phenomena, i.e., situations in which, say, the same perceptual response is made to different retinal stimulations and different perceptual responses are made to the same retinal stimulation.[4] In the former case, the behavioral environments must be the same and hence the same responses; in the latter case, the behavioral environments must be different and hence the different responses. All of the examples, Koffka concludes, lead to the same conclusion: in order to predict the behavior of a subject a psychologist must know the subject's behavioral environment.

Some learning theorists have objected to this Gestalt analysis as completely untenable.[5] The behavioral environment supposedly explains why a subject will respond in a certain way, yet one only learns what the subject's behavioral environment is by observing this response. The behavioral environment snow-covered-plain explains why the traveller walked over the frozen surface of Lake Constance, yet one only knows the former after the latter has occurred. Certainly this procedure is *ad hoc* and circular. I do not think this criticism will do, however. Even though one cannot predict the response from which he infers the subject's behavioral environment he can, knowing this environment, predict further responses of the subject. (Certainly he could predict the traveller's surprise and consternation on later learning the truth. Indeed, according to

Koffka's tale the traveller dropped dead on hearing the news!) Spence calls this sort of achievement the discovery of "response-response" laws in contrast to the learning theorist's "stimulus-response" laws.[6]

The learning theorist offers the following analysis of psychological lawfulness, in which, needless to say, the stimulus variables are physical or geographical (or social) ones:[7] $R = f$ (S, H, D, I). Take the characters 'S,' 'H,' 'D,' and 'I' to refer respectively to geographical stimulus, past learning, motivation, and individual differences; 'H' and 'D' being, at the present state of our knowledge, historically defined. ('D,' e.g., could be defined in terms of time of food deprivation, although this example should not suggest that 'H,' 'D,' and 'I' are always defined as functions of one independent variable; frequently they are functions of several or more.) Now if one knew a determinate function that relates the variables S, H, D, and I to the response R, and had different sets of values for H, D, and I with the same S, then he would be able to calculate and predict two different responses to the same physical stimulus S and thus *explain* 'how subject sees S.' It does not seem unreasonable to speak of the group H, D, and I as the "equivalent" of an allegedly irreducible behavioral environment because it is their different values which bring about the different responses, although strictly speaking the function involves values of all four variables (S included). I do not claim, of course, that all behavioral environments can be so explained in terms of stimulus-response laws; it is a matter of scientific success or lack of it —finding or not finding the functional relations, etc. However some "behavioral environments," as well as behavior, require explanations, and it is difficult to see how any light could be thrown on their production without some use of learning, motivational, and physical stimulus variables. The Gestalt theorists, on the other hand, insist that an S-R type of explanation is *never* possible and the puzzle is to explain this insistence. The Gestalters insist on it, we shall see, because they believe it is necessary in order to safeguard their tenets of psycho-physiological isomorphism.

The S–R type of explanation with its variable groups H, D, and I implies that learning and motivational factors are necessary for an adequate theory of perception. The Gestalters, however, are unwilling to admit this; they insist that perceptual groupings are "irreducible," that is, are prior to and independent of learning processes. They are, of course, willing to grant that perceptual organizations are modified by learning. Köhler writes that "Gestalt psychology holds that sensory units have acquired names, have become richly symbolic, and are now known to have certain practical uses, while nevertheless they have existed as units before any of these further facts were added."[8] E.g., Köhler writes that when we peer into the sky we see certain clusters of stars detached from their environment, Casseopeia and the Dippers, for example. "For ages people have seen the same groups as units, and at the present time children need no instruction in order to perceive the same units."[9] Then he goes on to argue against the Wundtian type of analysis through kinesthesis by pointing out that any "empiristic" (learning) explanation of visual organization in terms of eye movements simply *shifts* the problem of organization from one sense modality (sight) to another (kinesthesis) and does not *solve* the problem of organization itself. Moreover, as is well known, part of Max Wertheimer's famous article "Laws of Organization"[10] is devoted to anti-learning arguments of this type. *But why this Gestalt antipathy to any learning explanation of perceptual grouping?* The answer lies in their hypothesis of psycho-physiological isomorphism, by which they hoped to provide physiological explanations of psychological laws and facts. According to the Gestalt version of the isomorphism hypothesis, the "field" characteristics of the physiological apparatus are reflected in the organization of the sensory contents to which they correspond. Now, since the physiological apparatus is structured or organized to begin with,[11] the sensory or perceptual contents must be likewise. They must come from the very beginning not as elements but in perceptual groupings. The learning theories of the associationists, or the intellectual acts of the students of Brentano, can only modify what is there already—like traces modify the brain field, according to Koffka. Perhaps one might say, the genetic problem of discovering what part of sensory organization is an elementary perceptual fact and what part is learned appears extremely important to the Gestalt theorists because they think their notion of isomorphism requires that certain perceptual responses or givennesses *not* be generated by learning processes. There is a three-fold answer to this Gestalt view:

1. The learning theorist, clearly, is not primarily concerned with ascertaining how many "groupings" are innate and how many are learned. But he is interested in finding by experimental procedure, first, the laws *under which any learning occurs* and, second, in determining if perceptual responses, or in Gestalt terminology, perceptual groupings, are among those that can be learned. The answer to the second question is, one may say confidently, yes.

2. There is no objection to accepting unlearned relational responses into a learning theory; it seems that, as a matter of fact, not all relational responses are learned. Such unlearned relational responses are taken into account in several learning theories, e.g., Hull's postulate of "afferent neural interaction." On the other hand, some rather elementary relational responses on whose "innateness" the Gestalters insist appear, at least in principle, derivable from non-relational responses by means of the laws of learning. Spence, e.g., in a much quoted article,[12] has derived certain transposition responses from the principles of generalization and the cumulative strengthening of habit strength.

3. *Relations or groupings once learned may well be phenomenally "given" or even introspectively irreducible.* To assert the introspective irreducibility of a givenness at a certain moment is one thing; to say that it has, or has not,

been learned in a certain manner is another thing. The Gestalters, however, in their anxiety to protect the irreducibility of perceptual groupings, and since they blur the two notions, insist, in effect, on irreducibility in both senses, 'unanalyzable' and 'unlearned,' when, in truth, for the sake of their isomorphism, they need insist on the irreducibility of perceptual groupings only in the first sense.

The Gestalters' lack of clarity about the two senses of 'irreducible' can be explained, I believe, in terms of certain historical relations between Wundtian structural psychology and the new Gestalt psychology which rose in reaction against it.

For the Gestalt psychologists, a learning explanation of perception or "behavioral environment" cannot be right because learning theory is "elementaristic."[13] The first link in this verbal bridge between "learning" and "elementarism" is the Gestalters' identification of learning theory with "associationism." This connection between learning theories and associationism is of course justified; the English associationists, Ebbinghaus, and Thorndike all gave an important place to associationistic theories of learning and no others worth the name of a theory or explanation have so far been proposed. However, and this is the second link in the bridge, "associationism" means for the Gestalters also and mainly Wundtian associationism. And Wundtianism is "elementaristic" in the sense that it insists on the possibility of introspectively analyzing phenomenally given relations into non-relational elements.

Relational experiences, according to Wundt, can in this sense be built up out of non-relational elements, both sensory and affective. This is the hard core of Wundtian elementarism, and this is essentially the doctrine against which the Gestalters rebelled and on which, consciously or unconsciously, their whole thought is fixated. Thus because they are so anxious to safeguard the introspective irreducibility of relational givennesses they believe that they must insist on the unlearned nature of perceptual responses.

B. THE EXPERIENCE ERROR

According to Köhler, the correct formula for psychological lawfulness is this: receptor stimulation; organization of these stimuli by the central nervous system; and response to the product of organization.[14] Knowing only the receptor stimulation, one could not predict a subject's response; one needs to know how the subject apprehends or organizes the stimuli. Thus Köhler agrees with Koffka that the idea of behavioral environment is irreducible and indispensable, and from this standpoint he characterizes the S–R conception of stimulus as incorrect. Let us look into his argument in some detail.

Köhler proposes to label as the *experience error* the erroneous ascription of organization to a mosaic of receptor stimulation, e.g., retinal stimulation. "Physiologists and psychologists are inclined to talk about *the* retinal process which corresponds to an object, as though stimulation within the retinal area of the object constituted a segregated unit."[15] The facts are far otherwise, he believes. Say you see a sheep behind a fence. Now each element of the surface of the sheep and the fence reflects light independently. In this case two elements of the sheep's surface are no more related to each other than one of them is to an element of the fence's surface. "Hence, so far as retinal stimulation is concerned, there is no organization, no segregation of specific units or groups."[16] The autochthonous activity of the central nervous system is the organizing agent; its function, one might say, is to reorganize stimuli and thus recreate the relationships that were lost in the separation sieve of receptor stimulation. Or the nervous system may create relationships which do not even have a physical counterpart at all. In either case, the correct schema of lawfulness is this: receptor stimulation, organization of stimuli, and response to the product of organization.

How the S–R learning theorist goes wrong, Köhler thinks, should now be clear. He talks about the objective physical object as the stimulus for a subject. But this will not do, for the subject's proper stimulus is unstructured receptor stimulation which is turned into a structured stimulus by the central nervous system. Köhler writes that he once tried to convince a behaviorist that he should not refer to a female bird as "a stimulus" for a male bird because this way of talking ignores the facts of organization.[17] The behaviorist, however, Köhler continues, went on committing the experience error because he did not understand the importance of sensory experience for psychological theory. Moreover, Köhler says,[18] we are now in a position to see why the behaviorist's stimulus-response formula of lawfulness is mistaken, plausible as it might seem at first glance. The behaviorist simply uses the term stimulus in a loose fashion, applying it to an objective physical object which has already been perceptually structured.

The reply to Köhler's view is four-fold:

1. There is a deep lying philosophical confusion in this argument. Köhler, it would seem, forgets that in building the science of psychology one can use relational terms in the description of a stimulus without first accounting, within this science, for the perception of relations. We have here a confusion between a scientific "causal" explanation and the question of what is included in the level of undefined terms in scientific definition. Köhler confusedly thinks that one must generate the relational terms of the latter by a causal analysis before one may use them in describing a distal object as stimulus. When one realizes that relational terms are included among the undefined concepts in scientific definition and so are prior to any scientific study of perception, the groundlessness of the argument becomes clear and the charge of circularity, which Köhler implicitly makes against the S–R theorist's construction, is seen to be unjustified. And likewise un-

justified is what appears to be the Gestalters' implicit idea of the referent of the symbol 'S' in the S–R schema. Influenced by the fixation on Wundtian issues and by the other ideas we are now discussing, they always think of the referent of 'S' as an unstructured, non-relational "element"; distally, a monochromatic patch on a projection screen in a typical sensation experiment, proximally, the local retinal excitation produced by such a stimulus. Nothing is farther from the truth. 'S' like the other variables in the S–R schema may stand for a whole group of variables, including relational terms.

2. In this argument the Gestalters claim that receptor stimulation, not physical objects, is the "proper" stimulus of a subject; and they insist that retinal mosaics, not whole "macro" objects, are the "real" stimulus of a subject. Thus the Gestalters decide on *a priori* grounds what must be the locus of a stimulus and the units of its size. In fact, of course, the choice of the locus of the stimulus, the choice of units of description, and the inclusion of relations in it is not a systematic issue. The units one chooses in defining one's variables and the locus of them depend upon what sort of law is wanted. No type of law in itself is intrinsically good, albeit one might want a certain kind of law for systematic reasons. (E.g., an S–R law might explain an R–R one but the reverse could not occur.) Ever since the downfall of Wundt the tendency in psychology has been toward the use of physical macro units in the description

of stimulus situations. If one believes that this is fortunate it is only because at the present stage of knowledge the choice of such units is as a matter of fact more likely to lead to the establishment of laws. Neither it nor the Gestalt alternative is to be rationalized on *a priori* grounds such as Köhler advances.

3. Köhler seems to say that retinal stimuli exhibit no organization. But clearly they do. Although retinal stimuli are discrete and independent, they do exhibit relations such as contiguity and similarity. These relations, of course, Köhler would call "formal" or "geometrical," not "functional"—where the word functional means dynamic interaction—and would depreciate their significance. But the point is this: Köhler does not explicitly point out that the lack of "functional interaction" is not identical with a lack of all organization; consequently when he writes that retinal stimuli have no organization there is at least the silent implication that no relations are exemplified in the proximal stimulus pattern to which a response can be learned. Hence the *non sequitur* that no S–R schema of the constancy phenomena can be devised.

Actually the various retinal stimulations due to one and the same physical micro-stimulus object do of course exhibit relational invariances to which the learned response may be made. Let us elaborate this matter within the framework of the S–R schema for explaining certain constancy phenomena.

Let us call S the physical stimulus object and let

$$(1) \quad \begin{array}{l} s_1', s_2', \ \ldots \ s_n' \\ s_1'', s_2'', \ \ldots \ s_n'' \\ \quad \cdot \quad \cdot \quad \cdot \\ s_1^{(m)}, s_2^{(m)}, \ \ldots \ s_n^{(m)} \end{array}$$

be the m patterns of retinal stimulations corresponding to m different "views" of S. In retinal micro terms the stimulus is in each case not one elementary entity but a group of such, as I called it before; and, let me repeat, a group that may and as a rule will include relational traits such as, e.g., the spatial relations between the patches of homogenous retinal stimulation.

Thing constancy is then expressed by the following schema:

$$(2) \quad \begin{array}{l} R_1 = f(s_1', s_2', \ \ldots \ s_n', X) \\ R_1 = f(s_1'', s_2'', \ \ldots \ s_n'', X) \\[6pt] R_1 = f(s_1^{(m)}, s_2^{\ (m)}, \ \ldots \ s_n^{(m)}, X) \end{array}$$

The problem then is to find a function (complex relation) which remains constant for all the lines of (1). *Any* such functions can, by the logic of the case, serve as a cue for the macro response which, if verbal, may be thought of as "This is S." Which of the several possible functions of this sort is the actual clue is a matter to be determined by experimentation. To leave no possible doubt that there are such functions, consider the light waves coming from the same distal object. They give rise to different proximal stimulation, but they are all sections of the class of light beams which is reflected from the surface of the object. Inasmuch as the various proximal stimulus situations are all such intersections, there is a relational invariant to be responded to, like the ratio of frequencies in a tune.

4. Finally, Köhler and Koffka believe that 'S' can never be a physical stimulus but is always a perceived or apprehended 'S' because they are committed philosophically to a representative realism and thus acknowledge only mediate knowledge of physical objects. However, since their isomorphism hypothesis can be formulated in any epistemological system no particular one is *necessary* for it; and, as I have tried to show in the previous chapter, the grounds they advance for their representative preferences are a curious mixture of philosophical and scientific arguments.

C. VERSTEHENDE AND EMPATHY

Verstehende psychologists who follow Dilthey and Spranger, phenomenologists like Snygg, and various other psychologists who specialize in personality studies take the same view as Koffka and Köhler about the irreducibility of 'behavioral environment,' and the uselessness of a physical stimulus;[19] but they eschew the physiological explanations of the Gestalters and use instead behavior maxims which supposedly give empathetic understanding of the other fellow's behavior.

Recall the case of the traveller who walked over the frozen surface of Lake Constance. According to Snygg and certain *verstehende* psychologists,[20] the external fact is useless in explaining the traveller's behavior; one needs to know he sees it as snow-covered-plain. Then a behavior maxim drawn from everyday life connects this "internalized" stimulus with his response and thus explains it. The behavior maxim in this case, of course, is that people take the most direct line of action to get out of unpleasant situations. For the traveller the apparent plain offers the most direct line of approach or shortest route to the light of an inn; hence he takes this route. While this maxim explains his behavior it is not yet clear what is "empathetic" about it. The point is this: a behavior maxim is not "discovered"; it is immediately experienced as an understandable relation.[21] Thus the other fellow's acting on it—which explains his behavior—is understandable too: I have an empathetic feeling for him. The empathetic understanding, finally, does not come simply from the capacity to experience explanatory relations but from actually having them; if understanding is to occur, one must not simply be capable of having the same motives as another but must actually share them.[22]

The inadequacy of the empathy viewpoint is indicated in the fact that it is neither a sufficient nor necessary condition for explanations in psychology. First, incompatible explanations of behavior are usually equally understandable so one needs another criterion besides understanding to determine which of the alternative explanations is correct. This criterion, of course, is objective observation and experiment. We can make the same point by saying that empathy indicates only possible but not probable explanations. According to Theodore Abel,

> When we say we "understand" a connection, we imply nothing more than recognizing it as a possible one. We simply affirm that we have at least once in direct experience observed and established the connection or its equivalent. But from the affirmation of a possible connection we cannot conclude that it is also probable. From the point of view of *verstehen* [empathy] alone, any connection that is possible is *equally* certain. In any given case the test of the actual probability calls for the application of objective methods of observation. . . .[23]

Second, empathy is not a necessary requirement for psychological explanation either. There is a whole series of subjects which are, for most people, increasingly difficult to understand empathetically. At the apex would be a person like Hitler, certainly a legitimate object of psychological study. That Hitler's hatreds and ambitions are "experienceable" and in this most attenuated sense "understandable" or "human" is trivial—it follows tautologically from the existence of the subject. And if the explanation of Hitler's behavior consisted in experiencing his hatreds and ambitions, then he would remain inexplicable for most people. There is, of course, an explanation for Hitler's behavior; it consists in causal analyses of abnormal psychology, in which identification with the subject and so "understanding" of the explanatory concepts has diminished to the vanishing point. On the other hand, an unrepentant Nazi could give the same causal analysis but find the explanation perfectly understandable. Understandability, or the lack of it, thus, is not itself a part of the explanation of Hitler's behavior, does not tell us anything more about *him;* but it does express important information about the personality of the *explainer.*

Finally, it is not the case that external physical and social environmental factors are useless in psychological explanations, that the factors must always be "psychological" or "internalized." It is true that the psychologist usually explains his subject's behavior by personality factors—not necessarily, however, as we have seen, by understandable ones. If this were the only explanatory function of a psychologist, however, it would leave completely inexplicable those chapters in every serious study of personality which concern the all-important early "formative years" of the subject. The point of such chapters is to show the part that social and physical environmental factors play in producing those personality factors which, in turn, explain behavior. Personality, as well as behavior, requires explanation and in this explanation environmental factors, both social and physical, play an important role.

The psychologist's task of explaining how personality

characteristics came about is not confined to the youthful years, for every year is formative for those that follow. The psychologist is constantly trying to explain the continuous changes, large and small, which occur in the life of the subject. To neglect this task of explaining personality development is to produce a Theophrastian character, not to unfold a life with its mercurial flights, its shades and lights. The nineteenth century emphasis on processes, changes, and evolution has left its mark on the psychology of personality as on everything else.

F O U R

Psychoanalytic Propositions

THE RELATIONS between psychoanalysis and philosophy are complex indeed and much discussed. On the one hand, philosophers of science have been busily analyzing the logical structure of psychoanalytic concepts and propositions, and they have generally not been too happy with the result.[1]* Their criticisms are of two sorts mainly. (1) Many psychoanalytic propositions are meaningless—or, at any rate, pointless—because they are in principle untestable. Moreover, many others, even though meaningful and testable, cannot be accepted as confirmed since they do not yield any significant predictions. (2) The concepts of Freud's metapsychology, like Eros, Thanatos, Id, Ego, and Superego, and the hypotheses using them are fantastically vague, but even worse they are metaphysically queer. The

* For the notes to Chapter Four see pages 136-38.

very notion of unconscious motives as existing entities which *cause* slips of tongue, dream contents, *et al.*, seems ontologically odd to the point of being meaningless.

On the other hand, some philosophers accept psycho-analysis more or less *in toto* and bend it to philosophical purposes. Several have used it to explain the obsessive commitments of metaphysicians to "philosophical" statements which are allegedly meaningless[2] while others have used it for varying purposes in moral philosophy, either claiming that it establishes the traditional determinism position or that it reinforces the common-sense notion of self-determinism.[3] I shall examine the philosophical critiques of psychoanalysis in the present chapter and the philosophical implications of psychoanalysis for moral philosophy in the next.

A. ARE PSYCHOANALYTIC PROPOSITIONS UNCONFIRMABLE?

I shall examine first the allegation that psychoanalytic propositions are unconfirmable and hence scientifically meaningless—or at least pointless—and second, the contention that they are unconfirmed as a matter of fact. I shall finish by asking what sense the metapsychological notion of unconscious motivation, as a *vera causa*, might make.

If my watch runs slow and I explain it by saying a little blue devil gets his tail caught in the works, I must deduce some consequence and test it if this hypothesis is to be scientifically respectable. If I explain to someone who proposes unscrewing the back of the case and extricating the little devil that he can't because the little fellow is invisible, and moreover he is odorless, etc., too, then I protect my hypothesis from falsification by making it compatible with any state of affairs. Many philosophers of science have made precisely this claim about the nature of psychoanalytic propositions. They are framed and held in such a way that no evidence can count against them. Thus immune from falsification or disconfirmation they are also immune—although their proponents do not see it—from verification or confirmation. One writer cites Freud's concept of *archaic heritage* as a good example of this point.[4] Freud thought that dream analysis reveals "ideational contents" in the dreamer's unconscious which he could not have learned either from childhood or adult experience. Freud concluded that "we are obliged to regard it as part of the *archaic heritage* which a child brings with him into the world, before any experience of his own, as a result of the experiences of his ancestors."[5] But Freud's notion, of course, runs into headlong conflict with modern genetics; acquired characteristics cannot be inherited. But does the difficulty disconfirm the hypothesis for Freud? Not at all; he keeps the concept because "I cannot picture biological development proceeding without taking this factor into account." Thus this hypothesis is irrefutable and hence meaningless, or at least pointless. To be sure, most contemporary analysts do not accept this concept, but what then? If this concept of Freud's can be rejected and his others retained, *why could not this independence of theoretical notions be demonstrated to Freud himself?* Primarily because the concepts and hypotheses of psychoanalysis are so vague that it is not clear what is dependent on what, and what independent of what.

The answer to this criticism has several parts, but it is not very complex even so. First, psychoanalytic propositions are not all of the same logical type. So even if one type can be shown to be immune from disconfirmation and thus scientifically meaningless it does not follow that the other types also are. (Unhappily this implication is often present in the critic's argument.) Consider the following different types of psychoanalytic concepts[6]: (1) Eros and Thanatos; (2) psychosexual development, Oedipus complex; (3) fixation, trauma, etc.; and (4) Id, Ego, and Superego. The items in (2) are genetic concepts of development; the items in (3) are internal qualitative relations of these developments and processes to the demands of the environment; and the items of (4) are theoretical concepts —what I shall call intervening variables—which relate the concepts of (2) and (3). These are the inter-connected concepts of Freudian theory. The items of (1), Freud's instinct theory, to which the concept of archaic heritage belongs, are irrelevant to this body of imperfectly but decently related theoretical concepts. Thus, the critic's demolition of the concept of archaic heritage leaves the core of psychoanalytic teachings untouched. Second, to the question why the independence of (2), (3), and (4) from (1) could not be demonstrated to Freud, the answer is this: he was too close to his own theory and had more than rational attachment to all of his ideas, just as most of us do. One has no more right to assume that Freud could not see this independence because (1), (2), (3), and (4) are vague and blur together than he does to assume that Darwin could not see the irrelevance and untestability of his pangenesis theory because the concepts of natural selection and pangenesis are vague and blur together. Darwin's case is rather like Freud's in the sense we are insisting upon. Like Freud, Darwin was too close to his own work and more than rationally attached to his ideas to see the irrelevance of the concept of pangenesis. The existence of scientific societies and public forums attest to this universal fact of an individual's more than rational attachment to his ideas. It is gratuitous to ground one scientist's lack of insight on the vagueness of his own hypotheses when this lack would be explained in quite another way in other cases.

Another writer attacks one of the genetic concepts, claiming that it, too, and others like it, are in principle not testable and hence are scientifically meaningless. (Sometimes it is unclear whether critics are saying that analytic propositions are scientifically meaningless or simply pointless because of their alleged untestability.) Under what conditions, this writer asks,[7] is the psychoanalyst ready to admit that a child does not have an Oedipus complex? What kind of evidence is he prepared to accept to falsify the hypothesis that a specific child has an Oedipus complex?

Psychoanalysts have replied in the following vein. Unfortunately philosophers of science do not know much about psychoanalysis or they would distinguish between a fact of observation, the Oedipal phase, and a theoretical term, the Oedipus complex.[8] Then they give criteria which would falsify the claim that a child goes through an Oedipal phase. The criteria are complex but include this sort of thing[9]: if a little boy failed to express tender or romantic fantasies regarding his mother, if he failed to exhibit his penis, etc., if he were emotionally impulsive, if he had little identification with the standards of his human environment, and if he had little concern about others, then truly we could say he failed to go through an Oedipal phase. And there is a host of other criteria which could be appealed to for a decision. Philosophers of science counter this answer in the following way.[10] Is any one of these criteria *sufficient* to say that the Oedipal phase of development has not been reached? Or is each one *necessary* and the whole group together *sufficient?* But in this case the reference to a "host of other criteria" makes one wonder if there is such a finite list of necessary criteria. But this reply will not do. The psychoanalyst does not consider any one of the criteria as either necessary or sufficient, and he would consider the occurrence of all of them as staggeringly sufficient! The true situation, he believes, is

73

this: a child may not, and usually will not, have *all* of the specified characteristics, but he must have *some* of them; and the more he has, and the more continuously and intensely they manifest themselves, the stronger the evidence becomes for saying he is or is not in an Oedipal phase.

To this sort of defense, the following further criticism has been addressed: To be sure, terms like 'Oedipus complex' do mean something, but the semantical rules governing their use are so complicated and so complex that only a skilled and highly experienced psychoanalyst can apply them. So it follows that only an expert "really understands" psychoanalytic theory. "But then it is easy to see why a philosopher might be suspicious, might wonder, in view of these labyrinthine rules [known only to the expert], whether the psychoanalyst is really ever *using the theory*, and not, rather, *simply* relying on intuition."[11] The proper answer to this criticism is straightforward: (1) It requires considerable training, responsibility, and experience to apply correctly a term in any field which is both a science and an art, or skill; (2) in all such fields—medicine, engineering, testing—it takes intuition, or a "feel" for the field, as well; (3) in all such fields only an expert can really understand the theory; (4) but it does not follow from any of this that such an expert in whatever field is not relying on whatever theory he has. He may not be, to be sure, but the criticism we have been examining does not establish it.

This reply can be amplified and the source of the critic's

error exposed if we consider for a moment the nature of early experimental psychology, specifically Wundtian structural psychology.[12] Wundtian psychology depended upon introspective analysis under an analytic set, in contrast to the phenomenological set, say, of Brentano's act psychology. The introspective analysis of classical psychology required considerable training, responsibility, and experience on the part of a psychologist if he were to engage in it successfully. One, indeed, had to have a "feel" for it —gained only after much practice. Moreover, only "experts" in the use of introspective techniques clearly understood all their aspects and nuances. But it does not follow from any of this that such an expert did not know what he was doing or *that someone else who would go through all the prerequisites of training, practice, etc., would not get the same results.* In fact, structural psychologists on most issues had a high degree of agreement.

To be sure, one might argue against the conclusion in the following way. Classical psychology foundered on the image-thought controversy, a controversy over an untestable concept. May we not expect psychoanalysis to founder for the same reason? A closer look at historical facts suggests that this reply will not do. Classical psychologists wondered if "thought contents" always occur within "mental images." Some of them, on introspective analysis, always discovered a mental image present and operative in their thought processes; others did not. The latter, then, insisted that some thought, at any rate, is imageless.[13] The former, however, replied, not too graciously, that an image is always there if one is skillful enough in introspective analysis to discover it! Psychology, it seemed, had come upon evil times; the results achieved seemed to depend upon who did the analyzing. Now, of course, one or several such untestable notions, whether in classical psychology or psychoanalysis, would be neither sufficient reason for dismissing a science nor an adequate explanation of its demise if it did disappear. In fact, the demise of classical psychology was not caused by any untestable concepts or techniques; it died because research interest shifted from a desire to compile syndromatic-like inventories of consciousness to a desire to discover process-like explanations of behavior. Psychoanalysis, thus, couldn't fade away—desirably or not—on the same grounds classical psychology did, because it *is* a process-like series of explanations, and the only one we have, in the psychology of personality.

In addition to attacking the notion of Oedipus complex as untestable, philosophers have criticized many other genetic, structural, and theoretical concepts of psychoanalysis on the same ground (although one psychoanalyst points out in an *ad hominem* sort of way that it is no accident that philosophers are preoccupied with the Oedipus concept![14]). Counter-wish-fulfillment dreams, resistance to the analyst's interpretation, and unconscious hostility are just a few of the concepts which have come under fire. Philosophers have argued that all of them are immune to disconfirmation. Freud says all dreams are wish fulfillments. If a patient has a dream unconnected with any wish, does this count as disconfirmation? Not necessarily, the analyst replies, because the dream may fulfill the wish to produce a dream which does not fulfill a wish.[15] If a patient agrees with his analyst's interpretation, this response is taken as confirming its truth; but if he disagrees with the interpretation, this response is taken as a resistance to the true interpretation for unconscious causes.[16] Or, let us consider in detail the case of 'unconscious hostility.' (Everything said in this context holds for all three concepts and many more.) Suppose an analyst says a patient has an unconscious hostility toward his father.[17] What sort of findings would falsify this hypothesis? Supposedly if we observe that the patient acts with affection and solicitude toward his father. The analyst might deny that this evidence falsified his hypothesis, for the solicitude may be excessive and thus fit into the analytic hypothesis. Yet he is not, after all, protecting his hypothesis from disconfirmation altogether. If the solicitude is moderate and not excessive *this* fact would constitute genuine counter-evidence. Moreover, one might argue, this criticism is oversimplified since the hypothesis is only confirmed or disconfirmed by referring to a large range of facts. The hypothesis can be shown to be acceptable or not, only by referring to this total evidence. Certainly if a person, for example, does not tend to suppress and repress anger, never has dreams in which violence is directed at his father, never makes slips of the tongue which suggest abuse of his

77

father, never "accidentally" breaks his father's belongings, etc., then the hypothesis of unconscious hostility toward his father is rejected. On the other hand, ". . . if there are a fairly large number of affirmative answers, then the hypothesis tends to be highly confirmed."[18]

What troubles some people in this sort of answer is this: to be sure, there are a number of facts relevant to the unconscious hostility hypothesis, and they are interrelated by analytic hypotheses, but can any of them be *predicted?* If X has dreams in which violence occurs toward an object X associates with his father, if X makes a *faux pas* which is associated with abuse of his father, and if X "accidentally" breaks his father's possessions, can we predict, say, that X will generally avoid the expression of conscious anger and will not feel conscious anger in situations which would ordinarily arouse it? Or from all the rest of the relevant facts can we predict X will "accidentally" break his father's possessions? In short, can we find any reliable response-response law which allows us to predict one behavioral response from another or a behavioral response from some childhood experience? Some writers would answer all of these questions negatively and thus condemn psychoanalysis as hopelessly vague and untestable and, hence, meaningless or pointless. Psychoanalysts "explain" after the fact by interpreting analytic factors in a way which yields the observed result, but they cannot use these factors in a precise way to predict the result. Since the psychoanalyst thus always plays the role of Epimetheus his hypotheses are genuinely untestable and of doubtful worth. However, it does not follow that if a hypothesis cannot predict it is thereby not testable and, in fact, not a warrantable knowledge claim. Many sociological explanations, most historical and biographical ones, and all natural selection explanations in biology are of this *post facto* sort. A person could not possibly have predicted, say, George W. Curtis' bolting the Republican party in 1880. It is true, he hated the spoils system and Blaine stood for it, but, after all, Curtis was a staunch Republican and wasn't he a member of the nominating convention and thus bound to accept its choice? The situation is complex; many factors enter in. Which is strongest; how do they relate to each other? These questions could not be answered until the event had occurred. Then we know his contempt for the spoils system is the strongest motivation in his political decisions. Yet certainly his contempt for the spoils system *explains* why he bolted the Republican party even though one could not have *predicted* he would act in this way. Simply because a hypothesis or explanation could not have functioned as a prediction it does not follow that it is "untestable" or even that it is not a good warrantable knowledge claim. Indeed, in this historical case it is. But why cannot psychoanalytical propositions, too, be explanatory, and thus perfectly meaningful and even true, even though not predictive? Perhaps they are not meaningful and true but nothing in the present criticism tends in the slightest to establish this point, and without this point the criticism collapses. To be sure, if a series of propositions claiming to be scientific cannot predict anything they are certainly robbed of one of the best ways of being tested and perhaps confirmed, but they are not robbed thereby of meaningfulness and even confirmation. Or if they are, no one has shown why. Least of all in the present context. The whole point is simply taken for granted. Finally, this criticism assumes that psychoanalytic propositions are not predictive, but this assumption is far from obvious. Analysts think they predict a great deal. This point, however, takes us into the next section. And we are ready to proceed to it since none of the claims that psychoanalysis is in principle unconfirmable seems to be defensible.

B. ARE PSYCHOANALYTIC PROPOSITIONS UNCONFIRMED?

Most philosophers of science agree that psychoanalytical propositions are not confirmed. The claim here is this: while the propositions are testable and have some empirical meaning, we cannot tell whether or not what they assert is true. They simply have not been confirmed. I shall examine the major evidence for this conclusion in some detail and see what can be said against it.

The psychoanalytic interview is the method by which analysts arrive at their hypotheses and *by which they test them also*. In the interview, the analyst tries to discover the unfulfilled but repressed "wish" of early childhood, usually sexual in nature, which is causally effective, on the level of the unconscious, in producing neurotic conflict. The analyst tries to discover the nature of the wish and the neurotic conflict by interpreting the "latent meaning" of the patient's free associations, slips of tongue, and dream contents. Consequently, as Nagel says,[19] the crucial question is this: how do we confirm or validate such interpretations? Each "interpretation," one might say, is an analytical hypothesis; but the question is still this, how is it established as valid? Psychoanalysts, according to their philosophical critics,[20] would accept an interpretation as correct if it (1) is compatible with all things disclosed by the patient in the interview; (2) predicts specific consequences; (3) is an instance of a general law; and (4) is accepted by the patient as a true interpretation and has therapeutic consequences for him. However, the critics continue, analytical interpretations by and large are not confirmed: either a criterion is inadequate or else the interpretations fail to meet the criteria. (1) is an inadequate criterion. Simply because an interpretation is *compatible* with the facts does not make it a true explanation of them. The Ptolemaic hypothesis in a way was compatible with the facts but it turned out to be false even so. Moreover, it is a notorious fact that analysts themselves can give plausible alternative interpretations which are compatible with the same facts; but which, then, is the true one?

(2), (3), and (4) are adequate criteria but analytical interpretations do not really meet them in a significant way.

(2) What sort of predictions can the analyst make from his interpretation? Various reactions of the patient, apparently. The analyst, e.g., predicts the acceptance of an interpretation given and of sudden insight combined with the production of confirmatory details, such as the subject's recall of past experiences which he had been previously unable to remember, or substitute reactions of a wide variety. However, the critics say, this answer will not do. After all, the interpretation *itself* does not predict its own acceptance by the subject or an "insight" on his part. And it is difficult to see how the *acceptance* of an interpretation could ever be significant confirming evidence when it is a notorious fact that people often accept things for the wrong reasons. Moreover, the acceptance of an interpretation could not count as confirming evidence unless there is some information about negative cases. We need to know, after all, the percentage of cases in which similar subjects reject similar interpretations of their behavior, or the number of cases in which similar subjects do not have their behavior "illuminated" by such interpretations. Moreover, the 'recall of confirmatory details' is not without difficulty. It may well be that recall occurred simply from the overall prodding of the subject's memory during the interview rather than from the specific content of the analyst's interpretation. Furthermore, how do we know the object of recall—say a traumatic experience—genuinely occurred in the way remembered? When an adult recalls childhood events, he may well erroneously color

them in terms of his later experience, including that of the psychoanalytic interview itself.[21]

Finally, the analyst often has difficulty in making any objective prediction at all from his interpretations because he disturbs the interview situation by his own method of investigation. While the analyst is supposedly a passive hearer of his subject's "free-associations," as a matter of fact he often·directs their course.[22] The point can be made ironically by saying a patient seems to dream in the dialect of whatever psychoanalyst happens to be treating him![23]

According to (3) an interpretation is confirmed if it is an instance of a general law. The analyst believes that one can distinguish various types of neurotic personality and that each type is in fact related to a fairly distinct kind of childhood traumatic experience. Thus, when the analyst discovers by means of the interview to which type his patient belongs, his interpretation is supported by an appeal to the corresponding law.[24] But, the argument goes, there is something queer about these alleged psychoanalytic laws. First, it is unclear whether a regularity holds between neurotic symptoms and what actually happened to a patient in childhood, or between the symptoms and what the patient *says* happened to him in childhood. The second kind of regularity, of course, would be utterly unreliable itself and thus would not lend evidential value to any specific interpretation. But the first kind of regularity is not acceptable either unless there is something known again about negative cases. As Nagel points out, it may well be the case that children with such-and-such traumatic experience develop into certain kinds of neurotic adults. But such evidence is valueless unless it can also be established that *normal* adults have not undergone the same sort of childhood experiences. "In short, data must be analysed so as to make possible comparisons on the basis of some *control* group, if they are to constitute cogent evidence for a causal inference."[25]

According to (4), an interpretation is confirmed if it is accepted by the patient and has a therapeutic effect on him. Or better, there is some sort of confirmation bestowed on analytic interpretations in general if they *tend* usually to have therapeutic effects. To be sure, therapeutic success is not *identical* with confirmation of analytic theory but it certainly is *a part of* the confirming procedure. But, the criticism goes, even successful therapy will not help confirm analytical propositions. Granted that analysis is followed by therapeutic success, it does not follow that this success was caused by analysis. It might have been the result of suggestion, or simply the result of talking out a problem with a sympathetic listener.[26] Moreover, success often occurs without psychoanalytic techniques. General practitioners apparently have the same ratio of successful therapy as analysts do.

The upshot of this discussion is this: granted that the analyst's interpretations are *confirmable*—that is, they have some empirical content, however vague—nevertheless these interpretations, since they do not successfully meet the analyst's own four criteria of confirmation, must be taken as *not confirmed*.

I am not quite convinced by this critique of psychoanalysis and will suggest in some detail what I take to be an adequate reply to it. (1) No analyst would ever dream of saying that the compatibility of his theory with clinical facts is a sufficient validation of them; this condition, of course, is simply an obvious necessary one. But the analyst believes—and I think rightly so—that this necessary condition is only met by analytical theory and thus, whether or not it yields detailed predictions, analytical theory has a good degree of antecedent probability clinging to it. True, Copernican theory was not verified simply because it was compatible with all the facts; the Ptolemaic theory was also, but it turned out to be false. The important point is this: in this case there are significant alternatives while psychoanalytic theory is the *only* hypothesis that knits together widely divergent facts about personality development and neurotic behavior. This fact makes the analyst believe that the compatability of his theory with the facts gives his theory an antecedent probability; but he would not dream of claiming this compatability alone sufficed to establish the theory. Analysts themselves, it is true, often give plausible alternative interpretations of the same clinical facts, but what does this prove? It proves that they disagree about what analytic hypotheses to apply to a specific case for explanatory purposes; it does not show disagreement over the basic hypotheses. This same sort of disagreement occurs in any "geophysical" type science where laws discovered under artificially controlled conditions are used to explain some concrete, unrepeatable course of events.[27] The conflicting interpretations of historical, geological, meteorological, archaeological, and anthropological data are notorious, yet order gradually emerges from the chaos. And certainly no one would think of using the simple fact of conflicting interpretations of specific data to throw doubt on the basic principles—often quite exact—used in these intellectual enterprises. So why should the fact of conflicting interpretations throw complete doubt on analytic principles? To be sure, analysts of different "schools" hold *different basic hypotheses*, although they accept many in common too, far more, in fact, than non-analysts would ever suspect from reading philosophical treatises on psychoanalysis. The disagreement usually occurs on the level of theoretical terms and the ones which are held in common are generally genetic and structural hypotheses. Such hypotheses as these, then, would still retain their antecedent probability. (Moreover, one must not accept every *prima facie* conflict as a genuine one, and one must not accept every conflict as a significant one either. Some people still believe the earth is flat but this conflict does not upset geographers! The same can be said for the conflicts generated by "fringe" psychoanalysts—the literary, philosophical, and amateur dabblers in analytic theories. Their activity does not upset the working analyst.)

Psychoanalytic Propositions

(2) One must be very careful in saying what it is the analyst thinks he *predicts*. The analyst would readily agree that he does not predict as part of an analytical interpretation the patient's acceptance of it. Indeed, in some cases the interpretation, even though probably correct, is resisted by the patient. Then the analyst has the job of explaining this resistance. (Note well that the analyst does not explain every rejection of an interpretation in terms of the subject's resistance. To do so would indeed render such an interpretation untestable. Whether or not the analyst says the patient is resisting depends on the way the patient rejects the interpretation—out of hand and with considerable force or quietly and after consideration.[28]) But even though the acceptance of an interpretation is not predicted and often indeed is not accepted, does not the fact of acceptance offer support of some kind when it does occur? I think it does but only if the acceptance of the interpretation leads to uncovering forgotten events of childhood—for the existence of which there is some antecedent likelihood (knowledge of parental characteristics, environment, etc.), objective corroboration (documents, other people's memories, etc.), or lawful corroboration (exemplifying one of the genetic laws connecting a neurotic syndrome with specific childhood experiences). This sort of corroborating evidence, not really prediction in any sense at all, occurs in abundance in the clinical records. When it does not occur, then clearly the "memory" of a childhood experience does not count as confirming evidence for

the interpretation. (Certainly the analyst is fully aware of the treachery of his patient's "memory" in more ways than one! Freud saw more clearly than philosophical critics that some patients could not distinguish their fantasies from what actually happened.[29] Or through transference the patient's unconscious may submissively corroborate, through fantasies, dreams, and slips of tongue, a wrong interpretation. Or he may defiantly corroborate an interpretation *because* it is wrong! Obviously no analyst accepts such "memories" following the acceptance of an interpretation as confirming evidence—which, of course, is just another way of saying he does not take a remembered incident as confirming evidence unless it is corroborated.)

Furthermore the point about negative cases breaks down since comparable patients may well react differently to the same interpretation—some accepting and some resisting it. Then the analyst's job is to explain the resistance. (Certainly "comparable" cases cannot mean "identical cases." No analyst ever expects two patients to have identical syndromes and past experience! But if 'comparable' does not mean 'identical,' then two comparable patients may well respond quite differently to an interpretation, one accepting and one resisting it.)

Finally, it is true that the analyst *does* disturb the phenomenon under investigation but he is utterly aware of this as a part of his own theory. He has numerous corrective devices, including analytical knowledge of himself, and these devices have succeeded even in revealing observational error in other, more experimental branches of psychology.[30] Moreover, that some objectivity of prediction *is* as a matter of fact possible is revealed by the fact that a supervising analyst makes innumerable correct predictions about the development of a case and the appearance of certain specific material simply by using the record of a patient whom he has not even seen![31]

I have emphasized that the acceptance of an interpretation while it may be, under certain conditions, confirming evidence is not *predicted* by the analyst. What sort of thing, then, does he predict, if anything, and how do these predictions generally turn out? Do they tend to confirm or disconfirm analytical hypotheses?

Analysts using their genetic and structural hypotheses constantly predict in the following way. When they find some trait exhibited they can predict numerous different manifestations of it as well as closely allied traits and their resultant behavior. They also postdict the existence of certain childhood experiences associated with this syndrome of traits. Consider the following example cited by Jacob Arlow.[32] To the question "How long have you been married?" one patient replied, "Sixteen months, three weeks." From the overly precise nature of the response, Arlow assumed the existence of obsessional and compulsive traits. From this hypothesis he "predicted" the existence of a cluster of mental traits all of which, he discovered, did exist: the patient had a passion for accumulating money and keeping minutely detailed financial records; he was overly neat about his clothes, tidy in his habits; orderly, rigorously punctual, careful in meeting obligations, etc. Moreover, Arlow related this syndrome to a specific type of childhood experience in bowel training and interest in excrement, and again this "prediction" (postdiction) was verified. Such predictions, he concludes, occur hundreds of times in clinical cases—indeed they occur constantly —and hence cannot be simply the result of guesswork or intuition. Moreover, analysts constantly predict the kind of dream a patient is going to have, the kind of feelings he will manifest under specified conditions, and the kind of material he will produce,[33] and these predictions frequently hold true in fact.

Needless to say, there have been several criticisms of the significance and reliability of these psychoanalytical predictions. The negative case argument again: Even though these predictions are frequently true they do not significantly confirm an interpretation unless we know the frequency with which such predictions are incorrect.[34] But again this criticism will not do. Certainly no one would deny that these predictions often break down and this disconfirms the interpretation; hence the analyst has to *change* his interpretation. But if this is so, then it also follows that correct predictions tend to *confirm* a given interpretation.

Another criticism is this: analytical predictions are never precise, only approximative and often vague; thus they do not count much in the way of confirmation. The analyst may predict either overtly aggressive behavior or overly concerned behavior but cannot predict which specific one it will be. He may predict the form of a dream but not the content; he may predict types of behavior associated with traits but not specific acts, etc. Several replies to this criticism are possible. First, in some cases the predictions are, in fact, quite precise; these occur in the cases of uninformed children, naïve psychotics, and subjects under hypnosis. But it is true that in other cases the predictions may be only approximative and not at all precise. What then? One might say simply, psychoanalysis is only a protoscience; when its hypotheses are made more precise, its predictions will become more precise.[35] However this reply, while acceptable in a way, does not go to the heart of the matter. The best reason, I believe, for explaining why specific predictions are not always possible in ordinary neurotic cases is that learning and reasoning processes subsequent to childhood experiences require modification of the analytic hypotheses in ways not yet determined. Thus we need not simply greater precision of *analytic* hypotheses but also greater precision of learning hypotheses and greater precision in stating the ways in which they are both involved in interrelated ways in the explanation of ordinary neurotic cases. When we achieve this knowledge, then we will achieve more precise and not only approximative predictions in such cases. But the final point is this: although we cannot predict precisely the concrete course of a neurotic's life because we do not know how childhood and later experience mingle together to produce such a result, nevertheless it does not follow that our approximative and imprecise predictions fail to bestow *any* confirmation on analytic interpretations. Certainly if the approximative predictions turned out consistently to be wrong, this fact would go far to *disconfirm* the interpretations. Hence successful approximative predictions must tend to *confirm* them.

(3) Now we turn from criticisms of analytic interpretations to criticisms of the basic genetic and structural laws of psychoanalysis. From our discussion thus far it should be clear that these laws hold between neurotic symptoms and what actually happened to a patient in childhood, not between the symptoms and what the patient *says* happened to him in childhood. The laws themselves have been generalized from specific interview situations, and the analyst has of course constantly been on guard against accepting at face value what the patients report. As we have seen, patients often cannot distinguish betwen fantasy and fact and through identification erroneously recall incidents. Without antecedent probability and objective corroboration in the sense specified in the classic case histories, the laws themselves would never have come into being. Then, the laws themselves add their own confirming weight to subsequent cases where objective corroboration may be impossible to attain. To be sure, one would like always to get direct corroborating evidence—this would be the strongest sort of confirmation; but in the absence

of this, one still has *some* confirming evidence in the apparent applicability of a genetic or structural law.

But the negative cases point arises again for genetic and structural laws. We need a *control group* to see that there is not a significant percentage of men who undergo certain traumatic childhood experiences but nevertheless develop into reasonably normal adults before the fact that many men do have these experiences associated with later neurotic symptoms becomes a reliable law. At this point, the negative case argument must be taken seriously. It would be desirable, indeed, to have this information. Unhappily we are not likely to get it with the analytical movement isolated from the research advantages of academic institutions. It is, in fact, a good analytic question why most directors of such institutions resist incorporating any element of the movement in their offerings. Certainly as long as analysis occurs under the conditions it does—strictly as a medical enterprise with therapy as the immediate goal—we are not likely to get the statistical information about negative cases which is desired. But let us assume we have such information and that, as a matter of fact, there are numerous negative cases. *It still would not follow that childhood experiences were not the causes of the neurotic symptoms when they do occur.* Clearly experience subsequent to the early trauma effectively modifies results in some cases and not in others. The way such experience modifies the operation of analytic principles is the information we so desperately need to make the analytical principles *more* predictive and reliable. Again, this sort of knowledge is not likely to be forthcoming with the present status and restricted operation of analytical endeavor.

(4) Psychoanalysts themselves, as a matter of fact, generally depreciate the value of therapeutic success as confirming evidence for an interpretation.[36] Admittedly therapeutic success often occurs without analysis and hence its occurrence with analysis does not necessarily confirm an interpretation. But the analyst would point out, I believe, that according to analytical theory there is an *explanation* of his therapeutic success while this is not so with the success of the general practitioner. On the other hand, it is also true that therapeutic success sometimes does not result from using analytic techniques. Yet this fact need not be damaging since the analyst may have an acceptable explanation of a patient's resistance to a correct interpretation. But the gravest difficulty is this: even if success *does* follow analysis, how do we know it was the content of the interpretation that produced it? Perhaps it occurred simply from talking out a problem with a sympathetic friend, etc. To be sure, the analyst sometimes can explain under what conditions such "talking" has therapeutic effects and when not; but he realizes this reply is not a complete answer to the criticism. In any case, the analyst while making these various retorts for the purpose of clarification would agree that therapeutic success does not confirm his interpretations very much. But successful therapy is indirectly im-

portant. If he *never* had any success this would count heavily against his whole system of hypotheses!

The upshot of this long discussion is this: critics are not successful in showing that analytical hypotheses are simply *not confirmed*. True, they are not as well confirmed as some other scientific theories, but they do not lack confirmation altogether. They are, in my mind, sufficiently confirmed to make psychoanalysis a perfectly respectable proto-science.

C. METAPSYCHOLOGY

Psychoanalysts use the concept of metapsychology to refer to the mental entities "beyond" conscious experience, namely, the unconscious motives, wishes, *et al.*, which are causally efficacious in producing neurotic symptoms. They sometimes use the concept more specifically to refer to "the most general assumptions of analysis on the most abstract level of theory."[37] Thus 'metapsychology' refers to the "substructures" of personality, the ego, id, and superego. In either of these senses philosophers of science have been quite critical of analytic metapsychology. The criticism usually takes two forms: (1) The notion of unconscious motives and wishes as *existing entities* which *cause* slips of tongue, dream contents, *et al.*, seems ontologically odd to the point of meaninglessness. The same is true for the alleged struggles among these entities, characterized by the concepts of ego, id, and superego. (2) Moreover, if these notions are interpreted in a way which makes sense of them, namely as definitional intervening variables, then they do not have any explanatory value. They are merely convenient abbreviations and nothing can be deduced with their help which cannot already be deduced from genetic and structural hypotheses. This criticism was suggested as long ago as the early part of the century when Pierre Janet referred to Freudian metapsychological notions as *une façon de parler*.

I shall examine these criticisms in detail, see what the analyst says by way of reply, and draw my own conclusions. I will agree with the criticism about ontological oddity and claim too that the concepts must be interpreted as intervening variables. But I shall argue that the critics misrepresent the concept of intervening variable and that when it is correctly understood, the analyst no longer need object to this interpretation.

(1) Philosophers of science have charged that unconscious motives are like "ghosts in a machine."[38] Freud's theoretical mental apparatus, conceived as unobservable entities with causal powers, simply reduplicates on an alleged psychic level the (unknown) somatic mechanisms which carry the "traces" of early traumatic experiences. "Accordingly, though psychoanalysis explicitly proclaims the view that human behavior has its roots in the biophysical and biochemical organization of the body, it actually postulates a veritable 'ghost in the machine' that does work which a biologically oriented psychology might

be expected to assign to the body."[39] Psychoanalytical metapsychology is thus anthropomorphic, the protestations of the analyst to the contrary notwithstanding.

Psychoanalysts might answer in the following way. Physicists infer the existence of unobservable atomic entities from observed events; analysts in the same legitimate way infer the existence of unconscious mental causes from observed neurotic behavior.[40] Only a restrictive positivist or operationist would deny the ontological significance of such concepts. After all, how does a physicist operate? He observes, e.g., that low frequencies of vibration of a string are connected with low pitches and higher frequencies with higher pitches. Is pitch a monotonically increasing function of frequency of vibration? No doubt it is. But soon the physicist reaches a point where the vibrations that presumably accompany a pitch are no longer observable. Then, "assuming that the causes of the higher pitches are sufficiently *analogous* to the causes of the lower pitches to warrant description in terms of the same concepts 'vibration' and 'frequency of vibration,' "[41] he infers the existence of unobservable vibrations. But, the analyst continues, we follow precisely the same logical procedure.

> In psychoanalytic child therapy, for example, it is observed that a little boy exhibits just the sort of playing behavior that could be expected if he hated his father and sought to express this hatred through fiction, like painting a man and then splashing paint all over the picture. The boy fails to be aware of such

an evil emotion, so the analyst says that the emotion exists in unconscious, repressed form.[42]

But this answer will not do, philosophers reply, since the cases of unobserved vibrations and unobserved hates are quite different. The concept of unobserved vibrations is not ontologically queer since there is nothing about the meaning of vibrations which requires them to be seen. Thus in the phrases 'observable vibrations' and 'unobservable vibrations' the word vibration has the same meaning. But the case of 'conscious hate' and 'unconscious hate' is quite otherwise. To say "I hate X" implies, as part of its meaning, that I am aware of, or conscious of, hating X. Thus 'unconscious hate' is not a legitimate extension of the meaning of 'hate' but is a self-contradictory extension of the word. It is really discouraging to be told that you really hate someone but are unaware of it. It is like being told that you are thirsty but are not conscious of it. Anyone would insist that if he hated someone or were thirsty he would be the first one to know about it, not the analyst! True, the child may have had a traumatic childhood experience and this causes him, through a somatic trace, to act in subtly aggressive ways; but it is fatuous to say that he "really" hates his father although he does not know it. It is true that one can be *mistaken* about what he is introspectively aware of, but one cannot, in fact, be introspectively mistaken in the sense that he thought he did not hate his father but he was mistaken and really did.

We must distinguish between pure introspective awareness and such awarenesses plus a causal account of their genesis. I may say, e.g., that I hate X because he is an opportunist; but I may in fact be mistaken in my belief and really hate X because he has got ahead of me in salary and recognition. But in any case it is the causal analysis of why I hate X that is mistaken. The chance of being mistaken about hating X never arises since it is part of the meaning of hating X, like it is part of the meaning of being thirsty, that it is something we are aware of.

This sort of reply, it seems to me, effectively meets the analyst's reply to the philosopher's criticism and establishes once and for all the ontological untenability of the concept of unconscious entities which causally produce neurotic symptoms. But the analyst—sometimes, I suspect, even seeing the justice of the philosopher's criticism —still resists it. Why? The answer, I think, is this: the analyst believes if he relinquishes the notion of unconscious entities with causal powers, then he can only interpret 'unconscious motive,' *et al.*, and their "dynamic relationships" (ego, id, and superego) as intervening variables, in contrast to hypothetical constructs—which he is unwilling to do since he blindly accepts another of the philosopher's criticisms, namely, that intervening variables are merely convenient summaries or definitions and have no explanatory value.[43] Since the analyst believes his concepts *do* have explanatory value he believes he must reject the intervening variable interpretation of them and hold that they are hypothetical constructs. Hence he clings doggedly to his odd ontology. In the next section I shall claim that this interpretation of intervening variables is mistaken, that they do have explanatory value, and hence that the analyst need not desperately cling to his odd ontology in order to maintain the explanatory power of his metapsychological concepts.

(2) It is well known that the concept of intervening variable has long been used in psychology to refer to unobservable concepts "intervening" between observable stimulus and response events and explicitly defined by them.[44] In his learning theory, Hull, you recall, explicitly defines 'excitatory potential' as a function of 'habit strength' and 'drive'—$S^ER = f(S^HR \times D)$—and explicitly defines S^HR and D as functions of observable stimulus-response events. This terminology has spread throughout psychology, and 'intervening variable' has come to mean any non-model theoretical term in any area of psychology. Some analysts, in order to avoid the previous criticisms of ontological oddity, have wanted to interpret their own theoretical concepts like ego, id, and superego as intervening variables, and thus not referring to any entities with causal powers, but they have been deterred from doing so because they uncritically accepted the following interpretation of 'intervening variable.'

According to Meehl and MacCorquodale,[45] intervening variables are mere abbreviations and in principle eliminable. These terms, since they are only convenient summaries of thought and have no "excess meaning," are not helpful in deductively elaborating the hypotheses in which they occur. They distinguish from such variables what they call "hypothetical constructs." These "constructs" are not mere definitions but refer to actual entities in some model theory. Since they occur in a model theory they have the "excess meaning" which makes it possible to elaborate deductively the hypotheses in which they occur. However, the analyst need not be deterred from interpreting his own theoretical concepts as intervening variables instead of ontologically odd hypothetical constructs since this view of Meehl and MacCorquodale is clearly mistaken. Consider the notion of excess meaning. To be sure, the terms and hypotheses of any model theory must have "excess meaning" in the sense that it gives rise to deductive consequences other than the ones the theory was designed explicitly to explain. The kinetic theory of gases allows for the deductive development of consequences about gas behavior which were not anticipated by thermodynamic theory alone. But, of course, *the same can be said of any non-model theory, too.* Anything worthy of the name theory in science, in fact, has "excess meaning" in this sense. The essence of any non-model theory is twofold. First, fundamental laws describe the interaction of a limited number of variables in what is therefore called an elementary situation. Second, a composition rule, itself experimentally discovered, states how to form the laws of a complex situation in which many variables interact by conceptually decomposing it into elementary situations and reapplying a fundamental law to the parts. But intervening variables function in precisely the same way; they act as part of a non-model theory which predicts and explains behavior different from that on which they were based and thus have "excess meaning." Spence, as we have seen,[46] uses the concepts of cumulative strengthening of $S^H R$ (fundamental law of an elementary situation) and generalization (composition-like rule) to derive deductively certain transposition phenomena (which were not involved in the formulation of the laws). The derivation may not hold, as seems likely now, but this fact could not have been discovered unless the concept operated in a genuine theory with excess meaning. Moreover, Hull's concept of afferent neural interaction (despite its physiological sound) is again an intervening variable which has the status of a composition principle. The theoretical concepts of psychoanalysis too, conceived as intervening variables, can just as well have similar "excess meaning" in the sense of having explanatory power—at any rate, there is nothing in the notion of intervening variable that prevents them from having it. I am not claiming that psychoanalysis, in fact, does have fundamental laws and composition-like rules, but I am saying that it logically *can* have them while still interpreting ego, id, and superego as intervening variables. Indeed, the analyst may feel he does not have explanatory principles in these precise senses but still feel that his concepts genuinely have *some* explanatory value. This view, also, of course, is compatible with interpreting his theoretical concepts as intervening variables. The final conclusion, then, is this: if the analyst wishes to avoid odd ontological commitments by interpreting his theoretical concepts as intervening variables he is perfectly free to do so without thereby admitting that they have no explanatory function. I hope that the realization of this logical fact will convince more analysts to leave the dubious ground of "metaphysical science" and consolidate instead into a sensible whole their fascinating genetic and structural hypotheses with a scientific metapsychology.

FIVE

Psychoanalysis and Responsibility

I SHALL BEGIN with a rather lengthy statement of the traditional problem of determinism and moral responsibility in order to show clearly how psychoanalysis figures in its dialectical development. I shall argue, however, that psychoanalysis supports neither "determinism" nor "free-will," as different writers have urged; indeed I will contend that it is really irrelevant to this philosophical problem and that efforts to show its relevance tend to obscure the real import of psychoanalysis for moral philosophy. Finally I shall spend a good part of the chapter analysing what I take to be this real import.

A. THE DETERMINISM ISSUE

The problem concerning determinism and moral responsibility arises in the following way. Modern science seems to provide a notion of cause, quite distinct from Aristotle's final cause, which implies that if something is caused then it could not be other than it is. If I have a genuine instance of a cause (that is, if I am not mistaken), then a certain effect *must* occur. It could not be otherwise, for if something else *could* occur then the cause is still unknown. If the concepts of cause and determinism applied only to physical objects there would be no trouble, but these concepts also apply to human behavior and here the perplexities begin to arise. If human behavior, too, is caused or determined, then *it* could not be other than it is. But moral judgments of behavior, on the other hand, are meaningful only if it *is* possible for behavior to be other than it is. If I say, "You ought not to beat your wife," I presume, if this judgment is to be sensible, that you could either beat or not beat her, that you chose the former course, and that I am morally condemning you for making the wrong choice. Apparently, then, science and moral philosophy come into headlong conflict. If human behavior is caused, then it could not be other than it is; if human behavior is morally judgeable, then it could have been other than it is. Hence, either human behavior is not caused, or else it is not morally responsible. Or, putting the point positively, either human behavior is caused, or it is morally responsible—but not both.

This traditional way of formulating the problem of determinism and moral responsibility is still accepted by many scientists and philosophers, although, as you may guess, it has serious flaws. Accepting this formulation, a person apparently has only two choices: he may either say that behavior is morally judgeable so not caused, in which case he is an "indeterminist," or he may say that behavior is caused so not morally judgeable, in which case he is a "determinist." Indeterminists do not in fact generally hold that all human behavior is uncaused; on the contrary, psychology, sociology, and all the other human sciences tell us a great deal about what causes personality traits, group behavior, and so on. Nevertheless, in choice situations there is, finally, a decision of will, freely made, for which the moral agent is responsible and, hence, judgeable.

However, there seems to be a difficulty with this claim. If the indeterminist strictly means that choices are not caused at all then he must admit that the agent who acted one way under certain conditions may subsequently act in an entirely different way under the same conditions, even though he himself has not changed at all. But this way out of the deterministic dilemma is no help, for it does not introduce moral responsibility but simply straightforward caprice. Moral responsibility demands the presence of something positive, not simply the absence of determinism.

Determinism, on the other hand, seems equally as untenable as indeterminism. There are a number of reasons why this is so, but the simplest and most convincing is that determinism is self-destructive. If determinism were correct, "then our thoughts and the conclusions to which they lead would in every last detail be conditioned by factors which wholly antedated the thinking processes themselves. Evaluation or discrimination between better and worse, true and false, would be inexplicable and futile. Hence no rational defense of determinism would be possible. In short, if determinism is true, it is undemonstrable."[1]*

Since there is something artificial and untenable about both indeterminism and determinism, philosophers have come to suspect that the very formulation of the determinism issue which spawned them is confused. They have suggested that perhaps a further analysis of 'cause' and 'determinism' will dispel the whole problem with its strained alternatives. After all, behavior can be caused or determined in two radically different ways. Heredity and early environment are "external causes" over which we had no control but which nevertheless made us, in some sense, the way we are. To the extent that these factors control behavior—"by mechanisms behind the scenes"—a person indeed is not "free" and morally responsible. On the other hand, reason, imagination, and insight, along with a host of other subtle factors, are "internal causes" over which I have control and which quite obviously also

* For the notes to Chapter 5 see pages 138-43.

determine my behavior. To the extent that these factors control behavior, a person is indeed morally responsible. In fact, this notion of a reasonable being who can consider the consequences of his acts, unlike that of 'uncaused choice,' is the ordinary meaning of 'morally responsible.' Therefore, according to the present argument, while it is true that all behavior is caused, nevertheless some behavior is morally responsible, namely, that which is self-caused. This concept of self-cause can depend either on a complicated Kantian transcendental self or on a simple common-sense view that man is capable of acting on reasons rather than simply using them as rationalizations.

At this point in the dialectic of the determinism issue the cry has arisen that psychoanalysis shows that moral judgments are impossible or nonsense. According to this view, psychoanalysis annihilates the concept of self-cause, and thus this new way of salvaging moral responsibility comes to naught.[2] The psychoanalyst, after all, tells us that our behavior, including our so-called reasonable behavior, is really unconsciously determined and that conscious, reasonable life is merely a facade of rationalizations. "The unconscious is the master of every fate and the captain of every soul." However, it seems clear that this attempt to bolster determinism through psychoanalysis will not do. Psychoanalysts do not in fact usually claim that all *prima facie* reasonable behavior is unconsciously determined, for this view, of course, would deny that there are any objective or rational grounds for accepting the tenets of psychoanalysis itself—it would be self-destructive in the same way that traditional determinism is. The psychoanalyst's point is, rather, that much less behavior than anyone dreamed possible is free or responsible in the ordinary sense that it is consciously and reasonably shaped. However, this point is clearly irrelevant to the traditional determinism puzzle; for this puzzle simply disappears with the acceptance of the qualified statement, 'Most behavior is not free' or 'Very little behavior is free.' The puzzle only arises if all behavior is said to be determined in a way which implies it could not have been otherwise.

Some philosophers, on the other hand, have argued that psychoanalysis, far from annihilating the common-sense concept of self-determinism, actually provides the very techniques for deciding when and how much self-determinism or "freedom" a person has.[3] The analyst's techniques establish what behavior is obsessive, non-obsessive but unconscious, and rational—and, consequently, the argument goes, these techniques establish what behavior is nonresponsible and what responsible. And, after all, the point and frequent result of therapy is to produce freedom and responsibility where it did not exist before. More generally, some writers[4] argue that psychoanalysis, far from destroying the possibility of freedom, re-emphasizes the distinction between "reasons for action" and "causes of action" in its own employment of the "reason" or "motive" model of explanation rather than the efficient cause model. The analyst sometimes is misled by his hydraulic metaphors into thinking he has found efficient causes but only the physiologist with his palpable neurons can find the efficient causes of mental phenomena.

The common strain in all these views is that psycho-analysis reinforces or even establishes common-sense self-determinism and so salvages the notion of moral responsibility. This type of argument, however, misses the heart of the determinist's puzzle. Its irrelevance to the core of the puzzle is pointed up by imagining how a determinist would reply to it. He would say that he knows perfectly well there are common-sense tests which one uses to show a person could have done otherwise (by showing that he has the ability, displayed on other occasions, to do the alternate type of act and was under no duress to do the act he did) and scientific tests which one applies for distinguishing obsessive, non-obsessive but unconscious, and rational behavior; so that it makes sense both commonsensically and scientifically to make the distinction between free and unfree, responsible and nonresponsible acts; but nevertheless what he wants is proof that even in allegedly free acts we are not, without knowing it, being determined by neurotic or normal unconscious motivation beyond the range of our most careful tests to detect. This problem is the philosophical core of the determinist's position, since self-determinism, whether idealistic or commonsensical, plus the existentialist insight (namely, that in normal or non-neurotic behavior the point is not that man *is* responsible but that he *becomes* responsible as the price of maturity, of no longer being a child, and thus that he does *accept* responsibility for the consequences of his personality and character even though he had no control over their formation), easily avoids the original dilemma of the determinist. The determinist's real puzzle is the isomorph of a number of other philosophical puzzles. Even though there are accepted techniques for distinguishing veridical and illusory perception, how can I prove, or (Descartes's evil genius?) how can I be sure, that the allegedly veridical ones are not illusory or hallucinatory beyond the range of the accepted techniques—a crucial step in the dialectic of the issue over our knowledge of the external world. From this paradigm of philosophical puzzles, which in cludes science in its scope, psychoanalysis clearly cannot rescue us.

To be sure, one might argue that the issue which the determinist raises is spurious and the proof he demands nonsensical. He might try to show that the determinist's use of "free" in "For all we know we are really never free" is self-contradictory because the ordinary sense of "freedom," which he is apparently using (for otherwise the word is vacuous because he does not specify another meaning), is defined by the kind of thing which is evidence for the term's exemplification. Or one may cast his lot with common sense on other grounds, namely, that a property and predicate are "meaningful" over and above the tests of presence or applicability. In either case, however, the dialectic of determinism has eventuated in the dialectic of meaningfulness, which obviously antedates, logically, any empirical findings. Consequently, whether the issue the determinist raises is real or spurious, psychoanalysis has nothing to do with solving or dissolving it.

In this problem, psychology does not have philosophical results but philosophy has psychological results. When one realizes the true nature of the determinist's position (demand) his original perplexity is attenuated. What I have in mind is this. If one believes that the determinist's demand has not been parried successfully, he will admit, nevertheless, if he is honest with himself, that as a result of the dialectical drift he does not worry about the issue in the way that he did originally. He worried that the determinist had shown his ordinary views on freedom to be wrong, but it turns out simply that he has not proved they are right. But this ubiquitous problem—How can I be sure what I naïvely think to be true really is so?—is the paradigm of philosophical puzzles, and is not peculiar to a moral context, is not dependent on it for its formation. So the original perplexity and worry loses its force and urgency. A paradoxical way of saying the same thing is that a person worries less about determinism because he has to worry about the same problem everywhere. I think one could defend the view that therapeutic and casuistic positivists frequently confuse the attenuation of a philosophical problem with its dissolution and that the obvious fact that there is at least one philosophical problem that cannot be attenuated reflects the existence of the unannounced meaning criterion of the philosophical therapists and casuists.

B. THE REAL IMPORT

There are numerous other ways in which psychoanalysis and morality get mixed together to the benefit of neither and the obscuration of the real import of the former for the latter; all that one can do is be alert to the danger and concentrate steadily on the real import, which is the view, long defended by most forensic psychiatrists, that neurotic behavior is nonresponsible. Some philosophers, along with the forensic psychiatrists, have defended this view; and the argument usually relied on is, roughly, the following: Neurotic behavior is nonresponsible because childhood neuroses cause adult neuroses, which, in turn, eventuate in criminal or queer behavior. But since a person has no control over the formation of his childhood neurosis, and no control over what follows inevitably from it, he cannot be held responsible for these consequences. The point of therapy, of course, is to make it possible for the neurotic to accept responsibility in the ordinary sense of the word; but *prior* to therapy, or where therapy has not occurred or is unsuccessful, the "malevolent" nature of the neurotic's unconscious makes him nonresponsible for his behavior. One must be careful, at this point, not to extend the claim of nonresponsibility to normal unconscious behavior because this extension brings in a host of additional issues and usually culminates in the old confusion of making the general determinist claim that one is nonresponsible because he had no control over the formation of his personality, to which claim the existentialist position is again applicable.

The juristic view of legal and moral responsibility, however, is far from hospitable to the psychiatrist's claim that neurotic behavior is nonresponsible; indeed the struggles in court between lawyer and psychiatrist even in the rare cases where the medical psychopathologist represents the court and not the plaintiff or defendant, have become notorious.

On the juristic view of the matter, a person is legally and presumably morally responsible if, or because, he is able, or has the capacity, "to tell the difference between right and wrong"; if, or because, he "knows the consequences, both legal and moral, of his act." This rule is the famous McNaghten Rule the jurist relies on, the legal definition of sanity and insanity; but it simply incorporates what is apparently obvious common sense. In criminal law this view is again reflected in the concept of *mens rea*. Jurists speak of the mental element in criminal liability (*mens rea*) and by this phrase they mean knowledge of consequences, foresight, intention, voluntariness, etc. One can disallow the presence of *mens rea*, or mitigate it, or simply defeat the allegation of responsibility, only if he can present defenses or exceptions like duress, provocation, infancy, or insanity. However, since the neurotic person meets the requirement of knowing consequences, etc., and is not under duress, or provoked, or insane, he cannot be judged otherwise by the court than as legally and morally responsible for his acts.

The McNaghten Rule, it should be noted at the outset, not only prevents the psychiatrist from making a case for the nonresponsibility of a neurotic individual but even makes it extremely difficult for him to establish the nonresponsibility of the psychotic. A person plans his own death; he murders another intending to get caught so he will be executed. The judge in the case, applying the McNaghten Rule, held the man clearly sane and responsible because he deliberately acted in terms of consequences![5] This consequence of the McNaghten Rule amounts to a *reductio ad absurdum* and clearly points up the psychological naïveté of the legalistic view; a naïveté which, as we shall see, is again reflected in the deterrence theory of punishment; but it remains to give direct reasons why this view is naïve, and to present counter-stimuli which may help carry the day over deep-seated fears and anxieties. The forensic psychiatrists, I believe, are more successful in these endeavors than philosophical interpreters of psychoanalysis because they do not rest content, the way the latter do, with establishing the nonresponsibility of neurotic behavior by using the previous argument about origins—although, to be sure, this argument is important. A number of remarks would be necessary for complete clarity but two fundamental ones must suffice for now.

1. The McNaghten type rule is psychologically unrealistic because it is possible to know the consequences of an act without having any feeling for them and thus without understanding them. The flattening or dulling of emotional tone, or its complete absence—"the failure to feel" —results from many severe psychopathological reactions, and it plays an important role in many different kinds of criminal personalities. Within these personality types, a person understands emotional life only in the way a blind man "understands" color; he may know things *about* it, what causes it, what effects it has, etc., but he does not *experience* it. Such a person is incapable of *feeling* the force and import 'of consequences; he is like a person in a dream state or under the influence of drugs. In short, his reason—in the sense of knowing what consequences will follow from certain acts—and his feeling tones have split apart or disintegrated, and psychological trouble is bound to start. Such a breakdown opens the door to aggression of all types. According to a noted forensic psychiatrist, "the considerable diminution or absence of emotion, or 'affect' as we say, is probably the most virulent phenomenon leading to the paralysis of moral judgment. . . ."[6]

Psychoanalysts have known and recognized this fact for a long time yet our legal system has no way of taking it into account. And the fact is so little known generally that the public completely mis-reads the nature of this sort of criminal. They assess his emotional indifference as moral indifference, callousness, incorrigibility, and depravity and thus they become prey to all sorts of feelings of counter-aggression and to an eventual vindictively motivated desire for retribution.[7] Who does not feel revulsion when a child's murderer asks for comic books to read in his cell because he is bored? But the crucial point, of course, is this: if such a criminal were capable of experiencing regret he would not have the diminution of affect that made his crime possible in the first place. Such a person is not a fit object of retribution because he is not responsible, and he is not responsible because he is incapable, through psychopathic causes, of adequate feeling tones for the consequences he "understood" would occur.

2. Rules of the McNaghten type are psychologically unrealistic and pernicious in their effects because (a) they depend on fragmentary criteria where understanding of the whole personality is needed and (b) they utilize formal, universally applicable criteria where individual analysis and insight is needed.

(a) In a case previously mentioned, a man murdered a youth because he wished to be apprehended and hanged. The judge in the case declared that since he knew the *consequences* of his act quite well, he knew the "nature and quality of the act," the usual terminology of McNaghten type rules, and was thus responsible for the act. He was hanged accordingly, before which, however, the prisoner happily expressed his appreciation! Cases like this one, some of which are more refined and accordingly less dramatic, more than formal analysis, make it abundantly clear that one cannot infer that another understands "the nature and quality of an act," where this means its moral import, because he manipulated it or used it in a utilitarian fashion, or because he reacted to it with any other isolated rational or emotional response. The only way to understand how a person construes "the nature and quality of an act" is in terms of the harmony of his total personality—particularly when it is the insane harmony of a pathological mind or the queer harmony of a neurotic one.

(b) Rules of the McNaghten type are, technically, nonvague; they either apply or do not apply to every individual; but the psychological facts are such that make this application wholly arbitrary and itself immoral. The analyst finds that each individual case is not simply different but unique; he needs to know the whole historical background of an individual case in order to "diagnose" psychosis, neurosis, etc., and whether and what therapy is applicable and might successfully rehabilitate. Psychiatry by its very nature cannot be formalized either as a clinical system or as a therapeutic method.

When a formalistic clinical attitude is assumed in psychiatry, the psychiatrist loses his usefulness as a healer; but strange as it may seem, he may gain in stature as a psychiatric expert. For if he feels that he can classify mental diseases with precision, and if he feels he can look upon the individual as the sum total of so many logical categories, and formal principles, he can fit himself and his opinions perfectly into the mold of the verbal metaphysics of certain aspects of the law.[8]

Such a formalistic psychiatrist, of which there are few, can, in short, do what the law demands of him in court, namely, apply rules of the McNaghten type. But for the rest of the psychiatrists this legal demand is untenable. This untenability arises, it is evident, because the psychiatrist is asked to determine the applicability of universal legal rules by psychological methods which not only do not accommodate these concepts but repudiate them.[9] The crucial point is that if law is to make judgments about responsibility which are themselves moral each case must be judged in terms of its specific circumstances, the statement of which the Qualified Forensic Psychiatrist is alone competent to make.[10]

Now we have come to the heart of the conflict between law and psychiatry. The law insists that the essence of a legal rule is its universal applicability and refuses, and no doubt will continue to refuse, to have its judgments of responsibility usurped by psychoanalysts even if their science were perfected more than it is. To make every case a special case, they point out, is legally impossible and would lead to legal nihilism. Better to gas or electrocute a neurotic here and there than to have the legal structure collapse. The psychiatrist, on the other hand, feels indignation over what he rightfully takes to be unjust executions. The only solution to this impasse, I strongly believe, is to take the psychiatrist out of court procedure entirely—

he neither applies McNaghten type rules nor gives technical testimony about the peculiarities of a given case in order to establish responsibility or its absence—abolish capital punishment, and allow the psychiatrist to work for the rehabilitation of neurotically motivated criminals during the period of their incarceration. It seems to me that only the abolition of capital punishment can resolve the conflict between law and psychiatric knowledge, and this resolution is the strongest and most completely unsentimental argument in favor of the abolition of capital punishment. In the incarceration period, moreover, the law must not simply "allow" psychiatrists to work at rehabilitation. The law must give status to the psychiatrist's role here and make a massive effort possible. The expense would be great, to be sure, but the expense of not doing it is far greater. Moreover, a first rate psychiatrist would be the first to admit that not all criminals can be rehabilitated because they are not all neurotically motivated. The professional criminal has an ethic all his own and is entirely beyond the pale of the analyst. The analyst's recognition of this fact should go a long way toward dispelling the hostility the jurist and penologist take to what they think is a sentimental and soft view, namely, that all criminals are neurotics and, poor things, could not help themselves.

C. THEORIES OF PUNISHMENT

The present interpretation of psychiatry implies a rehabilitative "theory of punishment," the relation of which to the rival Kantian and utilitarian "theories" is usually far from clear. This traditional three-way classification, unfortunately, has more than one basis of division. If behavior is responsible, then Kantian and utilitarian theories are the significant alternatives (there is no rehabilitation to be achieved in non-neurotic behavior); but if behavior is nonresponsible, then rehabilitation and utilitarianism are the significant alternatives. Utilitarianism, unlike Kantian penology, is still a meaningful theory if behavior is nonresponsible because on this view punishment, and the pain it inflicts, is not intrinsically good but instrumentally good in preventing further more intense and overall greater pain. Punishment (preferably simple incarceration) achieves this end, the utilitarian believes, by protecting society and acting as an example that is effective in deterring not only the criminal himself from further criminal acts but also the potential criminal from acting out his wishes. Kantian and utilitarian theories are mutually exclusive theories of punishment if behavior is responsible. Protection and deterrence, for Kant, could never be legitimate reasons for punishing a person, but only desirable consequences of punishment. (One can, of course, try to show that both deontological and teleological justifications of punishment are exaggerations of different strands of common sense and that each in its own way is a "good reason" for punishment.) However, rehabilitation and utilitarianism are not mutually exclusive theories of punishment if behavior is nonresponsible; they are related in oblique ways, competitive in a sense but not mutually exclusive. For the person who believes that neurotic behavior is nonresponsible, the clarification of this oblique, and generally misunderstood, relationship is a most urgent need of penological theory.

The difficulty with the utilitarian example or deterrence view, the analyst feels, is not in principle, but simply that it does not do what it is supposed to do. Pickpockets plied their trade most avidly at executions, when all eyes were focused on the gallows, at a time when robbery itself was punishable by death![11] And comparisons among states which do and do not have capital punishment seem to indicate a lack of deterrence by harsh example (although there is sensible counter-evidence on this point).[12] This deterrence view is psychologically naïve because it does not take into account the neurotic roots of much crime, which renders rational deterrence irrelevant. And without the techniques of rehabilitation which do take these factors into account, straightforward punishment simply does not deter the criminal from repeating his behavior. "What the law . . . fails to see is that punishment alone inflicted from outside produces only a hostile response, an intensification of hatred, and consequently the diminution of those healthy, auto-punitive, restorative trends in man, which alone make man capable of inwardly accepting punishment and making salutary use of it."[13]

Rehabilitation and utilitarian social protection are in one sense obviously compatible. During rehabilitation the criminal is incarcerated and society is duly protected. However it follows that if the rehabilitation process appears successful the patient then has the *right* to be returned to society. Psychiatrists, however, meet great public indignation at either the idea or fact of the criminal's return. Analysts explain the vehement hostility of this objection in the following way. People identify themselves with the criminal's own impulses (who has not had them?) and are tempted to give way to the impulses. They become anxious and feel guilty, and are quieted by a sudden, unconscious denial of similarity with the criminal—and so react with great destructive hostility toward him. These causal analyses are usually justified but nevertheless one must not overlook the rational basis which underlies non-hysterical objections to returning the criminal to society—namely, a lack of confidence in the success and permanency of psychoanalytic therapy. Since psychiatry and psychoanalysis are not developed and certain sciences and since psychiatrists and analysts differ much among themselves on theoretical concepts, one must proceed cautiously, for the protection of society, in the return of rehabilitated criminals. One psychiatrist, in meeting the criticism of theoretic disagreement, writes that after all there is considerable disagreement in all areas of science, including the most rigorous—witness the disagreements of Einstein, Heisenberg, and DeBroglie—without impugning their reliability.[14] This type of defense, completely ignoring levels of disagreement, can only heighten the critic's suspicion that analysts are not always clear about what they are doing!

There is, finally, a regrettable tendency among certain

forensic psychiatrists to sentimentalize their antagonism to utilitarian views in a position they call "individualistic humanism." They condemn "legal utilitarianism" because it submerges the rights of the individual in a metaphysical entity, society, etc. A utilitarian, of course, is astonished at *this* sort of criticism because his notion of the greatest good is individualistic to the core—the largest amount of mutually compatible experienced goods. The psychiatrist's quarrel with utilitarian morality is a matter of detail, not principle.

NOTES

CHAPTER ONE
Wholes and Parts

1. In W. D. Ellis, *A Source Book of Gestalt Psychology* (New York: The Humanities Press, 1950), p. 3.

2. *Ibid.,* p. 1.

3. *Ibid.,* p. 2.

4. *Ibid.*

5. Wolfgang Köhler, *The Place of Value in a World of Facts* (New York: Liveright, 1938), p. 205.

6. Cf. K. Grelling and P. Oppenheim, "Der Gestaltbegriff im Licht der neuen Logik," *Erkenntnis,* 7 (1938), pp. 211-24.

7. Ellis, *op. cit.,* p. 2.

8. *Ibid.,* p. 12.

9. *Ibid.,* pp. 71ff.

10. Köhler, *op. cit.,* pp. 194ff.

11. *Ibid.,* p. 201.

12. Ellis, *op. cit.,* p. 4.

13. *Ibid.,* p. 2.

14. Kurt Koffka, *Principles of Gestalt Psychology* (New York: Harcourt, Brace and Co., 1935), p. 57.

15. Wolfgang Köhler, *Dynamics in Psychology* (New York: Liveright, 1940), p. 55.

16. Köhler, *The Place of Value in a World of Facts*, p. 254.

17. Mr. Nicholas Rescher has questioned my use of "analytic" in this chapter. (Cf. his "Mr. Madden on Gestalt Theory," *Philosophy of Science*, 20, 1953.) I believe my use is entirely clear but nevertheless offer the following by way of answer to him:

Wertheimer and Köhler have both described the procedures of science and have in certain instances found them wanting. Wertheimer wrote that science characteristically attempts to "isolate the elements [of complexes], discover their laws, then reassemble them, . . ." and Köhler wrote that in " 'analytical' science . . . the properties of more complex extended facts are deduced from the properties of independent local elements." They claim, however, that certain areas of science cannot be adequately described in these analytical terms but must be described in Gestalt terms.

As an example of the "analytical science" to which they have reference I described the classical Newtonian problem of n bodies, showing how a composition rule allows for the prediction of behavior of a complex configuration from the reapplication of the computation rule to the elements of a complex. This description constituted the analytical language of my chapter. In this language I tried to formulate certain Gestalt concepts—dynamic interaction, the whole is greater than the sum of its parts, etc.—and thus show that they occur already in "analytical physics" and are not, as the Gestalters believe, unique to what they call the non-analytical parts of physics. I hope this clarifies the use of "analytical" in this chapter, for without an understanding of it I do not see how any part of it would be clear.

My chapter is also "analytical" in a broader, less special sense. The designation of "analysis" or "analytical" in contemporary philosophical literature is usually 'clarification of meaning rather than ascertainment of truth or falsity.' Analysts, while they differ much in what they say and do, claim that the philosopher does not pass on the truth of common sense or scientific statements, but rather that he gives a more or less elaborate explication of such philosophical concepts as cause, substance, true, etc., and the sentences in which they occur. In philosophy of science the analyst clarifies such scientific concepts as variable, law, emergence, etc., and the statements in which they occur but himself makes no truth claim using these concepts. This analytical function of clarification rather than verification is the criterion which distinguishes the logician of science from the scientist. My chapter is analytical in this broad sense of "analysis" because I tried to clarify those Gestalt concepts and the statements using them which are relevant to scientific description and explanation by showing that they are already meaningful in the area of "analytical" physics.

Mr. Rescher writes that the "analytical" view is apparently taken as involving the denial of the Gestalt thesis that some perceptual properties of wholes are emergent relative to physical properties of parts and known psychological theories. However, this anti-Gestalt thesis is an assertion about psychological facts; it is a matter of truth or falsity which requires scientific ascertainment and so is beyond the pale of a logical analysis, such as mine, which clarifies systems of scientific sentences on whose truth it does not pass, let alone anticipate. To show that the meanings of specified Gestalt phrases can be rendered in a language which describes computation and composition rules which have been established is not to make any truth claims about where computation or composition rules will be found or to deny the breakdown of composition rules—emergence—in physics, psychology, or any area. The same things can be said about Rescher's statement that it could be claimed that the Gestalt thesis of emergence which he sketched is itself analytical. So we see that neither Mr. Rescher's statement of the Gestalt thesis nor its denial is analytical in the senses of "analysis" that are relevant to my chapter.

Considering Mr. Rescher's statement of the Gestalt thesis and its denial as truth claims in psychology, I have several brief comments to make. It seems pointless for psychologists to make either claim on *a priori* grounds, unless heuristically, when the answer depends upon scientific achievement or lack of it. However, the "analytical" view of psychology, as Mr. Rescher formulates it, seems to have a large assignment. According to him, this view denies that some perceptual properties of wholes are emergent. We may infer, then, that one who holds the view claims that no perceptual properties are emergent and consequently must show that all such properties can be deduced from description of parts plus a psychological theory. I wonder just which psychological theorists Mr. Rescher thinks are making this anti-Gestalt claim. The Gestalters bridge a long time span and theories opposing theirs have been many—Wundtian, structuralism, act psychology, contemporary S-R reinforcement theory, and non-reinforcement theory, etc. I think both Mr. Rescher and the Gestalters would find it difficult to show, say, that the S-R reinforcement theorists claim that *all* perceptual properties of wholes can be predicted from the description of their parts plus such notions as S^{H}R, D, etc.

Mr. Rescher utilizes the analysis of "emergence" formulated by Hempel and Oppenheim. I have not challenged the correctness of this analysis. Their formulation aims to eliminate the notion of absolute emergence by showing that emergence is only relative to some theory, and to prevent the notion of emergence from becoming vacuous—as it would, e.g., if it were a property of parts when suitably combined to produce wholes possessing certain properties—by requiring a statement of parts and attributes characterizing them. In this chapter, as a matter of fact, I urge the first of these points against Koffka's claim that "H, H$_2$, and H$_2$O have all different properties which cannot be derived by *adding* properties of H's and O's." I argued that it is an insufficient view of emergence to claim that one cannot predict one set of properties from another; I claim that emergence means an inability to predict a future set of conditions from a previous set plus some theory. The important thing is that, given this meaning, I did not claim that some specified property, whose status is in doubt, is or is not emergent relative to other specified properties and theories. I raised no issue about what is or is not emergent, as Mr. Rescher does in psychology, but considered the meaning of "emergence" in any case. To determine what is or is not emergent is the scientist's task, an interesting one, to be sure, but, for all that, not the philosopher's.

CHAPTER TWO

Isomorphism

1. E. G. Boring, "Psychophysiological Systems and Isomorphic Relations," *Psychological Review*, 43 (1936), pp. 565ff.; and R. W. Erickson, "Isomorphism as a Necessary Concept," *Journal of General Psychology*, 26 (1942), pp. 353ff.

2. Morris R. Cohen and Ernest Nagel, *An Introduction to Logic and Scientific Method* (New York: Harcourt, Brace and Company, 1934), p. 139.

3. Cf. E. G. Boring, *Sensation and Perception in the History of Experimental Psychology* (New York: D. Appleton-Century Co., 1942), pp. 34ff., 50. Cf. particularly, p. 37.

4. *Ibid.*, p. 89.

5. Further, Boring points out that the number of physical dimensions which a stimulus may have places no restriction on the total number of attributes a sensation may have, although it does restrict the number of *independent* attributes. Take the case where the physical stimulus is bi-dimensional and yields four sensory attributes. Suppose the functions relating each of the sensory attributes to the two dimensions of the stimulus are found through experimentation. Knowing these functions we would need only to know values of two sensory attributes in order to determine the values of the dimensions of the physical stimulus and finally to determine the other sensory attributes. The minimum number of sensory attributes which must be known, in addition to the functions, in order to determine all the rest of the sensory attributes, are in this sense *independent;*

and the number of independent attributes depends on the number of dimensions of the physical stimulus. As Boring concludes concerning Stevens' experimental results to which I have referred:

> The conclusion is that the [total] number of attributes of sensation is independent of the number of dimensions of the . . . stimulus. A bidimensional stimulus may yield a sensation with one or with n attributes. The sensation will also be bidimensional in the sense that any two of its attributes will then determine all the others. . . . [*Philosophy of Science,* 2 (1935), p. 243.]

In such cases the only one-to-one relation that could possibly exist is between a complete set of sensory attributes, on the one hand, and the complete set of physical dimensions that determine them, on the other.

6. E.g., in the theories of Johannes Mueller and Julius Bernstein.

7. *Gestalt theory* is much more comprehensive than a psychological theory; it is also an epistemology and metaphysics.

8. Wolfgang Köhler, *Gestalt Psychology* (New York: Liveright, 1947), pp. 6off.

9. Boring, *Sensation and Perception in the History of Experimental Psychology,* pp. 88-89.

10. Köhler, *op. cit.,* p. 60.

11. *Ibid.,* p. 61.

12. *Ibid.*

13. *Ibid.,* pp. 61-63.

14. Köhler, *Dynamics in Psychology* (New York: Liveright, 1940), p. 55.

15. Köhler, *Gestalt Psychology,* p. 61.

16. Köhler, *The Place of Value in a World of Facts* (New York: Liveright, 1938), p. 251.

17. Köhler, *Dynamics in Psychology,* pp. 49ff.

18. Cf. footnote 1.

19. Cf. Köhler, *Gestalt Psychology,* p. 57; and Kurt Koffka, *Prin-*

ciples of Gestalt Psychology (New York: Harcourt, Brace and Co., 1935) , pp. 61ff.

20. Cf. Köhler, *Gestalt Psychology*, p. 57; and Koffka, *op. cit.* pp. 61ff.

21. Koffka, *op. cit.*, pp. 33, 35.

22. *Ibid.*, p. 35.

23. *Ibid.*, p. 29.

24. Köhler,*The Place of Value in a World of Facts*, p. 108. Cf. Köhler, *Gestalt Psychology*, pp. 22ff.

25. Köhler, *The Place of Value in a World of Facts*, p. 109.

26. *Ibid.*, pp. 140-41.

CHAPTER THREE

Lawfulness

1. Kurt Koffka, *Principles of Gestalt Psychology* (New York: Harcourt, Brace and Co., 1935) , p. 34.

2. *Ibid.*, pp. 27-28.

3. *Ibid.*, pp. 32-33.

4. *Ibid.*, p. 34. Cf. Chapter VI in *Principles of Gestalt Psychology*.

5. Cf. Gustav Bergmann, "Psychoanalysis and Experimental Psychology," *Mind*, 52 (1943) , pp. 122-40. Reprinted in M. Marx, *Psychological Theory* (New York: The Macmillan Co., 1951) , pp. 362-63.

6. Kenneth W. Spence, "The Nature of Theory Construction in Contemporary Psychology," *Psychological Review*, 51 (1944) , pp. 47-68. Reprinted in Marx, *op. cit.*, cf. p. 75.

7. I use Clark Hull's learning theory as a paradigm, but Skinner's, Guthrie's, etc., would do as well as far as the present point is concerned. Cf. E. H. Madden, "The Nature of Psychological Explanation," *Methodos*, 9 (1957) .

8. Wolfgang Köhler, *Gestalt Psychology* (New York: Liveright, 1947), p. 139.

9. *Ibid.*, pp. 141-42.

10. Max Wertheimer, in W. D. Ellis, *Source Book of Gestalt Psychology* (New York: The Humanities Press, 1950), pp. 71-88. See, e.g., pp. 86-87.

11. Koffka, *op. cit.*, pp. 58-61.

12. Kenneth W. Spence, "The Differential Response in Animals to Stimuli Varying Within a Single Dimension," *Psychological Review*, 44 (1937), pp. 430-44. There is some doubt today about this derivation, but even if it is unsuccessful it does not follow that no relational responses are learned.

13. Köhler, *op. cit.*, Chapters 8 and 9.

14. *Ibid.*, p. 162.

15. *Ibid.*

16. *Ibid.*, pp. 161-62.

17. *Ibid.*, p. 166.

18. *Ibid.*, p. 164.

19. Cf. D. Snygg, "The Need for a Phenomenological System of Psychology," *Psychological Review*, 48 (1941), pp. 404-24; and Robert S. Woodworth, *Contemporary Schools of Psychology*, Revised Ed. (New York: The Ronald Press Company, 1948), pp. 249-52, for "The 'Understanding' Psychology." *Verstehende* psychologists like Wilhelm Dilthey and Edouard Spranger not only emphasize the empathy viewpoint but also stress the *uniqueness* of human events in contrast to the *repeatable* events of the physical world. Andre Maurois, in his *Aspects of Biography* (Cambridge, 1929), stresses this point and applies it to history and biography. According to Maurois, the historian or biographer is like a portrait painter; his goal is to create a likeness of an individual. And in his concern with the individual and the instantaneous he is unlike the scientist who deals with general repeatable phenomena. "If we have not clearly observed what

happens when sodium and water are brought together, we have simply to begin again and watch more closely the second time. But the proper function of biography is to deal with the individual and the instantaneous" (p. 86). Inasmuch as the biographer deals with unique experiences, which we can never behold again, he cannot use the scientific method (*loc. cit.*).

However Maurois' view that science deals with general repeatable phenomena while biography, *like all history*, concerns the unique, the individual, and the instantaneous—essentially Windelband's old distinction between the nomothetic and the idiographic—is an oversimplified dichotomy. Physics, for example, is not independent of singular statements, those which refer to individual objects and events. In prediction one uses not only laws but initial conditions—say, the description of the state of a particular system at a particular time. And the prediction itself refers to another such state. Further, the only evidence that one has for a law is its exemplifications in particular systems. Conversely, biography is not free from general statements, those which refer to repeatable phenomena; namely, the behavioral maxims of everyday life and, depending on their degree of verification, the universal hypotheses or laws of psychology. Maxims, universal hypotheses, and laws are used both in establishing biographical facts and in explaining how they occurred.

Consider, as an example of the former, Lytton Strachey's discussion of the Rousseau affair (*Books and Characters*, New York, 1922, pp. 203-15). The Encyclopaedists insisted that Rousseau was a villain. Madame d'Epinay's *Memoirs* confirmed this view. The original manuscript of the *Memoirs*, however, reveals corrections and notes in the handwriting of Diderot and Grimm. Apparently the *Memoirs* is not an independent confirmation of the Encyclopaedists' view but was altered to conform to it. Did Diderot and Grimm conspire to disgrace and humiliate Rousseau? No, Strachey argues. From all we know of Diderot from other sources, he was a fearless and noble man, and these traits are incompatible with conspiracy. Strachey's argument is a first order enthymeme. The major premise "Noble men do not conspire," although not explicit, is an essential part of the argument. One does not have to make it explicit because it is obvious. This obviousness and consequent suppression of the maxims of everyday life, which figure prominently in biographical explanation, probably help to produce the illusion that general statements play no role in historical and biographical inference.

Among the universal hypotheses or laws of psychology that the biographer uses in explaining aspects of his subject's personality those of psychoanalysis figure prominently. Strachey, for example, in explaining James Anthony Froude's attachment to Carlyle, and his consequent moralizing in the *History of England,* writes,

> Old Mr. Froude had drawn a magic circle round his son, from which escape was impossible; and the creature whose life had been almost ruined by his father's moral cruelty . . . remained, in fact, in secret servitude—a disciplinarian, a Protestant, even a church-goer, to the very end.

> When his father had vanished, [Froude] submitted himself to Carlyle. The substitution was symptomatic; the new father expressed in explicit dogma the unconscious teaching of the old. . . .
> (*Portraits in Miniature,* New York, 1931, pp. 193-94.)

This argument is another first order enthymeme. The law or universal hypothesis itself is not expressed; only its application to the particular case is made explicit. This procedure is usually followed when psychological laws are used in biographical explanation and, again, helps account for the illusion that biography and history are independent of general statements.

While there is in fact little explicit reference to psychological laws in biographical explanations, there is frequent reference to psychological "causes." The use of causal terminology, however, is a reliable sign that the explanation is enthymematic in nature. Causal explanations are usually applications of laws to individual events without an explicit formulation of the law which is a necessary condition for this application. This evidential problem must not be confused with the problem of the meaning of 'cause.' Whether 'cause' means nothing more than 'law' or involves, in addition, a compulsion between individual events, is a further question. Whatever the answer to it, a law whether expressed or not is still a necessary condition for asserting a causal relation between individual events.

There are, of course, many practical difficulties when the biographer uses psychological "causes" or laws to explain his subject's behavior. Maurois is quite right in insisting on them. No one is keeping a record of Bertrand Russell's dreams or Kurt Goedel's endocrine secretions so that the universal hypotheses of psychoanalysis and endocrinology may be used in explaining their behavior. Nevertheless where there are records to which psychological concepts are applicable it would be fatuous not to use them in explaining a subject's behavior.

Even though biography is not independent of general statements, either explicit or implicit, and singular ones do have a place in physics, we must not infer that Maurois' uniqueness argument is altogether misleading. The biographer *is* interested in individual events and is not himself seeking laws as is the scientist. In the explanation of individual events, it is true, he relies on laws, universal hypotheses, and maxims. However, these are not a result of his own investigations but are drawn from other areas, psychology and everyday life. In this respect biography is similar to geophysics. The geophysicist does not seek "geophysical laws" but tries to apply the laws of physics to the concrete course of physical events and so explain them.

The geophysics analogy is misleading, too, of course, because the geophysicist is interested simply in explaining phenomena while the biographer is interested in this and something else as well: he wants to satisfy the aesthetic interests of his readers. For the reader of biography the re-creation and reliving of past events has a charm all its own whether or not the events are explained. And this experience is a fundamental aesthetic value in biography. Still this aesthetic experience is not incompatible with an interest in explanation—which, indeed, has its own aesthetic value.

20. Snygg, *op. cit.,* pp. 404-24; and Woodworth, *op. cit.*

21. Cf. Theodore Abel, "The Operation Called 'Verstehen'," *American Journal of Sociology,* 54 (1948-49), pp. 211-18. Reprinted in

E. H. Madden, *The Structure of Scientific Thought* (Boston: Houghton Mifflin Co., 1960), pp. 158-66.

22. Cf. Andre Maurois, *op. cit.*

23. Theodore Abel, *op. cit.*, in Madden volume, p. 164.

CHAPTER FOUR

Psychoanalytic Propositions

1. Cf. Sidney Hook., ed., *Psychoanalysis, Scientific Method, and Philosophy* (New York: New York University Press, 1959).

2. Morris Lazerowitz, "The Relevance of Psychoanalysis to Philosophy" in Hook, *op. cit.*, pp. 133-56.

3. Cf. E. H. Madden, "Psychoanalysis and Moral Judgeability," *Philosophy and Phenomenological Research*, 18 (1957).

4. Ernest Nagel, "Methodological Issues in Psychoanalytic Theory," in Hook, *op. cit.*, p. 43.

5. *Ibid.*

6. Cf. Francis Gramlich, "On the Structure of Psychoanalysis," in Hook, *op. cit.*, p. 298.

7. Sidney Hook, "Science and Mythology in Psychoanalysis," in Hook, *op cit.*, p. 214.

8. Jacob Arlow, "Psychoanalysis as Scientific Method," in Hook, *op. cit.*, p. 208.

9. *Ibid.*, p. 210.

10. Hook, *op. cit.*, p. 217.

11. Arthur C. Danto, "Meaning and Theoretical Terms in Psychoanalysis," in Hook, *op. cit.*, pp. 317-18.

12. Cf. Kenneth Spence, "Historical and Modern Conceptions of Psychology," in his *Behavior Theory and Conditioning* (New Haven: Yale University Press, 1956). Reprinted in E. H. Madden, *The Structure of Scientific Thought* (Boston: Houghton Mifflin Co., 1960). Cf. particularly pp. 143-46.

13. Cf. E. H. Madden, *The Structure of Scientific Thought,* pp. 10-11.

14. Arlow, *op. cit.,* p. 208.

15. Cf. Wesley C. Salmon, "Psychoanalytic Theory and Evidence," in Hook, *op. cit.,* p. 264.

16. Cf. John Hospers, "Philosophy and Psychoanalysis," in Hook, *op. cit.,* pp. 339-40.

17. Salmon, *op. cit.,* p. 261.

18. *Ibid.,* pp. 262-63.

19. Nagel, *op. cit.,* pp. 48-49.

20. *Ibid.*

21. *Ibid.,* p. 52

22. *Ibid.,* p. 49.

23. *Ibid.*

24. *Ibid.,* p. 52.

25. *Ibid.,* p. 53.

26. Cf. C. J. Ducasse, "Psychoanalysis and Suggestion: Metaphysics and Temperament," in Hook, *op. cit.,* pp. 319-23.

27. Cf. Chauncey Wright, "The Logic of Evolutionary Theory," in *The Philosophical Writings of Chauncey Wright,* ed. Edward H. Madden (New York: Liberal Arts Press, 1958), pp. 28-42.

28. Cf. Hospers, *op. cit.,* p. 340.

29. Cf. Gail Kennedy, "Psychoanalysis: Protoscience and Metapsychology," in Hook, *op. cit.,* p. 274.

30. Arlow, *op. cit.,* p. 204.

31. *Ibid.,* p. 206.

32. *Ibid.,* pp. 206-207.

33. Lawrence S. Kubie, "Psychoanalysis and Scientific Method," in Hook, *op. cit.,* pp. 63-64.

34. *Ibid.,* p. 64.

35. Cf. Kennedy, *op. cit.*, pp. 275-76.

36. Cf. Hartmann's, Kubie's and Arlow's essays in Hook, *op. cit.*

37. Heinz Hartmann, "Psychoanalysis as a Scientific Theory," in Hook, *op. cit.*, p. 9.

38. Nagel, *op. cit.*, p. 47.

39. *Ibid.*

40. Arthur Pap, "On the Empirical Interpretation of Psychoanalytic Concepts," in Hook, *op. cit.*, p. 295.

41. *Ibid.*

42. *Ibid.*

43. Cf. the discussion of this point in Chapter I of the present book.

44. Cf. K. MacCorquodale and P. E. Meehl, "On a Distinction Between Hypothetical Constructs and Intervening Variables," *Psychological Review*, 55 (1948), pp. 95-107.

45. *Ibid.*

46. Kenneth W. Spence, "The Differential Response in Animals to Stimuli Varying Within a Single Dimension," *Psychological Review*, 44 (1937), pp. 430-44.

CHAPTER FIVE

Psychoanalysis and Responsibility

1. Lucius Garvin, *A Modern Introduction to Ethics* (Boston: Houghton Mifflin Co., 1953), p. 75.

2. The controversy between John Hospers and Herbert Fingarette is instructive at this point. Cf. John Hospers, "Free-Will and Psychoanalysis" in W. Sellars and J. Hospers, eds., *Readings in Ethical Theory* (New York: Appleton-Century-Crofts, Inc., 1952), pp. 560-75; and Herbert Fingarette, "Psychoanalytic Perspectives on Moral Guilt and Responsibility: A Re-evaluation," *Philosophy and Phenomenological Research*, XVI (1955), pp. 18-36. This controversy is an interesting one to analyze.

Hospers claims that one cannot legitimately be held responsible for the inevitable consequences of uncontrollable events (i.e., for the queer or criminal behavior which results from adult neuroses, which result from childhood neuroses, over the formation of which the individual obviously had no control). Fingarette denies this claim and, in addition, attacks what he takes to be another blunder in the philosophical interpretation of psychoanalysis, namely, that neurotic guilt is not real guilt. I suspect this conflict results mainly from confusions to which each author, perhaps, has contributed a share.

Therapy, Fingarette says, often consists, first, in making the patient aware that he feels intensely guilty. The second step is to find the ground of the guilt feeling which, in neurosis, is unconscious. The analyst tries to reduce, only *temporarily,* the burden of felt guilt so that the wish, to which the guilt is attached, finally comes into consciousness. The crucial point is that the patient rightly feels guilt over the wish. The guilt feeling is not disproportionate; the wish merits it. In the cases where the wish looks trivial it is, by and large, a mask that a fundamentally evil wish, which is unconscious, wears. And it is fruitless to say that the person is not really guilty because after all he did not *act* on his wish; for the wish itself is *morally,* albeit not consequentially, equivalent to the act. Consequently, the first step in therapy, when the guilt feeling becomes conscious, can be described morally by saying "the patient is enabled to face his guilt rather than to run away from it as he has in the past" (p. 27). And when the ground of the guilt, the evil wish, emerges into consciousness one can say, from the moral perspective, that the person has been forced to face not only his guilt but in addition the evil within him which is the basis of his guilt.

At this point in therapy the patient is able to reflect upon his evil wish in the context of his life circumstances and ideals, which context, through therapy, he sees more realistically than before. Appraising his wish within this context, he is at last able to reject the wish, modify it, or retain it, and even sometimes modify one of his fundamental ideals. As a result of therapy, then, the patient *accepts* responsibility; i.e., accepts as *his* the task of doing something about his wishes or suffering the moral and psychological consequences. "In spite of Hospers' assumption that we cannot be held responsible for the inevitable consequences of uncontrollable events, we seem to see in therapy an acceptance of responsibility for just such events" (p. 30). And this result unexpectedly lends support to the existentialist analysis of moral responsibility. It is not that we *were* or *are* responsible, as the existentialist says, but we must *accept* responsibility, by an act of will, of deliberate choice, as the price of maturity. True, it is hard to be responsible in the future for some of the things we are when we had no hand in so becoming, but nevertheless we must accept the hard reality that the world is not fair and just and assume responsibility in order sensibly to go about the business of living. Stop complaining; you are paying the price of no longer being a child. We can reach true humanity only by accepting the challenge to *make* the world just.

(1) *Guilt.* Clearly, I think, it is one thing to say an agent's wish or act is guilty in the sense that it is condemnable or morally wrong and another to say that the agent is guilty in the sense that *he* is condemnable. The second sense of "guilty" is the usual one, the sense which presupposes responsibility, and occurs in legal sentences like "not guilty by reason of insanity." Fingarette realizes that his use of "guilty" does not presuppose responsibility—we can be guilty when not responsible, he says, because guilt occurs very early in life, while responsibility occurs later—yet he blurs the distinction by going from "guilty wish" to "guilty agent" before responsibility occurs. The first step in therapy, when the guilt feeling becomes conscious, he writes, can be described morally by saying, "the patient is enabled to face his guilt rather than to run away from it as he has in the past" (p. 27). This type of blur occurs frequently; but it is not the confusion which leads to his dissent from Hospers' view.

(2) *Responsibility.* I can see no objection whatever in saying man *becomes* responsible or *accepts* responsibility as the price of maturity; and consequently that he does accept responsibility for the inevitable consequences of his personality and character even though they were not under his formative control. This claim effectively helps to meet the determinist's original di-

lemma. The point is, however, that in neurotic behavior this result only occurs after therapy. The forensic psychiatrist, on the other hand, is claiming that prior to therapy, or where therapy has not occurred or is unsuccessful, the "malevolent unconscious" makes an agent nonresponsible for his behavior; and we have seen above the type of reason he gives to defend this view. Hospers in some places in his article seems to be making the same point. However, if this is the case then his and Fingarette's views could not conflict because they do not even meet on the same ground; yet Fingarette offers his view as a devastating criticism of Hospers'. The only way to explain this state of affairs is that Fingarette interprets Hospers' view as if it were the traditional determinist's point that all behavior is nonresponsible because it is determined by our character but we did not have any control over *its* formation. That Fingarette interprets Hospers thusly is again suggested when Fingarette says that Hospers' analysis of psychoanalysis is not necessary or needed to make the point.

> It is interesting to note that we would indeed have a paradox, if we accept Hospers' assumption about moral responsibility. For in that case, even if we did not consider psychoanalytic doctrine but simply granted that, in some way or other, our present nature and behavior are the causal consequences of earlier states of the world, we would be faced with the problem of explaining how we could *ever* be responsible for *any* of our adult behavior. (P. 31.)

In view of some of Hospers' statements, Fingarette's interpretation seems legitimate; or understandable, at any rate, even if Hospers did not intend to hold the view. Hospers writes, for example: "An act is free when it is determined by the man's character, say moralists; but what if the most decisive aspects of his character were already irrevocably acquired before he could do anything to mold them?" (p. 563). "The unconscious is the master of every fate and the captain of every soul" (p. 572). Also Fingarette's interpretation is suggested in the way in which Hospers presents his analysis of psychoanalysis as if it were a necessary refutation of the Schlick-Russell type of dissolution of the determinism-responsibility issue when it is an (elaborate?) sufficient one. And bringing in the issue of the nonresponsibility of non-neurotic unconscious behavior I suspect is misleading, too, because it brings up additional issues to which Fingarette's and existential analyses are highly pertinent.

Hospers and Fingarette, it seems to me, each in his own way, slide psychiatry into the traditional determinism-responsibility issue; Hospers suggesting, in one way or another, that psycho-analysis reinforces determinism and Fingarette unequivocally holding that it reinforces commonsensical self-determinism and so moral responsibility. This maneuver, I believe, is unfortunate either way; and the real import of psychoanalysis for morality— namely, that neurotic behavior is not morally judgeable—is likely to be lost in the resulting confusion. The forensic psychiatrist cannot be anything but dismayed at this turn of events.

3. Fingarette, *op. cit.;* Stephen Toulmin, "The Logical Status of Psycho-analysis" in M. Macdonald, ed., *Philosophy and Analysis* (Oxford: Basil Blackwell, 1954), pp. 132-39; and Anthony Flew, "Psycho-analytic Explanation" in *Philosophy and Analysis*, pp. 139-48. Toulmin and Flew follow F. Waismann's distinction in "Language Strata" in A. G. N. Flew, ed., *Logic and Language, Second Series* (Oxford: Basil Blackwell, 1953), pp. 1-13.

4. Toulmin and Flew.

5. Gregory Zilboorg, *The Psychology of the Criminal Act and Punishment* (London: Hogarth Press, 1955), pp. 25-27. Other men whose work is particularly important in this area, and from whom I have profited greatly, are Winfred Overholser and Walter Bromberg.

6. *Ibid.,* pp. 71-72.

7. *Ibid.,* p. 32.

8. *Ibid.,* p. 126.

9. *Ibid.,* pp. 119ff.

10. Cf. David W. Louisell, "Review of Zilboorg's *The Psychology of the Criminal Act and Punishment*," *Scientific Monthly,* 79 (July-December, 1954), pp. 332-33.

11. Zilboorg, *op. cit.,* pp. 28-29.

12. Jerome Hall, "Science and Reform in Criminal Law" in Philip Wiener, ed., *Readings in Philosophy of Science* (New York: Charles Scribner's Sons, 1953), pp. 297-309. Text and footnotes.

13. Zilboorg, *op. cit.*, pp. 112-13.

14. *Ibid.*, pp. 118-19.

Index

INDEX

Index

Chapter One I still couldn't shake it.

I was standing at the toilet taking a piss, when the cell door opened wide with a metallic clang! Someone had invaded my space. I looked over my shoulder and saw none other than Silverstein, the most feared white man in the chain gang. He was the infamous leader of a white supremacy group known as the Aryan Brotherhood.

His presence filled the cell as he held his tool at his side, a two foot long shank. A sliver of light gleamed off its sharp edges. He was flanked by at least ten of his goons. White dudes with pink angry faces littered with tattoos, like scary clowns.

He took a step towards me and I felt my heartbeat accelerate; my pulse quickened. A trickle of piss ran down my leg and all over the toilet seat. Instantly, my body went into flight or fight mode. In the chain gang, it's called fuck or fight mode, but with Silverstein, it was more like fight or die mode.

I took several steps back, and searched for a way to fight my way out. There was none, and I didn't have my joint with me; it was stashed under the bunk. Silverstein had come for me, just like he said he would, and had caught me slipping, bad! We had a history and it was personal. We had never been friends, only foes. In the past, I had slaughtered two of his goons in revenge for him killing my nigga Lobo. Prior to that, Silverstein had killed half a dozen black men, and for good measure, when they placed him in Super Mix, a high security prison in Colorado, he killed two prison guards. It was inevitable that we'd cross paths, like two speeding locomotives headed straight for each other on a one way track.

As always, these were his type of odds: ten against one on a black man. I knew the only chance I had to defeat him, was to out think him. So I went for the mental gambit, his white Aryan pride.

"It takes all of y'all scary ass fake AB, crackas to come in here and fade me!"

I braced myself and looked Silverstein square in the eyes, "If it wasn't for them fake ass AB's helping your bitch ass, I'd fuck you up—."

Before I could get the words out of my mouth, his goons tried to rush through the cell door to get at me. He shoved them back; his enraged face was beet red. I had just disrespected their sect.

With his top lip snarled, teeth bared like some beast of prey, he raised his shank, and eased towards me in battle mode posture. I could tell by the arch in his back, and the way his muscles flexed, that he was studying me; my proximity, my vulnerability.

In a gritty tone that sent a slight shiver down my spine, he said, "Nigger it's just me and you, and I swear on my Aryan brotherhood blood, I'm gonna chop your black ass into so many tiny pieces. So small, that they'll use a broom to get your ass off the floor."

He charged me like a ram, and screamed his warrior cry as he swung the shank! It whistled past my head as I dodged and bobbed out of the way on the balls of my bare feet. I moved with agility, motivated by fear and the sheer will to survive.

I timed him perfectly, hitting him square on the bridge of his nose with a wild over hand right that sent him staggering backwards. Stunned and dazed, but unhurt, the punch opened up a gash on his nose that spewed blood. I needed to make it out the cell.

He charged me again, shank in hand, swinging wildly. We collided. His brute force was more than I had expected. I managed to grab his hand that held the shank as we tussled in death throes. My bare feet slid across the slippery floor. He outweighed me by at least fifty pounds, but somehow, I was able to use his weight to my advantage.

When he reached back to stab me, I grabbed his shirt collar, pulled him into me, and head butted him hard across his battered nose. Simultaneously, I kneed his nuts. His eyes exploded with pain. I heard him grunt as the impact of the blow lifted him off his feet. In my peripheral, I saw his goons inching close as he staggered away from me. I heard the ruckus made by their disgruntled shouting.

In my mind, I was thinking that I still needed a way out of the cell. Again, Silverstein swung the shank, this time he aimed for my face. In a nick of time, I threw up my arm to ward off the blow. The shank pierced my hand. Surging white pain ran through my body. He reached back to stab me again as he hollered with murderous rage.

I dropped low to the floor and scooped him high off his feet, just as the shank missed my face and hit the wall. I slammed him hard on the concrete floor, head first, like he had been thrown out a ten story window and landed on top of him. We fought like crabs in a bucket of blood, as blood began to pour from the back of his head

All the while, I could see his devil buddies inching closer; anxious and ready to pounce on me. Suddenly, I could feel Silverstein getting stronger as we fought to the death. He got off a blow, hitting me in the face with an open hand. Iron fingers like a dead man's claws, began to gnaw at my face. He tried to gouge out my eyes as I struggled to hold on to his wrist with the shank in it to keep him from stabbing me. My grip was slipping from the blood coming from the open wound in my hand.

The devils continued to inch closer...

He managed to land a right hand to my chin. I momentarily saw stars. My bloody hand was slipping off his wrist that held the shank, as he bucked, trying to throw me off him. He was still getting stronger by the second, as my hand continued to slip off his wrist.

I needed to do something and I needed to do it fast! I desperately tried a different tactic by stretching my body flat across his. I curled my leg under his. Using my forearm, I placed my elbow under his chin, onto his windpipe and pushed hard, cutting off his breathing. As he began to choke, gag and thrust, I saw it in the dark pools of his eyes; panic. Death was about to come knocking at his door. I wrestled the shank out his hand, this time it was me that roared like an African Warrior covered in gory blood. My conquest would be his demise.

Death!

I reached back to stab him, then it happened, his AB buddies jumped me. *I should have known!*

I struggled to get up and thwart their assault, but I was stabbed in the back, the face, and my neck.

Hack! Hack! Hack!

Death by a thousand cuts.

Butchered, battered and dying, I fought to no avail.

My screams were in muted silence. Like always, I never feel any pain.

My grandmother once told me, if you die in your dreams, you won't awaken.

Chapter Two

I awoke, drenched in perspiration, with Tamara's neck in a head lock, choking the shit out of her as she fought to get loose. I finally let her go. She was panting and struggling to breathe. When I opened my eyes, I was surprised to be in our bedroom, and even more surprised that I was choking her again.

Although I was no longer on death row fighting racist white boys that were sent at me by the Warden Scott, I was still tormented and traumatized like I had just come home from the war in Iraq.

As my eyes adjusted to the morning sunlight that filtered through the curtains, I was still expecting to see prison bars. Tamara sat up in bed and stared at me, as she rubbed her neck. I saw both hurt and compassion in her eyes; a duel of emotions emanated.

"I'm sorry, I had a dream again." I said softly, reaching for her.

"Naw'll you had another bad nightmare," she corrected me. Her voice was neutral, almost nurturing, as she continued to rub her neck. We were both nude, with the sateen sheets pooled at our feet.

I opened my arms. "Come here baby."

She hesitated, then laid down next to me. I could feel her heart beating fast like mine. With a delicate hand, she wiped the sheen of sweat glistening off my forehead, and attempted to coo at my nightmares.

"Innocent... baby, you are going to have to get help. Please."

I didn't answer, didn't trust my own voice. There was no manual or hand book on how to adjust to life after leaving five years of living hell on death row. My introgression back into society was terrible. I had experienced too much carnage, too much dying. Death had been my constant companion, always near me. I had murdered my own flesh and blood, my father, in retaliation for him brutally murdering my mother.

Somehow, I came out of prison a celebrity. Just about every place I went, people knew me. I had one of the most famous cases in American history. It has sparked riots and race wars with police and the criminal justice system as it relates to corruption. I had appeared on The Oprah Winfrey Show and several other high profile media programs. All the while, I wore a mental mask to disguise my shattered and tormented mind.

Prison had done something to me that I could never get back. A facet of myself, my soul, and my sanity had been stolen. To assuage my maladies, I sought refuge in what I loved most, a man's most prized possession; his family; my love, Tamara, the children, and my grandmother. Tamara is now my wife, and even though the twins, Knight and Dawn are not mine biologically, they belong to me, emotionally, and spiritually. So much so, that I gave them my last name.

They were mine to raise and to love, and that's what I intended to do.

I settled out of court with my lawsuit against the government for 1.8 million and bought a spacious five bedroom home in Stone Mountain, Georgia. I also bought Tamara a brand new 320 Benz, even though she still had a Benz truck and several other whips from her drug dealer ex-boyfriend, the twins' father Haitian Blue. As for myself, I copped a 320 BMW, and a motorcycle. I also purchased my beloved grandmother a home in Decatur, Georgia.

With some of the money I received from the lawsuit, I started my own real estate company. With $75,000.00 I bought old homes, remodeled them, and sold them at a significant profit. I doubled my money the first year. I expect to triple my money in the second year.

On the outside looking in, I was a perfect example of a success story. A brotha comes home from prison and succeeds, but on the inside, I was scarred like a bad wound that wouldn't heal. My mind wasn't right. It was like I was shell shocked. I tried my damnest to shake whatever it was that prison had done to me, but it was hard. There were certain gray areas that I was struggling with. Like when me and Tamara went out to a restaurant or club, I had to sit with my back against the wall, or I wouldn't let anyone stand behind me. It was a habit that I had unconsciously formed in prison in order to survive; warding off shank attacks. And God forbid, if someone were to stand behind me too close.

I once went off on a guy in a grocery store for standing too close behind me in line. I was about to fuck him up too, because he acted like he didn't understand what "YOU'RE STANDING TOO FUCKIN' CLOSE TO ME!" meant.

That day, Tamara stopped me from punishing dude. In fact, she apologized to him and everyone else in the store for my behavior, which made me feel like shit. What kind of got to me, was on the way home in the car, she nearly broke down crying as she tried to explain to me how I wasn't in prison anymore, and this was how things where in the world. So yeah, I had a few issues. I even had a weapon stashed in the bedroom that she didn't know about.

So, to compensate for all my flaws, I would make love to Tamara every morning and endless nights too. For some reason, all those years in prison gave me an insatiable appetite for sex, and Tamara loved that side of me. She had put on a significant amount of weight after giving birth to three children, but in my eyes, she was one of the most beautiful women in the world. I loved her that much, even though I knew she thought I was crazy as hell.

"What do you want me to do?" I finally said.

I did not want to engage her in any other battle but sex, as the humid scent of last night's lovemaking marinated between us.

"I want you to see a doctor... a psychiatrist," she said with emotion and struck a nerve on the surface of my manly pride, as only a woman can.

I did my best to understand, to comprehend. I tried my best to explain.

"We all change to some degree or another, Tam."

Out of habit, I eased my hands between her thighs and stroked her kitty. She flinched at first, and didn't really open her legs to give me entrance, like she normally would.

"Baby you don't laugh or smile unless it's with the children. You spend most of your time on the computer, or reading them damn books, or writing letters and sending pictures to dudes on prison. Let it go... I'm afraid you've become institutionalized." She snapped.

"What else is there to smile about or to do for that matter? I'm home with my family, with the woman I love. I'm free. As for prison, I left some good niggaz in prison—"

"Innocent you left your damn mind in prison!" she quipped.

Silence.

I removed my hand from between her legs, and stared up at the ceiling. God sure knew what he was doing when he created a woman and the balance of nature. She can irritate the shit out of a man. She may not be able to beat a man physically, but she sure as hell can crush him verbally, like Tamara was doing to me. I had been trying my best to adjust, but it was hard.

Tamara must have sensed my distress, because she eased close to me, and spoke with sympathy. I saw tears brimming in her eyes as she nestled against me. Fingers light as feathers began to trace the deep, jagged scars on my chest that ran all the way down to my chiseled six pack abs like tangent train tracks, hacked and battered. It was the horror of human torture; injuries I had suffered either before I went to prison, or while there. I was shot in cold blood by a racist State Trooper when I was eighteen, then framed, falsely accused of raping and killing a white girl, and sentenced to death row. When I went to prison, things got worse. Warden Scott placed a bounty on my head. Every day of my life, I fought for my existence. I fought to survive. I was lucky to be alive; to have killed, and to not have been killed.

"Innocent, I'm sorry. I know you're trying, but you need help," she cooed while caressing my chest as she spoke.

For some reason, I thought about my twin brother T.C. He made the ultimate sacrifice. It was only because of him, that I was alive.

She continued, "I'm not trying to hurt your feelings, and you're not the only one suffering, look at me and all my medications. Even your grandmother, Big Mama, has issues. Look at the twins, even little Tre. We are all suffering in some form or another, but you're the head of the household. If you lead, I will follow, but you got to get help to get deinstitutionalized."

I knew she was right, but I had to stand my ground. I wasn't going to see no damn psychiatrist just because she had seen one before. Then I thought about something she said.

"Deinstitutionalized!? Lemme tell you something, every real nigga I know that is doing time is institutionalized to some degree, but the thing is not to compromise your morals. Now that I'm out, it's just a process I'm going through. I'ma do better, alright?" I said, and eased my hand back between her legs.

She was moist. She gave me that look.

"Naw, you still act like you're in prison. For my birthday, you bought me a twelve piece set of butcher knives."

"What's wrong with that?" I asked.

With my other hand, I used my thumb and forefinger and started a circular motion around her nipple. She moaned softly and opened her legs.

"Duhh, I asked you for a Gucci handbag nigga, so I could have a full collection." She sassed.

"Okay, I'll get you another Gucci handbag. You want me to lick on your coochie?" I said with a grin, easing my finger inside.

"Ooh...oomph... in prison, you had a thing for knives. You hurt a lot of people... Hmmm." She bit down on her bottom lip, and threw her neck back as I played inside her sex box.

"A lot of people tried to hurt me. I was defending myself."

"Were you defending yourself when you butchered Bubba in the shower on death row?"

Mentally stagnated, I groped for words, and then regrouped. I used the only thing at my disposal, by easing my other finger in her vagina. She inhaled, sucking air like she was whistling backwards. I was speechless. I had killed Bubba Ray in the shower on death row, simply because he was the convict that had set me up to be killed; executed for a crime I didn't commit. It was all orchestrated by the Warden

Scott, a man I still hated and had nightmares about. Tamara was not supposed to know about that. I needed an excuse, something to keep her mind off my past.

"I'm not trying to live in the past. I'm living in the present, preparing for the future. Yeah, sure I had a body count in prison, but I've changed. I'm not institutionalized." I stirred her passion with my fingers and watched her face fight my fingers' rhythms. Somehow, she managed to give me a shrug as if to say that she was dismissing my argument. She reached under the mattress and pulled out the butcher knife I had stashed there.

"What is this, Mr. I ain't institutionalized?" She spat.

All I could do was stare at it, lost for words. I was tongue tied.

"It's... it's for me to protect my family." I tried to say with enthusiasm, but deep down inside, I felt like shit; humiliated.

She had known all the time that one of the knives I had bought for her birthday was stashed under the mattress.

"Humph," she grumbled under her breath while giving me a pathetic look and passed me the knife.

I placed it back under the mattress and heard her suck her teeth in contempt. I lay back down next to her and listened to the sounds of chirping birds, alerting me that it was time to do my morning workout. I needed an excuse to be away from her. Time to think for myself.

Is there something really wrong with me? I asked myself, as I ran my fingers through my shoulder length locks. I rose and prepared to get out of bed. Some mornings, I would run ten miles and then work out. That was how I dealt with stress in prison, and how I was going to deal this morning's conversation. She stilled me with an outstretched hand.

"Baby we're going to get through this somehow... I promise." I turned around and looked at her.

"Yeah, right. I need to go work out." I said plaintively.

That was my excuse to get out, and away from her and her mouth. Women can use words that cut like a sword, and hurt like hell.

She sat up in bed and grabbed my arm. With a passionate expression, she said, "Baby I'm sorry... You my man, I love you. Can we start over... please?" She pouted.

The poignant crescendo of her voice moved me in a way I couldn't explain. Since getting out of prison, my very existence on earth had been to please her and the children. It just seemed like I was failing miserably. That morning, I just wanted to walk away. I needed some time to myself, to think.

What the hell is wrong with me??

Tamara gestured, opening her arms wide like a pavilion beckoning. I just stared, hesitant and doubtful. I needed to be angry at her, I wanted to. She grinned sheepishly.

"Nigga get out your feelings... you know you want some of this good pussy." She taunted me teasingly. She spread her arms wider, "come here, you just gone to leave me hanging... I'll buy you a knife set for your birthday."

She giggled girlishly, then erupted into hilarious laughter at my expression, like she used to do when she was eight years old. I couldn't help but smile at her antics. She always had a way of making me smile when I didn't want to. Like now. I picked up a pillow and hit her with it. She ducked and reached for me. I fell on top of her.

I was already aroused when she spread her legs and kissed my forehead.

"I love you," she cooed.

I didn't answer. I needed to release some stress, I needed to be inside of her, my mental escapism. I licked and sucked on her neck, leaving a trail of saliva down her breast. I stopped for a fiesta, at her erect nipples with my tongue, while I eased two, then three fingers inside of her vagina. I stroked her like my fingers were searching for gold.

"Ooohhh," she crooned, seductively.

She was so wet. Slippery kitty making that gushy juicy sound of her succulent sex. Ever so tenderly, with my tongue and lips, I walked across her torso, licking, sucking, and kissing. Her sultry moans were my reward as I made a pit stop at her stomach and tongue fucked her navel, as I sped up the pace of stroking her kitty.

"Oooohhh, weeee, shit. Baby you just don't know what you do to me," she moaned. Her body let loose a light shudder.

I eased further down; the sweet scent of her sex aroused me. My fingers were full of her juices. I spread her lips and flicked my tongue on her clit. Licking on her labia, I buried my tongue inside of her womanhood. She let loose and her body began to shiver. As she grinded her hips, moving in a fevered fluent motion, she grabbed the back of my head.

"Shiiit, oomph...right there...right there... baby ohhh!" She grabbed the back of my head and began to fuck my face. I increased my pace, letting my tongue take a trek down south, then back up. I spread her lips and sucked on her clit, nibbling and lashing on it with a velvet tongue, like it was a delicious morsel of fruit. Meanwhile, I eased my three fingers back inside of her, stirring her passion. Her body began to tremble.

She let loose a moan as she began to grind faster on my face. "Ohhh, G...g...god, fuck! Fuck! 'm cuming I'm cuming..."

She thrashed and moaned, as she mashed my face harder into her pussy, like she was trying to suffocate me. I continued to tongue lash her. My strength was now her weakness.

"Hmmm, shiiit! mmm shiit! What are you doin' to me, ughhh, shiit slow ...down," she groaned.

That only made me speed up my rhythm and go faster and deeper as I spread her skin, licking every crevice, tongue boxing her clit. To my surprise, she began to scoot away from my tongue. I grabbed her firmly around her hips and pulled her back to me.

I pinned her to the bed and licked her gluttonously from the bottom of her anus to the top of her engorged pearl. She thrashed and moaned in ecstasy, making exulting sounds, and desperate facial expressions, I was certain she was going to break down in tears as her body went into convulsions. With the heel of her hand, she pushed against my forehead. As she climaxed, I continued to sip her juices, and suck on her clit with vigor. My tongue ravaged her hole wantonly as she panted, and squealed.

I stopped, and looked up at her over the patch of her heart shaped pubic hairs. Her breathing echoed and resonated as she stared down at me with wild lustful eyes, like she had just got off a roller coaster ride.

"Damn baby! You'll suck a bitch fallopian tubes out," she gasped, smiling awkwardly.

Her brow was still creased with a sex face. I almost laughed, instead I smirked. I had another idea. I tried to turn her over on her stomach. This was her favorite position, except when I don't take my time.

She resisted at first. "I.C. baby, go slow," The tone of her voice was like she was intoxicated, inebriated, high off my tongue.

I turned her over slowly and eased onto her back with my dick dangling and pulsating. It dragged against her thighs and butt cheeks as I prepared to hit it from the back. I was an Alpha male, long, hard, ten inches strong. It was the kind of dick that can do damage, a true testament to real black masculinity.

I tooted her booty up by grabbing her waist. I arched her spent, pretty pussy, glistening with cum dribbling down her leg. I eased the head of my dick slowly in. She was hot and wet. She gasped a whimper, then a groan as she grabbed the burgundy satin sheets. I eased in one inch at a time, and as usual, she was tight. I was starting to pick up a rhythm.

"Go slow," she intoned.

I always try not to violate that golden rule; the sanctity of our love making when she tells me to go slow. I honestly try, and I always fail. I palmed a handful of both cheeks, squeezed and spread them apart and thrust deeper, faster.

About five inches in, my dick bends. She is tight, friction scratches me. I spit on my hand and wiped it across her pussy. She does the same. Like a duel tag team, we maintenance her pussy with lubrication. My rhythm increases. I go deeper. She makes a noise between a scream and a moan. I fight against the torrid rage of lust, to go slow, but it's so hard. I ease a couple more inches inside of her. I watch her pull on the sheets so hard that I see one of her acrylic finger nails break as I go deeper. Long measured strokes that make her butt cheeks bounce. I smack her on the ass and she groans and attempts to move with me. Then, this erogenous feeling consumes me, a primitive expression that feels so good. I want to beat my chest and roar like a lion. Instead, I began to fuck her, thrusting deeper, faster, all ten inches go inside of her. She yells like I'm killing her, and tosses her head back. Her hair weave is matted to her forehead with perspiration

"Ugh...Shiit...go... Sloooow," she pouts and moans.

Her pussy is making that slurping slippery sound as I pound up in her guts. Her expression looks like she had bitten into a hot pepper as her supple breasts flung back and forward with each thrust. She reached back to slow me down. I grabbed her wrist and pulled her to me. I fucked her harder, drilling her pussy, while ignoring her clamorous pleas for me to go slow. I was like a thief, stealing the nectar out of the flower of her nooky. I pillage her pussy with frenzied strokes, and then I cum like I am having a seizure. I tremor like her pussy is an electric socket that my dick was stuck inside of and she was giving me a charge. I collapsed on her back, still grinding, still thrusting, eager to fill that insatiable void of a fevered fuck that only a good pussy can bring.

"You have no dick control." she said tersely as I half stroked her. Dick on idle time, to keep the pussy primed.

"My bad," I said with a grin.

She reached back and popped me on the arm. I rolled her over on her back. She laughed. I admired the way her hair cascaded over the pillow with her angelic face lying beneath me. Her heavy breasts swelled as she breathed. She gave me another one of her sex-faces, this one is quizzical. Her woman's intuition, she wants to know what is on my mind. What is wrong with me?

Delicately, I placed one of her legs on my shoulder, then the other one as I eased inside of her. This time, more determine to go slow, make it last forever. I just wanted to please her. I glided right in, stroking her lovingly, listening to her femininity whisper in my ear, like a melody. My strokes were measured, deliberate, intense good dick control.

Then she admonished "Fuck me! Fuck me hard!" She gritted her teeth, and then scratched my back as I fought another losing battle of dick control within the spoils of her luscious pussy. Our bodies were both saturated, covered with sweat, and then I did as she commanded. I fucked her hard. This time with deep penetrating strokes, causing our bodies to French kiss with sumptuous, salacious smacking sounds of lovemaking as the bed rocked and banged against the headboard.

Tamara clawed at my ass, fingernails erotically raked across my bare butt. This excited me more. We are lovers who fuck like prize fighters. Our boxing ring is our bed and each round ends with a fervid orgasm as we change positions.

An hour later, we are still going at it. Only now, it has turned into a track race and we are in a dead heat, until she races ahead of me to the orgasm finish line. I chase after her, grunting and fucking her into a frenzy.

The bed begins to bang harder against the headboard as she moans like an old Aretha Franklin song.

"OOOOHHH, WEEEE, Shiiiit! I'm cumming again!" She exhorts exhilaratingly. I cum in second place right behind her in oceans and streams as I bent her legs back to her ears and dived deeper until she shrieked in agony, grabbing her thigh.

"Awch!!!We tumbled off the bed onto the floor in a heap. Tamara landed on top of me.

She is a big girl. I hurt my back, but played it off. She laughed giddily. I did too. We were reminiscent of young lovers.

"I.C., boy, you bent my legs up like I am a damn pretzel. I caught a cramp in my calf. You be going too fast, trynna break a bitch back."

"You gone have my dick skinned up," I said.

She was still lying on top of me. One of my legs was partially on the bed. She looked at me with hooded eyes lidded with feminine mischief.

Something is brewing inside her head. Something I cannot discern. Then her demeanor changes like a chameleon. She shifts position and looks at me with goo-goo eyes as her fingernails rake across my six pack abs. In a raspy tone, her voice quivers. "Innocent... baby...I love you so much. Promise me you'll never leave me and the kids?"

Where did that come from? I wonder.

"Tam is there something you want to tell—"

"Shhh," she silences me by placing a finger over my lips.

Leaning forward, she kisses me like she is trying to suck the juices out my mouth. She caresses my joint, then pulls away and looks at me with enigmatic eyes, as a ball of sweat like honey rolls off her breast.

"Baby I need to talk to you about something."

"Talk to me about what?" For some reason she had me on edge, off balance.

Tamara has all kinds of shit with her, and yet, I was trying to dispel the proverbial myth: you can't change a hoe into a house wife. However, in my case, Tamara was once a hood rat and a bonafide hoe. She had been selling pussy out of both pants legs since she was nine years old, so my situation was two-fold. This was normality in the hood, it was known as ghetto love, and with ghetto love, anything was possible. It was sanctioned by God and had given birth to some of the most beautiful people the world has known.

"Talk about what?" I said cautiously and watched her gnaw at the carpet with her fingers, nervously.

"It's just something about our past that I need to talk to you about."

I could feel anxiety rising in my gut like an ocean tide. She refused to look at me as her hands gnawed faster at the carpet. Our silence lulls, stalls like a clock with no hands. Finally she gets up and sits on the edge of the bed. I follow her and sit down on the bed next to her. I can smell the humid scent of our sex. This is a sensitive moment.

"What's wrong baby?" I asked softly.

She placed a trembling hand on my thigh. I can tell in a minute, she is going to need her medication. Years ago, she had every bone in her face broken by her abusive baby-daddy. He beat her nearly to death while she was four months pregnant with the twins. They were born premature and in poor health. Since then, she's had several surgeries. She had been diagnosed with some type of mental illness with a tongue twister name I can't even remember to pronounce.

"Baby, I can't tell you enough what you mean to me and the children." She says wringing her hands together, a bundle of nerves.

"You're a great dad, and a great husband. You mean the world to us; I don't hurt for nothing..."

She got up from the bed as if she is disgusted with herself. She pads over to the dresser, opens up several bottles of her medication, and begins to swallow pills like they're the cure all for her problems.

"You still ain't tell me what's wrong, Tam. Talk to me Tam."

She turns around, her heavy breast swinging and her facial expression completely changed.

"Baby… from the bottom of my heart… I just want you to know how much I love you that is all."

I have a feeling she is lying, as I watch her standing in front of the dresser. I can see her reflection in the mirror. Even though she has gained a lot of weight, it's mostly in her hips. She now has a big ole ghetto butt that still turns heads whenever we go out. Something suddenly dawned on me as I look at the clock on the dresser, 7:03 AM.

"Shit!!" I cursed and rushed over to the computer. I logged on to CorrLinks, which is the email system for federal prisoners to communicate with the outside world.

Unfortunately, all of my partners had been slaughtered, killed in cold blood in a prison riot when Silverstein and his band of cutthroat goons took over the prison, killing and raping most of the guards. Miraculously, my dude Meatball had survived. Milkman was my homie from Chi-Town, his real name was Eric Brown and he was the only white dude in our clique. He had stood toe to toe and fought a many battle with the racist ABs. It was especially hard on him because he was a white dude raised in a black world; all he knows is black culture. Milkman didn't even date white girls, all he knew was black. In his heart and soul, he really was black.

Silverstein had placed a hit on his life, he called Milkman a race betrayer, and many times Milkman had fought off shank attacks by white men just for that. Now he was missing. He should have been out of prison months ago. I was baffled; I couldn't find any information on him in the BOP system.

There were no emails from Corrlinks that morning; which wasn't unusual. The prison stayed on lock down most of the time, due to killings or stabbings.

Next I went on Facebook. Someone had sent me a message in my inbox, it simply read,

You're going to have to find it in your heart to forgive me. Watch your back.

The name they used was Godsent. I tried to visit the sender's page, but it was private. I was contemplating the message and wondering if it was a threat, when Tamara walked over and stood behind me. Her breast rested on my back as she leaned against me to look at the computer. She smacked her lips as she read the screen.

"Who in da fuck is Godsent, talkin' bout you're going to have to find it in your heart to forgive them?!"

"I don't know—" Before I could answer, she bobbed me upside the head.

"Lemme find out you fuckin' wit some bitch. I'ma fuck you and dat hoe up!" All I could do was snicker at her antics.

I had over five thousand people on my Facebook page due to the publicity of my case. A lot of them were women and they were very flirtatious and horny. Tamara had access to everything, whether it is my phone or computer and she made it her business to let them know that I was married and she was my wife.

Next, I logged onto Safebabies.com, a software security system I had installed in the house. It allowed me to view every section of my spacious home. I could work the device either by my Motorola smart phone or computer. I was into gadgets big time.

Tamara continued to lean over my shoulder as I focused on the camera in the kids' room.

"They're gone!" She exclaimed.

I moved the camera at all angles in the room. It looked like a tornado had hit it. There were clothes and toys strewn everywhere. Tre and his toddler twin siblings, Dawn and Knight, were gone.

As I attempted to manipulate the computer to look at other areas of the house, Tamara moved away from me and asked contemplatively, as if talking to herself "Where the fuck their bad asses at?" I stood from the computer to face her and saw the concerned look on her face.

Chapter Three

"I'll go check on them—"

Before I could get the words out, there was a soft knock at the door, followed by children's giggles, then the door burst open intrusively. Then came the invasion of the Rug-Rats. Tamara and I, both naked, dived into the bed under the covers.

My son Tre led the pack. He had his toy gun with him as he wore his Spiderman PJs. So did his two year old brother, Knight. However, Dawn, his twin sister, was completely nude, in her birthday suit and proud of it. She beamed at seeing me with a child's jovialness. Both her and her brother Knight climbed onto the bed with us.

"Dada! Dada!" Dawn squealed in delight as she rambunctiously climbed into my arms, smelling like last night's urine. Knight snitched on her in a child's banter.

"Dada uh pee-pee in bed." He said while bouncing up and down.

I tickled Dawn's tummy, causing her to laugh and squirm in my arms like she is being tickled, and tortured to death.

"Girl, you pee-pee in bed again?" She giggles some more, looks up at me with doe-eyes and smiled, nodding her head like, *sure did and proud of it.*

I tickled her some more and was rewarded with the sweetest sound that God ever created; a child's laughter.

Dawn was a miracle baby. She and her brother Knight were born premature. Knight enjoyed good health, but that was not the case with Dawn. She was born with a hole in her heart, and she also had severe respiratory problems and a bad case of asthma.

Many nights, we had to rush her to the hospital and sit at her bedside praying to God not to take her away from us. Big Mama, my grandmother, took over after doctors told us that Dawn had less than a ten percent chance of making it. Big Mama used her old folk's remedies, and in the past six months, she had baffled doctors. Big Mama had single handedly nursed Dawn to good health with some type of concoction made from herbs and vegetables.

Dawn was born a sickly pale white. Big Mama would bathe her with olive oil; afterwards, she would affectionately rock her on her large bosom in the bright sun on her front porch, while humming a lullaby. The same lullaby she sang to me and my brother when we were sick. Dawn's sickly pale complexion changed to a beautiful brilliant hue of cooper brown like she had been tongue kissed by the sun.

The children continued to rumble on the bed, until Tamara yelled, "What do y'all want in my room, coming in here making all that damn noise!"

Of course they ignored her, like she was a figment of their imagination. Dawn wrestled loose from my arms and joined her brother, frolicking and jumping up and down on the bed. This drove Tamara crazy. She gave me an evil stare like she was about to go off. It amazes me that at such a tender age, children are innately a lot smarter than we give them credit for. They know that I will not allow Tamara to spank them, and they act on it.

My son Tre is the prime example. He is the elder. At seven, he is the designated spokesperson for the Rug-Rats. Gingerly, he walked up, play gun in hand. He focuses his attention on me. He too has become accustomed his mother's screaming. His hands fumble with the toy gun as he prepares words and speaks barely above a whisper. I have to strain my ears to hear him.

"Daddy we hungry. It's Saturday. You gone fix us some pancakes and watch cartoons with us?"

Knight and Dawn hear the word pancakes and jump up and down on the bed faster, doing their impromptu version of the Pancake Dance.

"Panny Cakes Panny Cakes dada!" Dawn squeals and nearly tumbles off the bed. I grab her in the nick of time.

She giggles with a child's delight as she lassoes her arms around my neck. I glance over at Tamara, she sneers her teeth at me; she was livid. For some reason, my relationship with the kids irks her at times.

Tre meanders over, and sits on the bed. He hits me with a child's pleading eyes that stab at the core of my love for him. I never had a father, never had a strong male in my life except for basketball coaches. So as a father, I made it a ritual to dedicate every Saturday morning to being with my children, acting goofy and watching cartoons. Hell, I'm the one that invented the Pancake Dance in the first place.

I ruffled Tre's hair as Knight falls on top of me. Dawn laughs at her brother. I steal kisses from both of them, then look at my son Tre and tell a small white lie.

"I was just getting ready to get up and fix y'all breakfast." Tamara smacks her lips, and rolls her eyes up at the ceiling.

I continue talking to Tre, "Lil man I want you to put some clothes on Dawn. I'll be out in a minute. Now go!"

I began to tickle the twins to get them off the bed. They laugh and continue to jump up and down. Tamara springs forward from under the covers.

"Y'all bad asses get, and that room better be clean when I come in there!" She then points an accusing finger at Tre.

"Boy you think you slick, coming in here asking your daddy for everything. You better have that room clean when I come in there."

He gives her a tacit nod, "Okay Mamma."

Dawn scrambles to get off the bed as Tamara reaches over and smacks her on her butt.

"Girl didn't I tell you not to take your clothes off again?!"

Dawn pauses as she climbs off the bed and looks at her mother in indecision. She is debating if the infraction on her butt was worth crying over. She then looks at me and frowns, pouting, lips pulled down as if to get my opinion. I smile at her. To my amazement, she smiles back, slides off the satin sheet and falls on her butt. She gets up and scrambles out the door to follow her brothers. I roar with laughter. Children are a trip!

Tamara elbowed me under the covers.

"You be spoiling them rotten. That's why they don't listen to me. And for some damn reason, Dawn will not keep her clothes on—"

"She get it from her mama!" I mimic the rapper Juvenile, playfully.

Tamara tried to swat me with her hand. I dodge her by scooting to the other side of the bed. I watch as Tamara gets out the bed and walk over to the dresser and fire up a blunt of purple kush left over from last night.

"Isn't it a little early to be smoking?" I said.

Tamara turned around and glared at me.

"Nigga I thought you was goin' ta fix some pancakes or s'umptin. It's Saturday, lemme do me."

Smoke curls from her nose and mouth like a dragon as she stabs the blunt out in the ashtray next to her bible.

She then strolled over to the full length mirror and examines her reflection. She grabs a row of flab on her stomach and asks. "Do you think I need to lose some weight?"

Of course, she means no harm, but this is a trick question. To answer incorrectly will get me crucified with no mercy and to plead the fifth is worse. I play it safe and lie tactfully.

"You look good baby. Maybe a few pounds here and there." She turns looks at me with giddiness and asks, "How much weight you think I should lose?" I pounder the thought, mindful I was on fragile ground.

"Maybe fifty or sixty pounds. Maybe if you ran the football field a coupla hundred times, and did some sit ups, you'll look good as new."

She spun around and looked at me with her lips pulled back over her teeth like an angry opossum.

"Nigga I ain't runnin' no damn football field and I sho ain't losing no fuckin' sixty pounds. If I get down to a size to a twelve, I'm good with dat."

Immediately, my mind goes into emergency mode. I don't know what it is about women and their bodies that make them so sensitive.

"Baby, like I said, it ain't no problem. I love you just the way you are."

She looks at me intently as if she's trying to decide if I'm lying, she then blushes placing an index finger under her chin as if in consideration.

"Okay, I'll tell you what, I'm going to get some liposuction, a tummy tuck and maybe a few more minor body enhancements."

"If it makes you happy Tam, do it."

She smiles, walks over and hugs me tightly.

Women, I think to myself.

The doorbell chimes. Tamara glances at the clock on the vanity.

"Oh, shit! I forgot, that's Big Mama, she must have come early."

"For what?" I asked.

"To pick up the kids so I can do some shopping and get my hair and nails done."

I watched her hurry around the room, putting on a headscarf and houserobe.

She rushes out the door, leaving me staring after her. Soon, I hear the clamor of voices coming from the living room as I lay in bed. Something about Tamara greatly disturbed me that morning. Something was wrong, and I just couldn't put my finger on it. The other issue was that she is a terrible mother and housekeeper. The dishes and the house would go unclean if it wasn't for me, even bathing the children was a task that I did. Big Mama said that Tamara would be a work in progress when it came to making her into a house wife. I mean, she tried, but considering the lifestyle she had prior to me getting out of prison, it was tough. She was working at the Meat Market, a high price whore house where she was earning anywhere from ten to twenty thousand dollars a week. Tamara was high maintenance.

I got up from the bed and walked over to the dresser. I fired up a partially burned blunt out of the ashtray and mellowed in my thoughts. As I put on my pants, I noticed something sticking out from under Tamara's side of the bed. I pulled it out, and at first I thought it was just miscellaneous papers, but as I shuffled through them, I discovered unpaid bills. Lots of them from department stores: Macy's, Dillard's, Tiffany Jewelers, and more... I even discovered several credit cards in my name that I damn sure had not applied for.

"So this must be what she was up to," I thought to myself as I opened another envelope and looked inside. My knees nearly buckled as my heart began to beat like a base drum in my chest. I had to sit on the edge of the bed as I ran my fingers through my hair in bewilderment. In the envelope, was a recent picture of Travon Harris. He was a childhood associate and Tamara's ex-boyfriend when we were in middle school. From six through eighth grade, we were both going with Tamara at the same time. Of course, she denied it, but every time we would break up, she would go to him. I once came over Tamara's house when she lived in the projects. I had a surprise for her, a ring that I had bought for her. I walked up on her and Travon kissing inside the pissy smelling stairwell. I was devastated

Now, as I looked at the recent picture of Travon, his features had changed. He was more masculine, more chiseled. Back in the day, he played quarterback for our high school football team. He was recruited by every major college in America. The girls went crazy over him, including Tamara. I was a point guard, the second leading scorer in the nation. We both were destined to go to the pros. After college, he had been drafted in the last round by the Chicago Bears. He played third string quarterback, I went to prison. We both wanted Tamara. She was a competition, like a sport.

Needless to say, I hated Travon Harris and Tamara knew it.

I seriously thought about balling the picture up and throwing it in the trash. Then I felt something else in the envelope, it was a letter. My hand trembled as I took it out.

What if she is cheating on me? I thought, as I unfolded the letter to read it. Suddenly, I heard a piercing scream followed by shouting. It made the hair on the back of my neck stand up. My first concern was the children.

I rushed to place the envelopes back under Tamara's side of the bed, just as I had found them, then I put on my pants and dashed out of the bedroom.

Chapter Four

They Invaded My Home

I entered the living room to see where the noise was coming from, and to my surprise, the room was filled with distraught chicks crying. Instantly, the smell of perfume overwhelmed me. Every chick that worked at M&M's was there huddled around the couch with somber expressions. They were all decked out in fabulous designer gear: Gucci, Prada, Versace and more, with lots of cleavage, ass, and tits galore. It looked like a high end fashion show gone wrong. Amanda, the white chick that had took over running M&M'c was decked out in a smoke gray and pink two piece Channel pantsuit. She was the first to see me when I entered. She stared at my chest, making me conscious that I had my shirt off.

Ebonyze sat on the couch as the rest of the girls stood over her. Kim, the Asian beauty, Carman and Tamara were comforting her. The children were huddled up in the corner watching intently. But what really caught my attention was the new girl, Jazzy Bell, who Amanda had hired. She was audaciously stacked and fine ass fuck! Bowlegged, thick as a muthafucka, with ass for days as she stood with her back towards me, bent over. Her long black silky hair cascaded down her back. She wore a chic black fishnet bodysuit that left little to the imagination. I could see her vagina lips bulging from the back like a furry monkey trapped in a fishnet cage. Her curvaceous body was adorned with a large Chinese dragon tattoo on her back. It hugged the symmetry of her curves and ran down across her right butt cheek and around her thigh, down to her calf and stopped at her ankle. I tried my damnest not to stare at her body, but as if caught in a trance, I couldn't seem to pull my eyes away from her.

"Innocent! Boy!" Tamara yelled at me. I tried to play it off.

"What the hell is going on in here?!" I asked tearing my eyes away from where Jazzy Bell stood.

At the sound of my voice, Jazzy Bell turned around looked at me. She was tall, regal in splendor, beautiful as a model, dark as an African princess; an amazon of a woman with stiletto heels on. She was every bit of six feet tall, with sable flawless skin, mouthwatering chocolate, like a Hershey kiss. She had hazel eyes that seem to penetrate right through me. I had to steal another glance, and I did. Jazzy Bell was the most beautiful woman I'd ever seen. She continued to stare at me as Tamara answered my question with indignation.

"Some punk ass niggas came into to M&M's this morning and jumped on Ebonyze and the security guys there!"

Amanda began to pace the floor as she ran her hand through her platinum blond hair in frustration. Both her wrist and fingers were icily bejeweled with large diamond baguettes, she was eating good off M&M. Something was deeply troubling her.

I walked over to Ebonyze and stood next to Jazzy Bell. I ignored her stare and the intoxicating scent of her perfume as I examined Ebonyze's face. Her lip was bruised, so was her eye.

"Who the fuck beat you like this?!" I asked, not noticing Tre and the Twins trailing behind me.

Ebonyze ignored me as she sniffled. Strangely, it was as if I was an outsider in my own home; a house filled with hoes.

"Aunty Ebony, don't cry. My daddy gone beat they ass fo- hitting you!"

"Tre watch your damn mouth boy!" Tamara screeched at Tre.

Dawn began tugging at my pant leg, whining for me to pick her up. There was so much commotion, everybody was talking at once. Tre walked over and wedged himself between the women and sat on Ebonyze lap. Rhythmically, she began to rock him in her arms as she sobbed solemnly. I am reminded that her and Tre are inseparable. She helped raise him in a whore house since he was a toddler, while I was in prison. She was twelve years old, turning tricks and babysitting for Tamara and the other girls who worked at the prestigious Meat Market.

Ebonyze was born in a war ravaged country in Africa, known as Darfur. Even at the age of seven, she possessed exquisite beauty that saved her life. Instead of being butchered and murdered with the rest of her family, her life had been spared. She had been turned into a sex slave by soldiers who had pillaged her village, killing her entire family. She was eleven when she was smuggled into the United States, and had already been infected with the AIDS virus. Since then, due to treatment and the help of various medications, she was now living a healthy life and the only woman at M&M's that wasn't turning tricks anymore.

"Damn, did they hit you with their fist?" I asked angrily.

Before she could answer, Kim the Asian beauty replied, "yes, when she fell they kicked her too."

Kim was dressed in a provocative black mini skirt and matching blouse that showed off her small perky breasts. She had a tattoo of a Scorpion on her neck, several eyebrow piercings and a tiny nose ring. Carman, the voluptuous Mexican chick was probably the thickest chick in the room, and the sexiest. She placed a comforting hand on Kim's shoulder, and as she did so, the spaghetti lace shoulder strap on her fuchsia colored Versace dress fell, exposing peek-a-boo cleavage of her double D breasts. They looked like ripe watermelons. I could see the outline of her quarter sized nipples protruding forward. She was top heavy, with a curvy hour class figure. She had a beauty mark on her left cheek that reminded me of an attractive Spanish actress whose name I couldn't remember.

"When the security guys came over to stop them from jumping on Ebonyze, they beat up the security too—"

"What dudes?!" I asked, irritated.

Dawn was still tugging at my leg for me to pick her up. Carman ignored me. Her fear was still tormenting her. I watched her expel a deep breath, causing her large breasts to swell as if they were going to burst out the confines of the sheer material of her dress.

"When they started beating up the security guards, that's when we snuck out the back door." Carman said, then paused and frowned like she was reliving a bad moment.

She then stomped her foot in a frustrated reflex motion and gave me a wary stare.

In a strained voice that sent chills down my spine, she said, "I think they followed us here."

The room suddenly became eerily quiet. For some reason, Jazzy Bell was watching me closely. Amanda stopped pacing. She turned and glared at Carman, like a warning to shut the hell up!

"What do you mean you think they followed you here?!" I said, instantly filled with rage as I reached down and wrestled Dawn off my leg.

"Hold on baby, Daddy gone pick you up in a minute." I walked over to the window and peered out the curtain.

A pellucid sun damn near blinded me as ardent clouds strobed the sky high above. Autumn leaves spread across the lawn. Amanda's Range Rover was parked awkwardly in the yard, blocking Tamara's Benz and my BMW. The streets were clear, all was good.

Then, just as I was about to close the curtain, I saw a suspicious black Lexus with smoked windows doing a slow creep up the street. I could feel it in my bones, in the pit of my gut. Something wasn't right with the car. I opened the curtains wider, and attempted to get a better look at the car, in hopes of seeing who was inside, as it passed. Suddenly, the car stopped, reversed and backed up. It sat idling in front of my house.

"What da- fuck!!" I scoffed.

The women walked up behind me and looked out the window. They screamed in chorus in my damn ear, like they were watching a horror film in HD.

"That's them! That's them!" Suddenly, pandemonium erupted, fueled by fear.

Someone was pulling on my arm. I looked over my shoulder and saw the twins crying. Tamara looked at me with apprehension and dread, and for some reason that angered me more. This was my family, this was my home.

Emboldened by my own anger, blinded by rage, I walked over to the door and yanked it wide open. I felt the autumn chill on my bare chest. I felt a thousand hands on me; fingers clawing at my back as they tried to pull me back into the house. I heard Tamara yell timorously,

"I.C. nigga get your stupid ass back in here! Are you crazy!" Yeah, I was crazy and it was all fueled by rage. *I wish I had my knife for these fuck niggaz!*

I opened the door wide and mean-mugged whoever the fuck it was that was bold enough to post up in my muthafuckin front yard. Slowly, the passenger window descended, and a billow of smoke rose. Someone was chiefing on a blunt. I could barely make out the silhouette of three people inside the vehicle. The only thing that I was curtain of, was that they were watching me watch them.

We stared.

Then in a flash, in what felt like a blink of the eye, they jumped out the car and were up on me. One of the dudes was dressed in all black, he wore a big ass platinum and diamond medallion chain with the letters NTG. His Atlanta Braves cap was turned around backwards. He had a chopper; an AK assault rifle. The gold grill in his mouth gleamed sinisterly as he gritted his malicious intent and rushed up on me. The other guy was much shorter, but, he too had on the same kind of NTG chain. He held a Chrome plated 9mm. He wore a white tee and jeans, and sported a thick beard that resembled a Muslim with sunglasses.

The Chopper was pointed at my head and I was shoved in the house. All hell erupted as the women screamed!

The small voice inside my head said, "You done fucked up now."

And I had, big time.

Chapter Five

Mayhem and Murder

The shorter of the two had a fiendish scowl as he looked at me. His face was oddly familiar.

"I got your bitch ass now," his lips hinted at a smile.

Uncannily, I recognized him from someplace, but where?

"Yo! Nigga I don't know you!" I said above the clamor of women and children crying. The guy with the chopper was walking around, waving the weapon, telling everyone to shut up. But what stood out in my mind was Jazzy Bell. She was screaming to the top of her lungs. Bellowing like it was personal with her, like she knew them.

"Bin! Cain! What are y'all doin'? Stop it Stop it!" She called out both their names. Her rage spewed like venom.

Bin was the goon holding the 9mm aimed at my chest. He looked slightly annoyed, but for some reason, he continued to focus his attention on me. His partner continued to harass the women by waving the assault rifle and shouting for the women to shut up. They all did, everyone except Jazzy Bell and the children. I looked down, and Dawn was at my feet tugging at my leg, crying for me to pick her up.

Cain strolled over to me and smirked like this was personal; like he knew me. I could tell he was getting some type of personal satisfaction from my humiliation, and seeing me suffer.

"Nigga, your brotha T.C., back in the day, ran up in my spot and shot up a bunch of my niggaz. He killed one of my dudes and touched us for a brick and a half—"

"I ain't got nothing to do with tha—"

Before I could get the words out, he reached back with the AK-and struck me upside the head, instantly opening up a deep gash in my forehead. I keeled over, seeing stars. Blood spewed like a faucet, spattering Dawn's amber face grotesquely red like a gory Picasso painting. I was determined not to fall, not to stumble. Somewhere in the dark abyss of pain, I heard Tamara scream my name.

"Innocent!"

She tried to rush over to help me. The girls struggled to hold her back. Cain chuckled derisively and took a step back, he let loose a barrage of bullets from the AK-47 up at the ceiling. It sounded like hell's fury on earth! It sent shivers throughout my entire body, causing my ears to ring. Large chunks of brick and debris came crashing down on us, leaving a gaping hole in the ceiling.

Lord, God! What have I gotten myself into? I thought.

Tamara continued to wail, crying hysterically, so did Jazzy Bell, calling out Bin and Cain's name.

"Small world, huh nigga?" Bin said taking a step towards me.

"Man what the fuck you want? You come into my home and terrorize my family. What the fuck?"

Jazzy Bell continued to yell their names. He glared at her, but kept his focus on me.

"Nigga, I know you don't remember me, but I remember you." I furrowed my brow, trying to remember where I knew him from, as blood ran into my eyes.

Bin sinisterly continued. "It don't really matter if you remember me, what does matter is I remember what you did to me and I'm finna punish your fuck ass for dat."

"Man, I don't know you!!" I yelled, as I wiped at the blood pouring from my head.

Dawn continued to hold onto my leg.

"Does dead man walking ring a bell?" He said, as he got more and more annoyed at Jazzy Bell screaming his name.

His words resonated in my brain and quickly took me back to another time, another place. Those were the words the COs used to announce whenever they were escorting a death row inmate out of his cell. "DEAD MAN WALKING". The reason I know, is because I had spent years on death row. *This nigga knew me from the joint?*

Bin laughed at the quizzical expression on my face, as if mocking me. He enjoyed toying with my brain. For the life of me, I could not remember where I knew this nigga from. One thing was certain, he knew me and he had come to wreak havoc.

I cast a glance behind me and saw Cain squeeze one of Carmen's breasts, then he walked over and palmed Kim's ass. It was obvious he had other things on his mind.

As Jazzy Bell's rage continued to grow, she was screaming their names so loud that an angry vein protruded from her forehead and neck. Finally, Bin had enough of her screaming. I saw him give Cain a conspiratorial nod as they both exchanged glances; a silent gesture.

With imperturbable calm, like the quiet before the storm, Bin walked over to Jazzy Bell.

"Stupid ass dumb bitch, fuck you keep callin' my name fo?"

She thrust herself forward, tears streaking her ebony cheeks. "Cus you ain't s'upos 'ta come in here!" She ranted defiantly. Saliva sprayed from her mouth indignantly.

To everyone's horror, Bin leveled the gun at her head. Her eyes bucked wide, in riveting fear. He shot her in the face at point blank range.

Blacka!

The 9mm exploded, blood splattered the walls. The women screamed as she fell. With malicious intent, he stood over her and shot her in the chest. Her body jerked. She landed on her back and instantly started twitching. She went into convulsions as her eyes rolled to the back of her head. Her blood soaked the carpet. It was a grisly scene.

I knew I had to do something.

———————

It dawned on me, that this was the dude that I had been hearing about, since I got home. He was known as a menace on the streets of Atlanta. The ghetto had a true to life hood-terrorist, and even though the Bin Laden of Al Qaeda had been killed, it was as if he had been reincarnated through Bin who just happened to share the same name. There were other formidable similarities that had earned Bin the infamous nick name "Ghetto Bin Laden".

In the hood, Bin was an official goon. He operated with a cadre of cutthroat thugs; ruthless niggaz that he had recruited. They specialized in mayhem and murder. His clique went by the name of Naptime Gangstaz and their street cred read like a resume for gangster's chronicles. Just like the Bin Laden of Al Qaeda, Bin's crew terrorized the city of Atlanta. They kidnapped in broad daylight, and they cut off body parts that were sent with the ransom notes. They held people and asked for exorbitant sums of money. Women and children were not exempt from their torturous reign of terror.

Rival drug dealers didn't have a chance. They either paid up or got fucked up. The Naptime Gangstaz had earned that name because they truly specialized in giving niggaz dirt naps, and bitches could get it too. Bin never discriminated on who qualified for pain. They seemed to always operate their ambushes above the law. It had long since been rumored that the Naptime Gangstaz had a high ranking police official in their pocket, because they always operated with lethal precision and proficiency. They seem to know when and where to strike. Their motto was: You paid up in cash or blood, it doesn't matter.

Violators got violated, in the worse way. It was simple. If Bin and his crew couldn't get the victim, they would settle for a family member or a loved one to kill.

Simply said, Ghetto Bin Laden and his band of cutthroat goons, the Naptime Gangstaz were official.

He stroked his beard as he looked at me deviously, "I.C. Miller, famous ass, celebrity ass, fuck nigga. Where dat million dollar lawsuit money at?"

I looked up at him through the blood that stung my eyes. *So that's what this is all about*? I thought.

"I don't keep money like that in the house."

WHAM!

Bin hit me upside the head with the gun. A rainbow of colors, like neon lights, flashed and exploded inside my brain, causing me to stumble and fall to one knee. Tamara released a blood curdling scream. The toddler Knight took off running to the other side of the room to his mother. Dawn, drench in blood continued crying. She tried to climb up in my lap as Bin stood over me with a gloating grin as he stroked his beard in contemplation.

All of a sudden, his partner Cain went berserk and shouted, "All you bitches get naked! Take off them fucking clothes!!"

I saw a smirk come across Bin's face. Cain walked around the room, frightening the women by shoving his weapon in their face as they began to strip naked.

On the floor in front of me, Jazzy Bell's body continued to twitch. Dawn began to cry and attempt to crawl in my arms. I resisted the urge to pick her up. Her hair and face are matted with my blood. It looked like a scene from hell.

I just happened to glance over to my son, Tre. He looked terrified as the women stripped in front of him. Cain began to pace the floor. His lustful eyes examined each and every girl's body as he felt them up. He made it known what he intended to do next.

Then I heard Tamara as she stood naked, Knight at her side. In barely a whimper she calls my name, and to me it sounds like she is pleading, begging for my help. I felt like shit, powerless to act on an invasion of my own home, wife, and family.

Cain barked an order to Kim as she stood nude and shivering. For some crazy reason, I remember thinking I could see her internal ribcage

"Hey, you Chinese bitch, bring your ass over here!!" Kim hesitated and moved too slow for his liking. He walked over and yanked her by her hair. "Bitch when I tell you to move. MOVE!"

He shoved her head hard against the wall, causing pictures to fall off the mantle.

"Now bend over and let a nigga see dat phat pussy," he commanded her.

Kim bents over and spread her skin. Together, Cain and Bin get a big kick out of this as they laugh giddily. All I could do was close my eyes, shut them tight, and pray that all this pain and misery would go away. Pray that I would wake up, and this would be another nightmare. I had lived in the devil's den, a small quaint corner of hell, better known as death row, and survived by fighting off racist white men. Only to come home to be tortured and possibly murdered by black people.

My own people.

Bin's words resonated in my mind like an evil incantation, my damnation.

I.C. Miller I know you don't remember me, but I remember what you did to me.... DEAD MAN walking...

Next, Cain strolled over to Carman and looked at her big breasts, then squeezed one as she stood stiff as a store mannequin, frozen with fear. Her mascara was smeared, running down her cheek as she cried softly.

"How about we have a little fun before we give 'em a nap," Cain said humorously, to nobody in particular, then called my son Tre. "Hey little man, come here, wanna touch a pussy? We got all kinds, Mexican, Chinese, African or white bitches." Cain said while gesturing at each girl by waving the assault rifle. Together, the two goons laughed heartily.

That was it!! I couldn't take any more. Right then and there, I decided I'd rather die on my feet fighting back like a man, than cowering on my knees, bleeding on my child, and not doing anything as my wife and children were being abused.

Emboldened, I rose to my feet, barely able to control my anger, ready to die. I gritted my teeth.

"Listen nigga, if you got a problem with me, then settle it with me like a man. Do what the fuck you gotta do, but leave the women and children alone!"

Both Cain and Bin looked at each other incredulously. Then, in a fit of rage, they jumped me. I don't know why they didn't just shoot me instead, and get it over with. Cain kicked me in my chest, then Bin hit me in the back of the head with his nine, and together, the two of them began to pistol whip me. But, still, I would not fall. Not in front of my wife and children. I writhed in pain, as I heard Tamara screaming as the girls held her back. Finally, Amanda yelled as she thrust herself forward in a near suicide mission to save my life.

"Bin stop it! Stop it! I got your money and more!" she yelled, flailing her chubby arms for them to stop beating me.

Her white skin was ashen pale and rife with horror; like she was at the borderline of sanity, about to cross over to insanity. Minutes later, the two goons stopped beating me. They were winded and tired, panting heavy and breathing hard.

"Where the fuck is my money at fat bitch?!" Bin asked, still trying to catch his breath. There was a sheen of sweat glistening off his brow.

I looked down at Dawn, and miraculously she was still holding on to my leg with a tight grip. She was no longer crying. She sniffed back tears, looking up to me as if to see if I was okay. The whole time, Cain was fuming mad, giving me a look that said as soon as he catches his breath, he's going murk my ass.

Then a phone chimes from somewhere, and Bin frowned as he snatched it out his pocket and looked at the number.

He answered. "Punk ass nigga you s'pose to be in here wit us. Bring the duct tape and trash bags and your fuck ass gonna get a violation pumpkin head—".

Bin stopped talking, and listened intently, his eyes grow wide. He quickly walked over to the window and looked out.

"Oh shit! We got company." He said to Cain with alarm in his voice, and for the first time I thought I saw fear in both their eyes as he cocked his nine, one in the chamber, fifteen in the clip.

Furtively, I leaned forward and stole a glance out the window. I saw the white Cadillac SUV I had bought my grandma parked behind the black Lexus. My heart beat faster like I was going into cardiac arrest. Instantly, my pain subsided, only to be replaced with more courage. There was no way in hell I was going to let my beloved grandmother come into harm's way, even if I had to sacrifice my life trying. I loved her and my family that much.

Through bloody eyes, I watched Cain walk over to Bin; together they whispered .I played more hurt than I actually was. They watched my grandmother get out her vehicle. I heard Bin whisper to Cain.

"We ain't leaving no witness, nobody lives. We'll duct tape, hog tie 'em and place their bodies in the trash bags, na'mean?" Cain gave him a nod.

I have to do something, and do it fast! I thought as I watched Cain walk away from the window and began to bark orders, telling us to lie on the floor face down. As he neared me, a voice inside my head told me to attack, NOW!

I raised like the Sphinx, using my elbow and every muscle, every fiber and sinew in my body. I slammed my elbow into his face, hard. I heard bone and gristle snap as the impact lifted him high off his feet. He was semi-conscious when we collided with Bin standing at the window. The Chopper was dislodged from Bin's hands.

Bin spun as we bumped into him. Startled, he fired off random shots that barely missed my head as we fell against the wall. He fired off more shots, the women screamed and ran for cover. There was even more pandemonium. I managed to grab Bin's wrist with the gun in it. Cain was wedged between us as we tussled and stumbled over a glass coffee table, causing it to shatter.

Somehow, Dawn was still holding onto my leg. Bin let loose more shots as I held on to his wrist for dear life. The next thing I know, like a pack of wolves, Tamara and her hood rat girlfriends piled on top of me, kicking and scratching, pummeling both goons!

Amanda sat on Cain's back, rabbit punching him in his face like a man. Carman broke a large glass vase over Cain's head. She then took the cord and began to choke him with it so hard, his eyes bulged out like they were going to pop out the sockets. Kim used her Jimmy Choo stiletto heel like a hammer, and simultaneously pounded both their heads.

Ebonyze raced over and pulled Dawn off my leg and whisked her to the other side of the room to safety with the other children.

We continued to wrestle, coiled on the floor like venomous snakes in a pit caught up in the calamitous throes of a death struggle. I heard a stifling sound, a muffled scream, it was coming from Cain as Amanda continued to pound him in the face with her fist as Carman strangled him with the cord. Tamara laid next to me on the floor, punching, biting and scratching Bin as we wrestled over the gun.

The front door opened and Big Mama walked in and gawked at the scene. Babies were crying, blood and broken glass was everywhere. Her eyebrows stretched wide as her mahogany cheeks dropped, mouth agape in shock at seeing me and the girls fighting the two goons.

When she realized we were wrestling over the gun. She dropped her purse and screamed. "Y'all get the fuck off my grandbaby!" She then rushed over and kicked at Bin, nearly falling. She grabbed for the gun, trying to help wrestle it out of Bin's hand. It exploded!

Blacka!!

Chapter Six

On Everything I Love

One single shot resonated, exacerbated, and shattered my life. I watched in what seemed like slow surreal motion, as my grandmother clinched her large bosom. There was a hole in her breast that spread crimson red like she was clutching roses. My grandmother's eyes scrolled down in shock, at the horror that besieged her as she stumbled backwards and fell. Glass crunched underneath her, she knocked over a chair.

I yelled at the top of my voice, "Grandma, NOOOO!!"

With strength unknown to me, I snatched the gun out of Bin's hand and punched him in the face. By then, him and Cain were already punch drunk and still getting pummel by the girls as they continued their vicious beat down of the two.

I raced over to Big Mama and sat on the floor next to a dying black girl with her leg still twitching. I cried like a three year old. My grandma is everything I love. I cradled her in my arms, doing my best to comfort her, oblivious to the gun that was still in my hand. I did my best to help her lie down, one of her legs was in an awkward position underneath, but she wouldn't budge. She just wanted to sit there, glassy eyed and distant, like she was looking into some faraway place. Her breathing was labored, like she was taking tiny sips of air. Her body began to tremble as she started sweating profusely.

"Somebody call an ambulance!" I continued to cradle her in my arms, I wiped at the perspiration on her forehead with my bloody hand.

Steeped in misery, my heart hurt like it was hemorrhaging. I had never experienced that kind of emotional grief before, not like this, not in my life, as I sobbed holding that old woman in my arms.

Ebonyze seemed to be the only person in the room with mental clarity. Somehow, she had redeemed her sanity as the children continued to watch. Wailing, with awe inspired terror, Tamara and the rest of the chicks continued to beat the thugs .Ebonyze reached into her purse. Removing her phone, she called for an ambulance. I'll never forget the way my son Tre watched me crying as I rocked rhythmically with Big Mama in my arms, gun in my hand.

The gun.

It suddenly dawned on me that I had a burner in my hand. The same damn burner that my grandmother was shot with. Bodies were entangled, spread across the floor in the precipice of madness when I aimed the gun with my bloody hand waving between Bin and Cain. I couldn't get off a good shot, the girls were obstructing my view.

When they saw the manic look in my eyes as I aimed the burner, hand trembling with rage, Tamara screamed my name as they all scramble to the other side of the living room. Bin and Cain were lying on the floor, beaten to a pulp. They were semi-conscious, but lucid enough to know what was going on.

Murder was about to be the case that they gave me. They were close enough for head shots to the dome as they both cowered at the sight of me holding the burner. Droplets of blood rolled off my wrist. My hand continued to tremble at what I was about to do. The vengeful anticipation of a death; a double homicide. I cocked and aimed.

The women screamed my name. Vaguely, I could hear Ebonyze on the phone talking with the emergency dispatcher. Just when I was about to pull the trigger, my Big Mama weakly reached for the gun and missed. Her tender word was as passionate as all my love for her as she begged me, wincing in pain. Her teeth were stained red with blood. Big Mama was everything I loved.

"I.C. baby don't shoot 'em..." she winced in pain. "Two wrongs don't make a right... do it for me, put the gun down..."

Again, she winced in pain, momentarily shutting her eyes as she began to mumble bible verses. In the distance, I could hear sirens blaring, signaling to me that the cops were coming. The clamor of women screaming, telling me to put the gun down fell on deaf ears.

The Black girl's legs jerked as she lay next to me in a puddle of blood

My son and his siblings continued to cry as they stared, horrified.

Big Mama pleaded for me to put the gun down.

I wiped the blood that had merged with my tears and sweat away from my eyes as I hugged Big Mama tight against me. The whole time, I sparred with rage; a duel in my confused brain. These niggaz had invaded my home, terrorized my family and shot my beloved grandma!

Fuck that. They had no right to live. I couldn't give them a pass.

My hand continued to tremble when I said ruefully, "Grandma I'm sorry."

I aimed at Bin's dome and pulled the trigger.

Chapter Seven

Tamara

Crazy ass niggaz!!

Click! Click! Click!

The gun was empty. I didn't realize I had been holding my breath. Both Bin and Cain looked at Innocent in shock, as if they were surprised they were still alive. I'm sure Bin had shit all in his pants. I know one thing was for sure, we beat the hell out of both of them.

As Innocent held Big Mama propped up against his chest, his hand trembled with the empty gun. Sirens blared. Cain and Bin gathered themselves up off the floor on wobbly legs. They were both badly beaten and bloody like they had been mauled by a lion.

Bin glanced at the Chopper on the floor, we all did; everyone except Innocent, he was too busy crying and holding Big Mama. Just as Bin reached for the weapon, Kim still holding the bloody stiletto shoe in her hand, with feline quickness, beat him to it and snatched the Chopper up off the floor.

"Ah, uhh, muthafucka!!" Kim screeched, her hair was splayed in her face. She looked wild and untamed as she breathed heavily.

"Chill ma!!" Bin said throwing up his hands and walking backwards. He almost slipped in the puddle of blood draining from Jazzy Bell's body.

On the other side of the room, Innocent stopped rocking Big Mama in his arms. It hurt me to my core to see him like that, bloody and torn and suffering. Red tears streaked his handsome face as he yelled like a mad man.

"Shoot 'em! Shoot 'em!"

Startled, Kim turned slightly, waving the assault rifle in our direction. We all ducked for cover, that's when both thugs, stumbling and bumbling, slipping on blood and broken glass, made a mad dash for the door. Kim turned and fired a fusillade of shots that badly missed both bandits, as bullets tore through the walls, windows, and the floor, knocking her flat on her butt. Both Cain and Bin managed to hobble out the door.

Now, my home resembled a battleground. It is bedlam everywhere. Everyone was running around frantically, either trying to resuscitate Jazzy Bell or comfort Innocent who was rocking Big Mama in his arms. I'm afraid she is already dead.

Dear God help me! I prayed as I looked around the room and saw nothing but disaster and ruin as Ebonyze did her best to quiet the children. I walked over to Innocent, tip toed across broken glass, barefoot on a battlefield of emotions as he continued to cradle Big Mama tight in both of his arms. He cried hysterically, rocking her back and forth. I had never seen him like this before.

Never!

He howled. "Noooohhh, Nooooohhh, God, please noooohhh."

I turned my head and wiped at my eyes with the heels of my hands. The heavy stench of blood and death was in my nose. I was overwhelmed with so much grief and dismay for my man, that I would have traded places with him if I could. All around me, my girls frantically rushed about.

I happened to look to my right. Ebonyze was tugging on Tre, trying to get him and the twins out the room. Tre wouldn't budge; he just stared at his dad crying. It was an eerie scene, it unlevered me more. For some reason, I lost it.

"Tre get your ass outta here!!!" I screamed so loud, it felt like I nearly broke one of my vocal cords. He still didn't move. Then it dawned on me, what held him so spellbound. Big Mama had died with her eyes wide open, as Innocent continued to sob, rocking her in his arms. It was a sad sight. I walked over and accidently bumped into Kim as she applied a towel to keep the pressure on Jazzy Bell's wound. Miraculously, she was still alive.

I bent down next to Innocent and talked with tears in my voice.

"Innocent, baby, she's gone...she's in heaven..." I suppressed a sob that wasn't just for Innocent, or Big Mama. It was for this fucked up world.

I reached out and waved my hand across Big Mama's beautiful face, shutting her eyes. Innocent cried harder, howling a man's cry. She was his love, she was his everything. I almost crumbled to pieces right there. I wished that I could take his hurt and place it in a bottle and throw it into the sea, but I couldn't. I got up and walked to the corner of the room and broke down crying

"God, please help me. Please."

Then I heard it, the roar of a helicopter and sirens blaring. It dawned on me as Innocent rocked back and forth with Big Mama in his arms, that he still had the gun in his hand, the same gun that shot both Jazzy Bell and Big Mama. That was all the police needed for probable cause, hell that was all they needed to come in here and kill him.

I rushed over and wrestled the gun out his hand, then picked up the chopper off the floor where Kim had dropped it. In all the panic and upheaval, no one was paying me any attention. No one seemed to realize that when the police come, they bring with them their own version of hell, in the form of racism. I know this first hand, and I also realize the abuse that a single black man, my husband Innocent, could face, especially in his current state of mind.

I stood right there in the middle of the living room and watched as Amanda propped the dying girl's head up on a pillow. I yelled above the clamor of voices with guns in my hand.

"Don't none of y'all tell the police no names, only tell them what happened or what you saw." Amanda nodded her head in agreement.

She knew like I did, that Bin and his goons would be paying her a visit at M&M's, and not just that, the police will get a bitch killed just by making it looked like we cooperating with them. They're often worse than the criminals, because some of them are criminal as it relates to black people. We are guilty til proven innocent. I know this to be true, because the last time Innocent cooperated with police, he ended up on death row. All of that would have been cool, but considering the Meat Market is an illegal prostitution brothel and most of the customers are kingpins, public officials ,and celebrity ballers; it caused a major problem for everybody.

I rushed out the room and passed Dawn, she was crying and reaching for Innocent as Ebonyze dabbed at the blood on her face. I ran upstairs and stashed the guns in a fake compartment in the attic where I had a lot of other shit hidden from Innocent.

———————

Minutes later, I rushed back downstairs to the living room and glanced up at the gaping hole in the ceiling. I could vaguely see the police helicopter hovering above. I heard its mighty rotors reverberating as debris stirred in the room. To my utter shock, in the commotion, Tre and the twins were on the other side of the room, sitting next to Innocent as he continued to cry sorrowfully.

Dawn had her arms around him. To my left, Ebonyze, who had seen more dead bodies at the age of seven than most Iraq war veterans, had finally broken down sobbing uncontrollably. A ball of snot ran from her nose. Her eyes were blood shot and swollen. It was obvious she had reached her breaking point.

Suddenly, there is a loud knock at the door as the sound of the helicopter lowered. A deep baritone voice bellowed.

"POLICE!!"

Then the door came crashing in and the madness rushed in tenfold as a platoon of Swat Team members rushed inside the house with an arsenal of weapons locked and loaded. All of them, trigger happy rednecks. We all screamed, yelling, telling them not to shoot, but they don't hear us.

We are told to lie on the floor and place our hands where they can see them. In the chaos of madness, I was shoved to the floor face down. I can see Innocent still holding Big Mama's lifeless body. He is screaming at them as they bark commands, telling him to lie down. In their eyes, he is resisting. He will not place his hands where they can see them. He is the sole black man in the room and for some unknown reason, all their attention is focused on him. Guns are pointed at his head. There is no doubt in my mind he is about to get shot. Atlanta police have a notorious history of killing unarmed black men.

"Innocent, lie down and show them your hands!" I yell from across the room as police continue to storm the house.

"She needs a fucking ambulance! Get me an ambulance!" He screams at them, rocking faster as Dawn holds on to him. Tre and Knight stand next to Innocent. I am afraid they will be shot because to the police ,and their idiotic training, he is resisting arrest.

"Put your fucking hands up or I'm going to put a bullet in your fucking head!!" A cop yells.

I later learn that his name is Sergeant Nelson and he is a real asshole. He has angry red lines creased in his forehead as he bounces on his feet. He wears enough police armor and paraphernalia that when his body moves, there is a loud metallic sound. I can tell he is nervous, antsy and trigger happy. Like Innocent is a blatant threat. I realize that the tiny red lights that dot Innocent's body are coming from the various assault rifles pointed at him.

"Lawd-haf-mercy." I mutter.

Then I hear the words that make my soul shudder as the rest of the girls shout to the cops telling them we are unarmed. Which should be obvious because we are all completely nude.

A cop yells, "HE'S GOT A GUN!!"

Instantly, my heart pounds in my chest so hard, I can't catch my breath. *WHAT FUCKIN' GUN?? THE CRACKAS DONE PLANTED A GUN ON INNOCENT!!!*

I reared up to look, as the tactical unit surrounded him. The staccato sound of weapons being cocked, aimed, and prepared to shoot as they assumed a military stance permeated the air. Then some asshole slammed my head down so hard on the carpet, I was seeing stars. A foot came to rest on my back, causing me to screech in pain.

At the time, I didn't know that underneath Innocent's leg was Tre's toy gun. The police thought it was a real gun. Innocent is about to be shot, or worse.

Sergeant Nelson speaks into his radio, "There is a black male suspect in the home. He is armed with a gun and resisting arrest. I am about to use deadly force to disarm him."

That was his documented excuse for murder. Then he takes aim, and barks orders regardless of the fact that my fucking children are right next to Innocent. I attempt to belt forward, I scream to thé high heavens above. I was violently shoved back to the floor.

Then, my girl Amanda raises off the floor, her blubber body is ashen pink and nude. She is big as a whale, three hundred pounds plus, strong as an ox, and angry as hell as the police attempt to grab her. A barrage of fists and night sticks bounce off her head and body.

Two police are knocked to the floor as she rumbles forward like a linebacker, placing herself in front of Innocent and the children; a human shield. Even though Amanda is my girl and I love her to death, in my heart and soul, I know that if she had of been a black woman, they would have shot her. As a white woman, she was the complexion for the connection. I am certain Amanda knows better than I do, the benefits of being white. I am thankful for her.

Tiny red lights from the assault weapons strobe across her body as she scooped up Dawn and Knight in her arms. I saw a green angry vein protruding from her neck as she kicked the toy gun from under Innocents leg.

"That's a toy gun you ASSHOLES!"

She then pointed at Big Mama and shouted, "Somebody came in here to rob us! They shot that old woman. He is in shock! That's his grandma, she died in his arms." She nodded towards Jazzy Bell, "And that girl was shot, she needs medical—"

The aggressive white cop shoves her and she nearly loses her balance with the twins in her arms. They are able to manhandle her and pull her to the side of the room. For some reason, this cop is determined to harass Innocent, who was still holding Big Mama in his arms and crying poignantly as Tre stood by his side. I can see some semblance of sympathy in the other officers' faces now that Amanda has explained to them the situation.

A young white cop who looks to be barely in his twenties walks over and picks up the toy gun and announces, "It's a toy gun Sergeant Nelson."

Still, we are not offered help or medical attention. In fact, I noticed several of the cops looking at our naked bodies. Their weapons are still trained on Innocent as if they had every intention of shooting him. It is then that I wonder about the blatant relationship between angry white cops and young black men.

Tre is standing next to his father. He has a stern expression, the expression of a stubborn child. For him, this is his rite of passage in the ghetto, into police, racism and brutality. The first encounter is like an indoctrination into something he will unwillingly inherit; a sordid legacy of black boys that have come before him.

Like his father standing before him.

Not if I can help it!

"TRE! BOY! Get yo- ass over here. NOW!" I shout above the commotion of police walkie-talkies blaring, women crying, police yelling senseless commands.

My son, a seven year old child, turned and looked at me with splotches of dried blood on his face and Spiderman P.Js. His bottom lip trembled in a way that breaks my heart.

"Mama I'm standing wit my daddy right here." Tears welled in his starry eyes.

I felt like an outsider looking in, not understanding the relationship between racist cops with big guns and naïve black boys with even bigger hearts.

"I'm going to ask you one more time. Put your hands up." The cop said to Innocent.

"I need a fucking ambulance!!" Innocent rocks Big Mama's body in his arms and yells. This agitated the cop even more. He takes a step forward.

"TAKE HIM DOWN!"

Tre is violently snatched away from Innocent's side kicking and screaming. It isn't until a cop placed his hand on Big Mama's lifeless body that Innocent completely lost it and went berserk. He punches the cop in the jaw and drops him. I watch nearly twenty irate cops pile on top of Innocent and beat him.

Amanda screamed with me for them to stop. She placed the children down on the couch. Her chubby cheeks are flushed with anger, there is no doubt in my mind that she is about to jump into the melee. And if she does, the rest of us are going to join her, because that how me and my girls roll.

Suddenly, a plain clothes black detective walks in. He was immaculately dressed in a beige two piece suit and Stacy Adam shoes. He was tall, handsome and light skinned with what black folks call good hair. He had an aura about him that commanded authority. I noticed several of the other cops nudge their partners, alerting them that he was in the room as they distanced themselves from the beat down.

"Okay, that's enough!" He raised his voice, while taking in the scene.

The cops looked up and saw the detective, and instantly stopped their assault of Innocent; all but the aggressive white cop and a few of his pals. One of them had his foot on Innocent's neck while two of them twisted his arms so far behind his back, I was afraid they are going to break.

Innocent looked as if his entire body had been dipped in blood as he continued to resist. I am sadly reminded that he is twenty three years old and angry at the world.

The detective takes a step forward, his eyebrows knot up as he does another visual sweep of the room and sees Jazzy Bell lying on the floor. Her leg continues to twitch as Carman and Kim frantically attend to her. He then gazes up at the big hole in the ceiling, staring in bewilderment.

"Good Lord. What the fuck happened in here?" He gives the aggressive white cop an indignant glare.

The cop still has his foot on Innocent's neck, applying pressure. It becomes apparent that the cop has rank because he doesn't heed the detective's command to stop. The black detective's eyes flashed anger as he walked over and squatted down next to Innocent, who continued to thrash and struggle in a losing battle against a lethal submission hold.

The detective places a comforting hand on Innocent's shoulder.

"Stop resisting, you're only going to get hurt." I am surprised by the gentleness in the cop's tone, like he really does care.

Innocent doesn't obey. It's obvious the other cops are enjoying themselves brutalizing him. Finally, the detective stands, he has seen enough.

"Let him GO!" He is talking to the angry cop that has his foot on Innocent's neck.

"Huh!?" There is an authority challenge that lingers like a confrontation about to happen, as the white cop glares back at him.

"I said, take your fucking foot off his neck." There was another kind of tension on the room.

"He assaulted one of my men." The cop said, while still balancing his foot on Innocent's neck.

"You telling a muthfuckin' lie!!" We all yelled in chorus from across the room as the two cops stared each other down.

Finally, the cop removed his foot, as the rest of them follow his lead and step away. Innocent just lay there on the floor, his body heaving with emotions as he cried pitifully. Between sobs, I hear him call out Big Mama's name.

"Fuck!" I hang my head and swallow the dry lump in my throat. I fight the overwhelming urge to walk over to Innocent and hold him, but I was scared.

The detective goes into action, barking orders. "Get some goddamn clothes on these women and get the medics in here. Now!!" He shoved the young white officer and snatched the radio from another officer as he barks an order.

"We need paramedics in here, and possibly an air lift." The officers scurry about, following his commands.

Again, he looks over at Big Mama, then at the dying Jazzy Bell and wipes his face with a weary hand. It is then that I put back on my housecoat and rush over to Innocent as medics rush into the house, bringing with them their own urgency. The babies wail. Dawn is struggling to get out of Ebonyze's arms to come to Innocent.

The Detective walks over as I bow down to talk to Innocent. Police technicians arrive. They pick up spent bullet casings and ask questions. A short white man wearing latex gloves begins to dust for fingerprints.

"Hi, I am sorry for your misfortune. This is truly a tragedy...my name is Bryce McKnight. You mind telling me both your name and what happened here?"

Just as I was about to speak, Innocent looks up at him. His face was scarred, bloody with an ugly gash on his forehead. He mustered the courage to speak.

"My name is I.C. Miller..."

The cop's eyebrows rise at the sound of Innocent's name.

"... this is my wife Tamara, and this is my home. Those are my children—" Innocent pointed with a bloody hand and then stopped talking.

He was staring at something. I turned around to look. Big Mama's body was being placed on a gurney. The white sheet was pulled over her head. Innocent frowned and I saw something sinister in his eyes. The last time I saw that look was when he was on death row, after he had killed a man.

"That's my grandma they are taking away..." he stopped talking.

He blinked eyes as he inhaled deeply, his demeanor had completely changed. He spoke with grit.

"Some niggaz came in here and tried to rob us. I ain't seen no faces. I don't know nuttin'!!"

The detective made a face. If that's the way you want to do it, then I'm going to haul all of you down to the station for questioning."

"That ain't goin' ta bring my grandma back, that ain't gonna stop what them niggas did—"

"Yea, but you can't take the law into your own hands. I'm familiar with your case, I know what you did on death row. I'm a cop; your case shook up the entire police force. Cooperate with us, let me help you."

"Fuck the POLICE!! Innocent yelled. I wanted to crawl my fat ass under the carpet. The one man that was trying to help us, Innocent was going off on.

A cop from the other side of the room said, "We oughta take your ass down to the station for assault on an officer."

"Fuck you too and I'ma charge all you muthafuckas with police brutality!!" Innocent shot back.

McKnight glowered at him as he absentmindedly fumbled with a button on his suit coat.

"You need to check yourself, because from this point forward I'ma be on your ass watching every move you make and you don't want that to happen."

Innocent sighed with a shrug of his shoulders. "Man, do what you gotta do, and I'ma do what I got to do."

Somehow, Dawn managed to get away from Ebonyze. She was at Innocent's side, tugging at his pant leg. He looked down and picked her up, just as one of the technicians took a picture. The camera flashed on both Dawn and Innocent, smeared with blood and dried tears. They were a sight to behold, something straight out of a creature feature horror movie.

Then, Detective McKnight barked. "This is a crime scene! I want every area of this place cordoned off, and every nook and cranny searched. All the witnesses will be brought down to the police station." He then turned to Innocent and added, "willingly or unwillingly, you coming!"

My heart leapt into my throat. I had stashed the guns in the attic with Innocent's and my prints on them.

Innocent and his big ass mouth!

Chapter Eight

From Bad to Worse

Eighteen Hours Later
Grady Hospital Emergency Room

We had been interrogated, investigated and subjected to all types of their bullshit for twelve fucking hours. By the time we were released, the police still hadn't learned much more than they had in the first place. That aggravated the hell out of Detective McKnight. The first thing I did when I got back home was check the attic for the guns. They were gone. I nearly had a heart attack. They had found them and were not saying anything. I reasoned, they were waiting until they could do ballistics and fingerprint checks and then have probable cause to lock our asses up.

We all were going to be in big trouble, especially Innocent. His fingerprints were on the murder weapon; we would have a lot of explaining to do.

A bitch had buzzard luck. I was speeding against time for a lick I had been setting up for months; it was a big lick too! I was asking for a million dollars and I was gonna get it. I just had to get this situation with the hospital over with, and then I was going to race over to get my money. Or so I thought.

I changed clothes, into a fly Gucci outfit. I was rockin' the whole attire, including the handbag, shoes and the intellectual slim shades that made me look so sophisticated.

The medics had worked on Innocent and cleaned him up. Ms. Harvey, a family friend had picked up the children and we all, as agreed, met at the hospital to check on Jazzy Bell. For some reason, Innocent wanted to go to the hospital with us. Big Mama was in the morgue, and Innocent was no longer grieving, at least not on the outside. It was his inside I was worried about. I didn't have a chance to tell him about the guns the cops found. I wanted to wait for the right moment; he was still under a lot of stress.

We sat in the hospital lobby with the sick and suffering. Grady is a poor folk's hospital. They could do a reality show off of it. People were coming in with gunshot wounds, knife wounds, and a white dude had swallowed a screwdriver. How in the hell do you swallow a screwdriver?

Innocent sat next to me, his face was bruised and bandaged, but I know his ego and his heart hurt even more. As soon as we entered the emergency room waiting area, the TV was on CNN news. The media was having a field day reporting on the home invasion that resulted in one murdered and another critically wounded. As expected, Innocent's past was an issue with the media.

"The once promising athlete I.C. Miller, who was falsely accused of murdering and raping a young Caucasian woman, is back in the headlines again...."

The anchor reported, and then to everyone's shock, the photo of Innocent bloody and battered, holding Dawn appeared on the screen. She looked like she had been dipped in blood. I saw the shocked faces of the people in the visitation room as the broadcaster continued.

Innocent turned away from me, I reached out and held his hand. At a loss for words, my silence was a barrier, a bridge that neither of us could cross.

Carman, Kim and Amanda sat across from us, while Ebonyze paced the floor in the crowded waiting area. People milled about with somber faces. The scent of antiseptics and death seemed to permeate my nostrils as I tried my best not to stare at other people. Gloomy faces that matched my own.

Suddenly, the emergency room doors swung open, and pandemonium erupted like a violent storm, as paramedics and police rushed by with a young black boy on a gurney. He looked to be in agony. He was handcuffed to the rails, his eyes wide as if in shock. The lower portion of the gurney was covered with blood, his guts where hanging off the sides of whatever it was that the medics had used to get him to the hospital.

A black woman walked briskly behind them, crying. She looked like the boy's mother. I heard one of the medics tell the doctor the boy was shot twice in the abdomen with a twelve gauge shotgun at close range as he tried to rob a liquor store. They left behind a trail of blood in their wake. An elderly woman was standing nearby; she looked like she was going to pass out.

Unconsciously, I squeezed Innocent's hand. As I turned to look at him, his mind was somewhere else. That's when I noticed the young girl with the baby. She couldn't have been more than fifteen; she had another baby at her side in a stroller.

Then I saw the dude a few seats away. He was dressed in an all-black T-shirt and jeans with a baseball cap pulled over his eyes. Maybe it was my imagination, and then again, it could have been the pills. I had just popped an OxyCotton along with my medication.

Ebonyze stopped pacing, and said with alarm in her voice.

"Jazzy Bell has no family, only her son, Snoop. Who's going to look out for him?"

"Who is Snoop?" Innocent asked.

"Snoop is Jazzy Bell's son. He runs the streets. He's about twelve .She had him when she was eleven from her stepfather. I used to babysit for Snoop and Tre at the same time." Ebonyze said.

Innocent shook his head and muttered, "damn, she had a son?"

Amanda nodded her head. Crestfallen, she looked like she had aged ten years, even with her designer Dolce and Gabbana gray skirt suit. Her hair was a mess, and her face looked naked without makeup. She had bags under her eyes.

Reluctantly, she said, "I'm gonna give Bin the money and close down the Meat Market—"

"Money?? What money? You owe the nigga money?!" Before she could answer, Innocent added angrily, "So why in the fuck did he come to my home acting like he know me? Acting like he was at y'all, but he know me."

"Well I'm going to pay him," Amanda said.

"You ain't paying him shit!" Innocent stood. Amanda cringed like he was going to slap her.

"You got his phone number, or a way to get in contact with him?" Innocent raised his voice. People began to watch us, especially the dude dressed in black.

"No, I was just going to put the word out on the street." Amanda was lying and we all knew it.

"Well, you ain't paying him shit!!! I'ma handle his fuck ass real soon—"

I leapt from my seat when I heard him say that. Innocent wasn't a street nigga, or a hood like his brother, T.C., or his notorious uncle, the shot caller for the Black Gangsta Disciples were before they died. And he damn sure wasn't no match for the Naptime Gangstaz.

I chest bumped him. "You stay outta this!"

He made a face, like I was stupid as fuck. We were drawing attention. As he sat back down, I saw metal gleam off his waistband.

Good-Lawd! This crazy ass nigga done bought a butcher knife into the hospital. My fuckin' birthday gift.

Just as I was about to confront him, a doctor came into the visitation area. He had on a blue smock, and a surgical mask around his chin.

He removed a pair of latex gloves and asked, "Is there a McMillan family here?"

We all jump up and chimed "yes" at the same time.

"Follow me." The doctor said.

High heels and mini-skirts with protruding asses went sashaying behind him as people stared.

I looked over my shoulder and saw Innocent linger behind. His eyes were intently fixed on something. I follow his stare. Innocent was focused on the dude dressed in black. He was walking behind Carman, casually staring at her big butt, acting as if he is with us. He stepped to the side to avoid a collision with a patient being pushed in a wheelchair by a nurse. That's when I saw his iced out chain with the initials, NTG. I knew that stood for Naptime Gangstaz. It was the same type of chain Bin and Cain had on.

Maybe it was a coincidence. *I just wish I could convince Innocent of that,* I thought as I looked at him.

He had that crazy ass look in his eyes. He was locked in on dude like a rocket launcher missile about to take flight.

As we followed the doctor into the emergency room, more heart wrenching drama and despair awaited us. Faces looking like zombies, patients lying on stretchers, loved ones crying. I was instantly overcome by the smell of decay, a poor folk's hospital filled with death and dying. I glanced back over my shoulder just as dude dressed in black passed me. Innocent was right on his heels.

"INNOCENT!!" I yelled his name.

My words came out lethargic and slurred as I reached out to grab his arm. He dodged away from me. His eyes were still focused as he walked behind dude like a predator about to attack its prey; about to kill. This was the perfect environment for him to operate out of. An institution with hallways and rooms, lots of people to conceal his actions and his dirty deeds just like in prison.

I looked ahead in the crowded emergency room. I lost sight of Innocent and dude dressed in black.

"Fuck!" This nigga was ruining my high

Suddenly, I heard Kim exclaim, "Snoop! Here he is over there!"

She pointed to him sitting in a chair. We all hurried over.

Ebonyze was the first to get to him. He looked up to see her. Snoop is an extremely handsome man-child. Tall for his age at six feet, he was dressed in the latest Jordan's and True Religion jeans. Both of his ears have big diamonds in them. His hair is in dreadlocks down his back. He wore a crispy white t-shirt that read. "Obama for your mama".

Make no doubt about it; ever since Snoop was a shawty, he has been selling something. When he was ten, I once caught him selling weed in the bathroom at M&M's. His mama was selling pussy in another room. Now I suspect he's selling cocaine. What the hell. That was life in the hood.

As I looked at him with bloodshot eyes and a face full of dread, the only thing I could do was watch him and Ebonyze embrace as the rest of the girls looked on. Then, we each individually hugged him. No matter what, he was still our baby. Even though the reality was that the streets had long since claimed him.

The doctor cleared his throat to get our attention. He clearly looked uncomfortable as he speaks. We all huddle around him.

"She is in critical condition. She has lost a considerable amount of blood. However, I was able to stabilize the bleeding. As for her wounds, the bullet wound to her face shattered her lower cheek bone. Fortunately for her, the bullet entered the right side of her jaw and exited. As with the gunshot wound to her chest, the bullet hit no vital organs. However, her lung was punctured and she has two broken ribs."

The entire time, the doctor talked, I watched Snoop's facial expression. He looked disconcerted, but strong, like anger is building a fortress inside his soul. I see revenge brewing in his eyes. I can't help but wonder. What are the streets doing to our young boys?

"I think this is nothing short of a miracle, and she should make a full recovery. However, I won't be able to remove the bullet that struck her in the chest; it is too close to her spine for us to operate."

The girls all mob Snoop. It's a happy situation in a grim place. Snoop is still not showing any emotion.

Then something suddenly dawns on me, because I was a little slow, the pill had me like that. I turned around to look for Innocent.

I spotted dude with the NTG chain. He was intently watching us from the other side of the room. That's when I noticed him adjust his jacket. I saw that he was strapped with a gat, and directly behind him, Good Lord!! Innocent stood close, real close, so close dude should have felt him breathing down his neck, maybe about to slit his throat with his twelve inch butcher knife. I almost pissed in my panties.

Just as I was about yell for Innocent to stop, I heard someone say my name in a deep baritone voice that sent shivers down my spine. I looked up, and it was detective McKnight entering the emergency room with several other cops.

"Oh, shiet!" I hissed.

I thought about the guns. I just knew the police had come to arrest us. I happened to look up and see Innocent follow the guy into the restroom. My knees nearly buckled as I peered over at Detective McKnight. He and his men still didn't see us in the crowded area.

I dodged behind a crowd of people as I walked backwards, keeping my eyes on the po-po. I accidently bumped into an old man in a wheelchair. My boot hit him in the face as I nearly stumbled into his lap.

He grabbed my ass, acting like he was helping me off his lap. He smirked with a toothless grin like he had just won the coochie lottery. I wanted to slap fire from his old ass, but instead I made a mad dash for the men's bathroom.

Chapter Nine

Prepared to Catch a Case

As I entered, I saw Innocent standing outside the bathroom stall listening to a conversation on the other side. As soon as he saw me, he mean-mugged me, gesturing for me to LEAVE!

I gestured back. "NO!!"

I flailed my arms, signaling to him that the police were right outside. We were like two deaf mutes arguing, using sign language.

I was determined to stop his crazy ass from doing something stupid that he would regret, and going back to prison. After all, the police were standing right out in the hall looking for us. From the looks of it, he was just determined to wreak havoc and go back to prison.

Besides, the dude with the NTG chain could have been an innocent bystander, I reasoned, until I heard the snarky voice resonating from the other side of the bathroom stall.

"Yeah Bin, I'm at the hospital... I overheard the doctor tell them Jazzy Bell is gonna make it. What you want me to do?"

Silence was heavy, as once again, Innocent gestured, waving his hand for me to leave. I gestured back, and mouthed to him as I pointed at the door, "POLICE!"

The snarky voice continued, "Yeah, the old bitch, his grandma is dead, that shit been all over the news. His bitch ass is here at the hospital somewhere. I saw him earlier."

Innocent turned to me with an enraged face! Honest to God, I knew dude was a wrap right then and there. So I did what a bitch is supposed to do in a situation like this: prepared to catch a case with my nigga!

I signaled to Innocent that I wasn't going anywhere, as I wedged my foot and my body against the door so nobody could enter.

Ride or Die!

The voice on the other side of the stall continued with a giggle, "Yeah, I got the needle full of cyanide right here in my hand. I'll sneak into the bitch room and poke her. Tonight, we go back to his crib and finish where we left off. Just like you said, the children get it too."

Before he could finish his sentence, Innocent slammed the stall door in with his shoulder, hitting dude in the face. Catching him by surprise, the impact of the force knocked him against the toilet. A syringe and phone fell to the floor as Innocent punched him in the face three times, then hit him with a vicious elbow to his chin as he swept him off his feet.

Grabbing his shirt collar and using the momentum, he slammed the guy hard on his head on the tile floor. The sound resembled a bowling ball making a strike. The guy was hurt bad, as Innocent landed on top of him and began to pound his face with brutal, punishing blows. The guy screamed for help.

Innocent grabbed his Adam's apple and squeezed, choking him and silencing his scream. Panic stricken, the guy tried to plead for his life. Innocent wrestled the gun from his waist and struck him upside the head with it.

"Fuck boy. I'ma give you a chance to save your life, tell me your name and why Bin out to get me. Where does he live? Where can I find him? Innocent growled and placed the gun to the guy's head.

"My name is Malcolm...." he winced in pain, struggling to breathe. "Him and the crew like to hang out at... Foxy Lady... Bin has a hideaway, somewhere in Marietta Georgia. I don't know where."

Innocent cocked the gun and shoved it into his mouth.

"Wrong answer! You die."

I screamed, "Noooo!"

Someone pushed on the door and tried to enter.

"Okay! Okay, Pah-leeeze don't kill me!" The guy pleaded.

Innocent squeezed his throat, and applied more pressure, cutting off his wind supply. The guy thrashed and kicked and struggled to breathe. Innocent struck him again, this time in his temple, it shook his brain.

"Talk!!" Innocent shouted. His voice echoed.

Someone began pounding on the door.

"Bin... just... told us... that you know him from his past .... and he needed to get you out the way."

"What past?!" Innocent choked him harder, then wacked him in the jaw with the butt of the gun.

A gold tooth careened across the floor. The guy began, crying, whimpering, and begging for his life like a bitch.

"I... swear I don't ...know...don't kill me..."

Innocent punched him again, slammed his elbow into his face and began to pound his head against the floor again and again. The sound was maddening, the punishment was brutal. I had to turn my head.

The guy was punch drunk and dazed, still, Innocent continued to punish him. He pounded his face, and took him to the la-la land of semi-consciousness.

Someone was still knocking on the door. Innocent reached over for the phone and picked up something else I couldn't see. A tranquil sinister claim washed over Innocent's face as he spoke deliberately.

"Hey Bin, I got your man Malcolm right here with me."

Innocent listened to the voice on the other end of the phone, then replied, "Nigga don't worry about who I am. I'ma make sure this nigga mama dress his ass up in a nice suit for his funeral. As for you, nigga, I'll get at you real soon, even if I gotta kill every one of them Naptime niggaz till I get to your fuck ass. I'ma find you, and that's on my dead grandma you killed." Innocent snapped the phone shut and placed it in his pocket. The guy began to squirm on the floor.

"Pleezz... don't kill...me. I swear to God, I didn't have nothing to do with –."

Innocent stomped his face, the guy's head banged against the floor with a loud thud. I winced. Someone was still pounding on the door.

"I'm not going to kill you." Innocently finally said.

I expelled a deep sigh of relief as I continued to push back on whoever was pushing on the door.

"Thank you... Thank you." The guy said through a bloody mouth; happy to have his life spared.

"Come on baby, let's go!" I shouted as I held the door.

The last thing a bitch needed was an accessory to murder charge. I needed to get going, I had a lick to hit.

Innocent spoke to dude like he was an old friend, as he lifted him up to his feet.

"Naw'll I ain't goin' ta kill you nigga. I'ma let this cyanide do it."

I hadn't noticed when Innocent picked up the needle off the floor, but I saw when he slammed the needle into dude's neck and pushed the plunger. The guy instantly started going into convulsions as his eyes rolled back up in his head like he was having a seizure. His lips turned purple as white foam started coming out his mouth. As he slumped, ready to fall, Innocent grabbed him and sat him on the toilet.

"Oh, shit!!"

I had just witnessed my first murder! I watched Innocent pull down the guy's pants, making it appear that he was taking a shit. Innocent moved carefully and methodically. He wiped his prints off the stall, tucked the Glock 9mm in his pants waist, moved the butcher knife to the spin of his back, then snatched the dead guy's iced out medallion NTG chain off and placed it into his pocket.

As we prepared to exit the bathroom, I explained to him the situation with the guns at the house and that the police were outside in the hallway looking for us.

Innocent almost bugged out, but then calmed himself. I had almost forgotten that he was a cool, calculated killer in prison. I was about to find out what he was on the outside world.

As he took my hand, his knuckles were bruised.

Innocent said, "I swear to God, I ain't never going back to the joint".

He then placed his hand on the burner in his pocket and snatched the door open. I felt like his damn hostage.

And there stood detective McKnight waiting on us. A trickle of piss ran down my leg, and there went my high.

Chapter Ten

Cold Busted!

Detective McKnight was in a heated argument with Amanda and the girls when we stepped out the restroom. As two elderly men brushed by, they looked at Innocent with disdain. I heard one of them mutter, "Trifling fat bitch!" as he rushed by like he was about to shit in his pants.

I grabbed Innocent's elbow and tried to steer him away from the cops. So far, Detective McKnight hadn't noticed us, and Innocent was walking with his hand on the strap. The exit was only ten yards away when the cop called our name.

"Mr. and Mrs. Miller!!"

We stopped.

Innocent said to me, "Stand back away."

I jerked his arm and whispered, "Don't do nothing stupid!"

By then, my nerves were fried. I needed another pill, bad. The cop walked up, bringing with him what looked like the arm fucking forces of police.

I had on high heels and I remember my leg shaking so bad, one of my heels nearly turned over and I almost fell. My girls followed the cops. People in the emergency room watched us like a cinematic thriller movie where action is about to pop off. They all gathered around us.

The cop gets up front and in Innocent's face. "I'm going to need for all you all to come down to the station and be finger printed."

"For what?" Innocent asked.

"Don't play dumb with me. I could have had a warrant issued for your arrest. You know damn well what it's for. The guns we found in your attic. Somebody has got a lot of explaining to do. For now, we're running more tests on the guns."

As McKnight talked, I watched the restroom. *God, please don't let one of them old ass men come running out the bathroom hollering about a dead body.*

"And ballistics will be back soon."

For the first time, I could actually see Innocent weighing his thoughts on the cop. The scenario had changed, and I guess Innocent must have realized that. The cop could have been an asshole and ran us all down to the station again.

"Okay, we'll come down to the station...I'll talk to you. First, let me get the situation taken care of with my grandma's funeral," Innocent lied. The cop went for it.

"We just want to know what happened; if you cooperate, we can get the culprits off the streets."

Innocent nodded his head solemnly as he mopped at his bruised face with a bloody hand. I noticed the cop's eyebrows rise as he took a step back and glanced at us. He took out his notepad and jotted something down. I can tell his mind is sharp.

"Actually, we also came here to check up on Jazzy Bell. We had a tip that someone was going to make an attempt to kill her."

Innocent acts shocked, so do I. In the back of my mind, I am reminded that I had suspected that Jazzy Bell had something to do with the house invasion by the way she continued to call Bin and Cain's name, like it was personal. Innocent knows this too, it's the reason he wanted to come to the hospital in the first place.

The cop hands Innocent his card and walks off with a trail of his men following him. As soon as he leaves, I steal another glance at the restroom. The old elderly man comes shuffling out, wiping his hands with paper towel.

I pull Innocent's elbow to tug him out the emergency room as Carman and the rest of the girls go back to talking to Snoop. Amanda was on the other side of the room, frantically calling Bin's phone.

I popped another pill. Swallowed that bitch dry, felt it crawl down my throat like a serpent invading my belly. Instantly, the euphoria of flying on a cloud took over and eased my nerves. Ever since my baby Innocent came home, I had relapsed on an addiction of P.D.S which stood for pills, dick and shopping.

I had completely stopped going to church. It's amazing what a big ole dick, a honey wet clit and a bank full of money can do to a chick's mind. It actually gets worse. Innocent came home traumatized like one of them dudes from the army. He needed to see a shrink in the worse way. Many nights, he would have nightmares and I'd wake up and he would be sitting on my chest choking the shit out of me. He came out of prison with this crazy ass fetish for butcher knives, the big razor sharp Knives like Freddy Kruger used to chase people with in Nightmare on Elm Street.

I glanced over at Innocent in the crowded hospital. His demeanor was still calm and aloof, not like he had just murdered a man in a restroom, and dropped his pants to make it appear like he was taking a shit.

I gave my girls the heads up, it was time to bounce. We left the hospital with the quickness, taking Snoop with us. The girls piled in to Amanda's Range Rover.

Finally alone with Innocent, my mind plotted and conspired. I needed to drop Innocent off at Ms. Harvey's where she was babysitting our children at her home. I was running late. I needed to pick up a shit load of money, so I could deposit the thousands of dollars I had been spending out of our joint bank account.

The entire time, Innocent was babbling inaudibly, trying to reason in his head as I zoomed through heavy traffic. There was a dark overcast in the sky, threatening rain. Mary J Blige sang on the radio as I reflected back on my dreary past that threatened to run me down and destroy me and my family. Things seemed to have gotten worse with the murder of Innocent's grandmother. I looked over at him. He was still talking to himself. My heart ached. My eyes filled with tears. To my surprise, Innocent reached over and held my hand. I kept driving, didn't want to look at him, look at what we had become, what I had become. My dirty secret.

A few months ago, a childhood friend, Travon Harris, who now plays pro football for the Chicago Bears, contacted me out of the blue talking about Tre was his son and he wanted to spend some time with him. He was going on a reality show and he wanted all of his baby mamas to be a part of it. He said I could make as much as ten thousand dollars an episode. I flatly denied that Tre was his son and reminded him that Innocent was Tre's father.

I had forgotten all about the fact that Innocent and and Travon were not just enemies, but they had always competed for me since I was a little girl. Travon was back with animosity. After I told him not to call my house no more, I asked him where he got my number. He said from my mom. I called my mom to give her a piece of my mind and was shocked to learn that my mom actually thought Travon was my son's real father.

She went on to explain the reason why she asked me to name the baby Tre, was because he looked like him. I was fifteen when I gave birth to Tre. Yes, I was having sex with both of them at the time, when Innocent went off to college and ended up on death row. To be honest, I loved only Innocent with all my heart and soul, and I didn't want to take a paternity test as Travon had been asking in his letters to get the drama on his reality show.

"HELL TO THE MUTHFUCKIN NAW'LL." To be truthful, I wasn't certain who the father was. I know one thing was for sure, I damn sure was not going on a damn reality show. Ever since, Travon had been writing letters and calling me non-stop. He even sent me pictures.

However, I did find a rainbow at the end of it all. The twin's real father was a despicable man, Willie Scott. When I worked at the prison, a scandalous ass ex-girlfriend of mine named Kenisha snitched on me about a lick I pulled on an identity fraud caper. That's how I got the job. The warden threatened to have my ass locked up if I didn't have sex with his old wrinkled white perverted ass. I needed to keep my job. I needed to be near Innocent while he fought for his life on death row.

At the time, I worked at the prison as a security guard. Needless to say, I relented and let him have his way with me. And that's how I got pregnant with the twins. There was no doubt in my mind, if Innocent found out, he would be crushed beyond repair. He hated Scott more than any man in the world; well I take that back, maybe not more than The Ghetto Bin Laden.

Now, I was about to come back with vengeance. The tables had turned; it was me blackmailing his old white ass. It's awesome what chick can find on Google. After all, he was my babies' father, like it or not. As soon as I found out his wife was Senator Rothschild, and her father was an oil tycoon worth millions, and Scott's ninety one year old father was Rupert Scott, a media mogul whose media empire was worth billions with a capital B, I was on his ass like white on rice. A bitch couldn't tell me my damn children did not have a right to at least a few million.

I pulled in front of the Yacht Club; it was located on the affluent side of downtown Atlanta. There was nothing but expensive whips in the parking lot: Bentleys, Jags, Lambos, and a bunch of other exotic cars whose names I couldn't pronounce. There was money here and I damn sure came to get my share. As I looked at my reflection in the mirror, a tumultuous clap of thunder erupted in the sky. I checked my Marc Jacobs diamond studded watch. I was right on schedule and dressed to impress for the occasion. As usual, I was fly, rockin' a black silk Fendi dress and high heels. I rushed out the car and tip toed across the parking lot at a brisk pace. The last thing I wanted, was to get rained on.

I walked inside the plush restaurant. The place was elegant. A guy played a piano, a nice sensuous jazz melody. A waiter seemed to appear from nowhere as I stared at the palatial splendor of the place.

"Do you have a reservation?" The waiter asked.

"Yep, I'm here to see my baby-daddy, William Scott." I said loud enough for all the patrons to hear.

The waiter arched his brow, a tight line formed across his face. He looked at the reservation papers in his hand twice, then back at me.

Of course I gave him that look, like *is there a problem*.

"Follow me," he said and turned up his beak nose.

As I followed him to the rear of the restaurant, I was conscious of every eye in the joint watching me. I was a big girl, full figured, however, I dressed my ass off. I was always complimented on my clothes. My plan was after I got the money and replaced what I had borrowed from our bank account, I was going to get me a tummy tuck, liposuction, breast enhancements and some more touch ups just like that fake ass Kardashian chick.

I spotted Scott seated at a table in the rear of the restaurant. He had on a gray suit, with no tie. He had aged a lot since I had last seen him. As I approached him, I felt my pulse quicken. I was about to be one million dollars richer. For some reason, I couldn't help but chuckle to myself as I passed a table with a group of people that merrily sang happy birthday. Their jovial laughter seemed to envelope me.

As soon as I sat at the table across from him, he snapped, "you're fucking late!!"

He was full of rage, pouring a heavy dose of anger on me.

I ignored his wrath and tried to stay calm, cool, and focused, even though my heart was beating fast. I did my best to keep my composure. It wasn't every day that a chick like me was able to make a million dollars.

"I'm sorry, an emergency came up. Did you bring the money?" I said, looking around.

I tried not to sound desperate, but I was jittery. My palms were sweaty; my heart was racing around in my chest. He placed the briefcase on the table in from of me. I couldn't take my eyes off of it, couldn't stop staring at it.

With his jaws clutched tight, he hissed, "I don't appreciate you blackmailing me."

For some damn reason, he struck a nerve and I found myself getting all ghetto with him, as I snapped my neck and shook my finger in his face.

"Fuck you mean you don't appreciate it? You was the one started it, that's how I fuckin' got pregnant in the first place, remember asshole!?"

"If it wouldn't have been me getting you pregnant, it would have been some other poor soul. You people breed like rats and then get on welfare. What happened, Miller didn't give you none of the welfare money he was awarded from the courts?"

"Hold up partna, you got me fucked up! Fuck you mean we breed like rats and welfare?! All the fucked up shit you did and you got the nerved to call somebody a rat. You testified against your own buddies in court, just to stay out of prison, and all that corruption you intentionally did to people with them clan rednecks friends you snitched on. That money was rightfully awarded to Innocent."

He shot back, "Innocent is nothing more than a coward. He killed Innocent people."

"He killed the people that you sent to kill him!"

"I wonder what he would think if he found out I was the father of your children." Scott smirked with a gloating grin.

"I don't know, but I have you and your wife's address. I can tell him, perhaps he can come by, pay you a visit one night and you and him can talk about it."

The smirk died on his face as I watched his skin pale to the color of rotten fruit.

An attractive brunette appeared; she had large breast and beautiful teeth, like a movie star. I decided that I would also get my teeth done with the money.

She asked to take our orders. I declined.

Scott ordered a T-Bone steak, rare with the blood running out of it. I frowned and took a trip down a nasty memory lane and thought about the disgusting times his old freaky ass forced me to let him eat my coochie while I was on my cycle.

Ugh!!

The waitress walked off. I grabbed the briefcase like it was my life support system. He took a sip of his drink and stared at me over the rim of his glass, like he was contemplating my existence. He looked at me with fiendish eyes.

"Suppose I wouldn't have paid you. Suppose I would have let you take your story to the media and let you ruin my life, and starved you and them bastard ass children along with your coward husband."

As he spilled his anger, I popped open the latch on the briefcase and peeped inside.

Bingo!

All I saw was a bunch of Benjamin Franklins. I give him a curt smile, rebuked his anger and rebelled against his hostility as I whispered above the merriment of voices celebrating.

"You need to be real careful that you don't piss me off. I ain't stupid. I could have asked for much, much more money and got it. Now if you want' ta spend more for unwanted sperm donations, just keep running your fuck—"

He grabbed my arm with surprising strength, causing pain to shoot through my body as he pulled me close. His fetid breath was hot on my face, dentures big as horse teeth, he snarled, "Bitch suppose I don't want to pay your welfare whore ass—?"

I reached into my purse and fumbled around. I pulled out my nine, and shoved it under the table into his ribs.

"S'pose I blow a big ass hole in your chest if you don't take your fucking hands off me, crackah."

I watched his anger turn to fear, then shock as he released his hold on my arm.

I picked up the briefcase and couldn't help but smile at his fear as I placed the gun back into my purse. This was the same man that used to rape, abuse and humiliate me. I instantly felt a surge of energy, like a pent up release as I got up and looked at his sorry old ass. I couldn't help but smile as I strutted off, one million dollars richer.

Then he did the strangest thing, he smiled back and waved at me. Then he began to laugh a dry cackle.

––––––––––

As I approached the door, I looked over my shoulder and the two men that had been sitting at the table where leaving too. At first I thought it was a coincidence, until I reached the parking lot and they were still behind me, walking at a brisk pace. One of them was wearing a black windbreaker jacket. The other had on an army coat. He had his blond hair cut into a Mohawk. He wore dark sunglasses. The air had turned damp and cool as a misty rain had begun to fall.

Fuck! Scott had outsmarted me.

I sped up my pace to nearly a trot, my high heels scraped the worn out pavement. As I passed a minivan, I could vaguely see their reflection in the window. I heard their footsteps running behind me.

Think fast! Think fast!

My mind churned. With no choice, I reached into my purse, pulled out my gun and spun around. They had their guns drawn too, and by then, they were on both sides of me.

Too late!!

Shots were fired! Then I heard someone shout. "POLICE!!"

Chapter Eleven

A Serial Killer

Marietta Georgia

In the confines of a modest home in a plush quiet residential area on a cul-de-sac street, the outside painted a placid and serene picturesque view in this upper class neighborhood. However, on the inside of the brownstone, things are quite different. A Money machine blares as the 72 inch TV is turned up loud to tune out the horror that lurks within.

Steve Jackson is nude, tied to a folding chair. A rope is fastened tightly around his balls and tied to a doorknob on the other side of the room. It's apparent that Steve is in excruciating pain. His face is severely disfigured; both eyes nearly swollen shut, discolored purple and blue.

Punisher is six feet four, three hundred pounds of brute force and pure muscle, fortified by years of prison life. He is Bin's chief enforcer, responsible for issuing violations. Punisher towered over Steve. The Punisher's brawny body was dark and sable black. Sweat glistened off him, it resembled dark coffee. He too is nude, his massive dick dangles long like a third arm as he reaches back. Massive muscle coils and flecks as he punches Steve again, this time the blow is so powerful, the chair teeters back and nearly topples over.

A feminine voice cheers with gaiety, followed by applause with a child's excitement.

"Twenty-two!"

Steve is receiving what is known in the gang as a "Pumpkin Head Deluxe." One hundred blows to the head, ordered by Bin for Steve's failure to aid them with the home invasion.

WHAM!

"Twenty-three!"

Bin sat on the couch feeding large stacks of money into the money counting machine as his side chick Samantha stood over him pampering his face with a cotton swab, dipped in alcohol. Bin winced and cursed. His face was badly bruised along with the rest of his body.

Samantha's loyalty was carved in stone; she had been with him for years. She had a beautiful, caramel complexion with a sleek body, large breasts and an ass so big and voluptuous it made her body look deformed. She was bisexual and enjoyed kinky, outlandish sex. That's what attracted Bin to her the most.

At twenty two years old, she was drop dead gorgeous. She had a slight Bugs Bunny overbite that gave her sex appeal and long naturally curly black hair that cascaded down to the middle of her back. However, what Bin secretly enjoyed about Samantha as well, was that she would cater to any and all his perverted sexual fantasies even though Bin was married with a wife and daughter. When they arrived home that day with Steve, the white girl, Stacy, a sadomasochist sex fiend was there.

Bin didn't even ask how Samantha was able to pull it off, and to their surprise, Stacy delighted in seeing Steve receive his unmerciful beat down. Stacy specialized in pain, both mental and physical. She enjoyed working as a prostitute, being abused, and abusing her clients that reached all gambits of erotica including human bondage, torture, role playing, and deep anal penetration.

In one video in particular, Bin watched and masturbated as three burly white men beat the shit out of Stacy while having sex with her. They had huge dicks in her ass and mouth. What really turned him on, was that she really truly enjoyed being slapped and beat; punished. Forced to suck a dick far down her throat while violently being fucked in her ass and strangled to the point of nearly passing out. Those were the only ways she could achieve an orgasm.

Bin first saw Stacy on Craig's List where she advertised as a Massage Therapist. He tried to pay for her services and she flatly turned him down. Bin knows for a fact that it was because she did not do business with black customers. Bin had watched her sadist webcam video where she dressed in black leather thongs and ten inch high heels.

Cain lay on the carpet; his face looked like he had been bit by a thousand bees. He picked pieces of broken glass out of his head. His shirt is off, he is tatted up, but that day, even his tattoos seemed to hurt. He had so many lacerations and bruises, he didn't know which one to tend to first.

Across from him was Stacy, she clapped and applauded as she sat nude. Her double D breasts bounced and seemed to clap as she moved animated and hyperactive. This was more than she could have ever asked for as she sat on the carpet, her long athletic legs crossed Indian style. Pink pussy glistening and sparkling with blond public hairs and pre-cum as she sat positioned directly across from Cain, giving him more than an eye full. Somehow, looking at the attractive white girl made some of his pain subside.

If she only knew what was in store for her, Bin thought.

"How did you manage to get her here?" Bin asked under his breath, over the whir of the money counting machine.

"I offed her triple the money and assured her that she would receive all the sexual gratification that she desired or I'd pay her even more money. This is her first time doing this with black men."

Samantha stopped talking and watched as Stacy clapped and applauded more as she delighted in Steve's brutal beat down.

Samantha added, "It was icing on the cake to bring Steve here for his violations, she is getting a big kick out of it."

"You can say that again, look at the cum running down her thigh." Bin replied as he fed more money into the machine.

He leaned forward and took one of Sam's nubile breasts into his mouth and sucked on it. Samantha purred seductively and wet her hands and began to stroke Bin's tiny four inch penis. She got on her knees and took him in her mouth whole.

Suddenly there is quiet.

Stacy, the sex manic was frowning.

Punisher has knocked Steve out cold.

Bin yells from across the room, "Wake his ass up!!"

He then snatches Sam up by her hair off his dick. She scowls with a face of dismay; lubricious pouting lips form a question mark.

"Go wake his ass up!"

Samantha got up off her knees. Her ass shakes as she picks up the bottle of rubbing alcohol off the table, stomps over and splashes it in Steve's face. He screams in agony.

WHAM!

"Twenty-four!"

Stacy stands and applauds louder. Her large pendulous breasts bounce and sway as her round plum ass jiggles. Cain can't keep his eyes off the white girl and the luscious gap between her legs. His dick is hard as he unconsciously strokes himself. Stacy notices. She likes his lascivious stare. Secretly, she is excited about her first ménage a trois with black men.

Sam sashays back over to Bin, drops to her knees and attempts to stroke and suck his effeminate penis to an erection.

"So Stacy," Bin asks nonchalantly, "tell me, what is your specialty?"

Punisher stops what he was doing and watches the white girl as Steve moans painfully. Stacy picks up the rope tied to Steve's balls; she examines it with fascination and speaks in a voice brimming with sexual desire.

"I do it all; I'm the best in the business. You name it, I do it, oral, anal, double penetration, triple bondage. As you probably already know, I have a high tolerance for pain." She said as if bragging.

She placed a tuft of blond hair behind her ear as she shifted on her feet.

"So you're basically a big freak." Bin said and squirmed slightly as Samantha sucked on his dick.

Stacy nodded her head in agreement as she stared at all the stacks of money on the table, then back at Steve moaning and groaning in the chair with a rope tied around his nuts. She was impressed, but would never admit it.

"I do it all; being a freak would be putting it wrongly. I go way beyond the boundaries of freakiness," she said and inserted a finger in her pussy.

"Is this your first time providing your service to black men?" Punisher asked in a deep voice.

"Yes, this is my first time." She said, stroking her clit faster.

"Why is that?" Cain asked.

Stacy stopped stroking herself and looked down at his dick, mile high long and thick as a coke can. She expelled a deep sigh.

"Because what I do is abnormal, it's considered bizarre, and if you really want to know the truth," she smiled nervously. "Black people are not into S&M, exhibitionism and pain the way I like it. Besides, you guys don't like to pay." She giggled girlishly.

Samantha looked up from giving Bin head and replied, "Bitch I just gave you ten thousand dollars."

"I wasn't talking about you all." Stacy tried to cover her blunder, but it was too late.

Punisher walked over to her, his massive dick swinging with a pink uncircumcised head. Even with a soft dick, he had the biggest dick she had ever seen in her life.

"What you say about being dominated and pain, three way penetrations?" He asked in a deep intimidating voice.

She gazed up at him and replied, "As long as it's painful and brutal, I can handle it."

"Have you ever been fucked with a dick this big?" Punisher asked whimsically with a sheepish grin as he stroked himself. His dick instantly rises, long and mammoth for the occasion.

The white girl does a double take, giggles, then laughs out loud and finally admits, "noo, how long is that thing?" she said in a giddy voice while absentmindedly, her hand reaches out to touch it.

"Let me just put it like this, when I was in the joint for all them years, I had a bunch of blood and shit on my dick from muthafuckas not being able to hold their own."

Stacy frowned. "Whaat?!

Bin chimed in. "We got a whole bunch of sex toys. You got a problem with that?"

Stacy crinkled her nose, still looking at Punisher with almost disdain, then she replied curtly, "No... I have no problem with that... Like I said, the more painful, the better."

Punisher snickered, "You ready then, bitch?"

She gave him a terse nod. And then added timidly, "After this is done, uh... hmm, can I pull the rope tied to his testicles?"

She was talking about the rope tied to Steve's balls. Everyone in the room erupted with laughter at the white chick, everyone accept Punisher.

He finally asked with a smug expression. "What da fuck is a testicle?"

More laughter.

Punisher got angry.

"Enough of the bullshit, let the games begin." Bin said and began to give orders.

He stood up and winced in pain.

"Punisher, you hit the bitch from the back doggy style, straight asshole. Cain you get underneath and pound that pussy. I'm finna get my money' worth."

Punisher lassoed his hand around her long blond hair and yanked it hard.

"Bend the fuck over bitch, on the couch!"

"What about lubrication?" She asked with concern.

"Bitch you said you like pain. So I'ma give it to you raw, nigga pain."

She made a face, a repugnant stare, then retorted. "But with anal penetration, especially with a dick that size—"

Cain cut in, "Bitch you worried about his dick, you need to be worried about this hard nine I got hangin' over here."

She cut her eyes at him and checked out what he was working with.

The entire time, Steve continued to moan and babble about a white SUV. In the background, Stacy said, "just give me some lubrication."

WHAM!

Punisher punched her in her thigh, instantly producing an angry red bruise; the imprint of his large fist.

"Bitch that's your lubrication, now bend the fuck over!!"

The white girl grimaced in pain and began to rub her thigh like it's on fire as she sucks air, inhaling deeply. Then she grabs her breasts and began to squeeze them.

Everyone is surprised when she blurts out with her eyes closed, as if savoring the moment. She hums, and moans, "oomph, Fuck! Fuck! I like that a lot Pun- is- her." she pronounces his name liltingly, takes a step back and bends over.

Her wide curvaceous ass spreads, she bounced it, slaped it, and spread her butt cheeks wide, showing them her glistening pussy and asshole. She has an earring on her pussy lips. She made her asshole wink, twice.

Punisher takes a hesitant step back as he peers down at the white girl's ass. Cum shimmers in the light as it runs down her inner thigh. Just that fast, she has received an orgasm. Everyone in the room exchanges wary glances, fascinated by the weird white girl.

Everyone, except Cain. He rushed over, dick in hand, slightly hobbling in pain, but eager to please, fully intent on fucking Stacy into submission. He swept a glob of cum from her glistening clit and rubs it across her anus. Then he stuck his forefinger deep in her asshole, causing her to thrust her hips. She backs up, leans forward and grinds her ass against his finger while moaning wantonly.

Cain takes his finger out, licks it, then gets down on all fours. He maneuvers his body underneath her and spread pussy lips with his dick, he plunges all the way inside of her on the first thrust. Stacy gasps, her eyes buck wide as she screams.

Cain reaches up and slaps her hard three times across the face. The sound echoed in the room as he began to jack hammer fuck her. Then he started strangling her so viciously that she struggled to breathe. Her face turned beet red. Riveting panic showed in her face.

Punisher smiled to himself mischievously, as he stroked his dick. His manhood is long, thirteen inches strong, nearly as thick as a baseball bet. He is prepared to do serious damage to the white girl's tiny pink anus as he watches Cain drill her so hard her body bounces up and down like a rag doll.

Bin walks over; he has a fixation as well with seeing women and children abused sexually. His penis is fully erect as Samantha walks in front of him and drops to her knees. She too is excited; she likes to see people abused just as much as Bin and Stacy does. In fact, it was her idea to tie a rope around Steve's nuts and tie it to the doorknob with hopes of being the one slam the door.

"Hurry up Pun, I gotta see this bitch take all that dick up her ass."

"Me too!" Samantha said excitedly.

Chapter Twelve

Punisher smiled, then hauled back and punched the white girl in her buttocks causing her to wail in pain. She reached back to rub her ass, just as Cain slapped the shit out of her again and continued to jack hammer fuck her. Punisher hawked up a wad of spit on the crack of her ass as it bounced. Just as he aimed his ramrod hard dick long as a pole at her ass, Bin's phone chimes.

"Hold up!" Bin threw up a finger.

Samantha continued to take Bin in her mouth. Irritated, he thumped her on the head, then spoke into the phone, "Wuz up?"

"This is Malcolm. I'm at the hospital like you told me to do. The chick Jazzy Bell is still alive."

"Wha-da fuck do you mean she is still alive? I shot that bitch. What about the fat bitch?"

"That was his grandma. She died at the scene."

"Good, you still got the syringe with the cyanide in it?"

"Yea, I'll sneak into her room first chance I get and stick the bitch and bounce. No witnesses. No problems."

"I wanna deal with dat nigga Innocent on a personal level and the bitch Amanda too that runs the Meat Market."

Samantha was back to sucking his dick, she had inserted her finger in his ass. Bin liked that.

Suddenly, Bin heard a violent crash and lots of commotion like there was violent struggle going on at the other end of the phone. He heard a painful grunt and what sounded like a stifled scream. He took the phone away from his ear and frowned quizzically.

He looked over at Punisher, who was holding his massive dick throbbing in hand, waiting for Bin to give him the word to fuck the shit out of the white girl, and that's what he literally intended to do.

A raspy voice came over the phone, "I got your man, bitch ass nigga, right here—"

"Who in the fuck is this!? Put Malcolm back on the phone!!"

"Malcom is busy right now, nigga. Don't worry about him, I'ma make sure his mama dress his ass up in a nice suit for his funeral. As for you, nigga, I'll get at you real soon, even if I gotta kill every one of them Naptime niggaz till I get to your punk ass."

The phone went dead. Panic stricken, beads of sweat suddenly appeared on his forehead as he frantically pressed redial.

No answer.

"Muthafucka!" Bin yelled, enraged.

Punisher mistakenly took that as his cue to fuck the white girl. He spit on the head of his dick, long and sable, blue black it shined like a serpent as he aimed for her ass, as Cain continued to pound her. Somehow he managed to thrust his dick in her tiny ass hole. Stacy squealed and bucked, wiggling her butt trying to adjust her asshole and pussy to accommodate both men as they sandwiched her, slamming in and out of her body, a duel of ravaging dicks.

Cain continued to choke and strangle her. Punisher delved thirteen inches of dick all the way into her rectum. Stacy SCREAMED in agony, as together, they pillaged her pussy, molesting her body at the same time. Stacy had never experienced anything as violent as this.

"God...Jesus..." she cried as her body was being flung forward and backward to the succulent sounds of deep penetration, resonating with the rhythmic smacking sounds in rapid motion.

"I'm about 'ta... cum... again!" She snarled, her teeth like a rabid crazed animal.

As if in a trance, while Samantha sucked his dick, finger fucking his ass, Bin thought about the phone call. A shiver of fear ran through his body.

That couldn't have been Innocent! His mind raced.

He pulled away from Samantha and walked to the corner of the room and dialed a number. For a fleeting second, he looked over at Steven, battered and bruised. Steven was has brother-in-law. He was his wife's brother, and that was the only reason he even allowed the soft ass nigga to function with the Naptime Gangstaz in the first place.

Sam walked over and takes a partially burned blunt out of the astray and lit it. The entire time, her eyes are fixed on the white girl getting pounded.

True to her word, Stacy the sex fiend can take a dick. She can take punishment, or can she? Samantha thought as she padded over.

Bin dialed another number. Samantha took a deep pull off the blunt, then smiled mischievously as she burned Stacy on the thigh, causing her to scream in pain. At the same time, Cain bit down hard on her nipple, drawing blood, then slapped her twice.

Stacy screamed, more like a complaint, like a sex manic fully engaged in the forte of pain. That's when Cain stood up; his dick looked like it was a mile high. He grabbed a handful of her blond hair and shoved his dick deep down her throat.

She gagged a little, but managed to swallow him whole and began to suck on his dick masterfully, rhythmically, bobbing her head, slurping him up and down his elongated shaft. Cain was losing the battle, he was about to explode in her throat. He closed his eyes and continued to deep throat her mouth.

Bin was on the other side of the room watching everything, but yet he wasn't; his mind was elsewhere.

"Nigga I'll get you real soon even if I gotta kill every one of them Naptime niggaz…"

Innocent's threat resonated in Bin's brain. He dialed the next number, his mind raced with the dilemma of how to get rid of Innocent. That was the only solution.

"Hello Nelson, can you talk?" Bin asked as he watched Punisher flip Stacy over, place his foot down hard on her neck, and fuck her asshole frantically.

"Yeah, go ahead and talk." Sergeant Nelson said.

He was the irritated cop that showed up at Innocent's home. Nelson is on Bin's payroll. As he drove his unmarked Caprice, he frowned at the phone with disdain.

"I just got a fucked up call from one of my dudes at the hospital, I'm not sure, but it sounded like Innocent had him and was roughing him up pretty bad."

Sergeant Nelson had an attitude. "That should be the least of your worries. You again placed me in a fucked up situation, because by the time I got to Innocent's residence there was a dead body and a gunshot victim."

"That wasn't my fault. One of my dudes was out of place."

"Well, I can't keep cleaning up behind your mess."

"That ain't what the fuck I called you for. Where is Innocent? One of my dudes is missing!"

"There is a lot of shit going on with that case, for one that girl is not dead. That is going to cause you a problem."

"I know. I will take care of her. Don't worry about that."

"The other issue is Innocent. I tried to make up an excuse to put a bullet in his brain. Was gonna use the age old story that he resisted—"

"Well what happened?!" Bin raised his voice as he watched Cain choke and spank the white girl silly.

"Detective McKnight, the guy that runs homicide walked in. He's an asshole."

"What about the hospital? Can you have one of your men check up on my dude for me?" Bin asked and winced when Samantha walked over and spit in the white girl's mouth and they swallowed it.

"Yea, sure I'll have one of my men check the hospital out, but I wanna tell you this. Me and several of my men used physical force on Innocent, this guy is strong as an ox. And not just that, he is not all there. I mean REALLY not all there."

"What you expect? We invaded his home and killed his fucking grandmother."

"No, I'm not talking about that." Nelson said, and pulled the car over to the side of the road on Peachtree Street.

Nelson continued, "This guy suddenly got cool, calm and meticulous like the quiet before the storm. I went back to the station and checked up on his prison records. The guy is a cold blooded killer. He had this thing for knives."

"So! I am a killer!" Bin suddenly got angry.

"Yeah, but you let him get away. You should have killed him when you had the chance.

Silence.

Bin recovered, "I'll get him next time. Shit just went wrong. Them bitches at the Meat Market gonna pay with their lives and Innocent's entire family; his bitch and them ugly black and white ass kids gone die too!!"

Sergeant Nelson suddenly got angry, "Listen buddy, I don't fucking kill children!"

"Did I ask you to kill 'em!? You just do what the fuck I'm payin' yo crooked ass to do. And I'll handle the loose ends."

"Well, speaking of loose ends, you left a nine millimeter and AK 47 at the crime scene. I hope you didn't leave your prints on the weapon."

Once again, Bin looked over at his brother in law, Steve, and thought about blowing is fucking brains out. He felt like Steve had made his crew like look idiots for being so dumb in the botched house invasion.

"Fuck naw'll our prints were not on them! Fuck you think, I'm stupid?"

"What you did was stupid. There is just too much going on in my district with you killing and kidnaping drug dealers and yesterday there was another dead white girl found. I hope you ain't had nothing to do with that?!

There is a pause on the phone as Bin glanced over at Stacy. Punisher still had her in a crazy position, fucking her in her ass with his foot stretched on the back of her neck as Cain continued to slap her face.

Bin instantly got an erection.

"Naw'll , hell naw'll I didn't have nothing to do with that white girls murder. You need to stick to the script, that's what the fuck I'm paying you for."

Bin catches Steven looking at him and flinches like he is going strike him with the gun. He watches him writhe, helplessly bound in the chair with his balls tied to the rope connected to the doorknob.

A white pigeon landed on the hood of the patrol car. Nelson takes that as a good omen.

"Keep an eye on Innocent, watch him closely, learn his moves, his routine."

"Okay, I got you, but I have a bad vibe about his guy. He's weird and he ain't all right in the head."

"You think I give a fuck about that! Just do what I'm payin' you to do!!" With that said, Bin struck Steven upside the head with the butt of the gun.

CRACK!

"Twenty-five nigga!" Bin counted.

"What was that?" Nelson asked.

"None of yo-muthafuckin' business. You just make sure you get somebody down to the hospital to check on my dude Malcolm, and stay on top of Innocent. In a day or two, he'll be a dead man—"

"Don't you think you're taking this too fucking far?" Nelson interjects as he watches a prostitute walk by.

"You can never take revenge too far. You just do your fuckin' job and let me do mine!" Enraged, Bin threw the phone on the couch and walked over and shot the white girl in the back of the head while she had Cain's dick in her mouth.

Involuntarily, she clamped down hard on Cain's dick with her teeth. Blood from the gunshot splattered everywhere as Cain yelled in excruciating pain and Punisher jumped away, startled. He fell and scrambled away, looking at Bin in shock.

At first they thought that Bin had accidently shot Cain as he stood with a full four inch erection, until they saw him snatch his dick out her mouth as she fell. Cain hopped around the room, holding his dick in agonizing pain.

"My bad dawg," was all Bin said as he looked at the dead girl.

Then he barked orders at Samantha and Punisher, "Get the plastic wrap and towels, I don't want no blood n' shit on the rug!"

Cain and Punisher glanced at each other apprehensively, like *that nigga crazy for real* as Samantha stood as if frozen in time.

There are tiny splatters of blood on her breast.

Bin strolled over to Steven. "Pussy ass nigga, you abandoned us, got a nigga all fucked up."

"No! No! I'm telling you it was a white SUV that spooked me."

Bin cocked the gun and placed it to his head, "Nigga dat ain't no fuckin' excuse. Your fuck ass s'pose to be family and you pull dat fuck shit—"

"No, man! We is family, I swear it was a white SUV that throw me off, give me another chance." Steven pleaded through swollen bloody lips as they all watched.

"Yea, that's right you are family." Bin smirked fiendishly and reached down to pick up the rope connected to Stevens's balls. He walks the length of it to the doorknob and caresses the door handle. Steven's eyes bucked wide as he realizedwhat was possibly about to happen. He began to whine like a baby, new tears and blood smeared his cheeks.

"Naw'll man, Naw'll man, pah-leeze don't do it." Steven pleads.

Samantha covers her mouth as both Cain and Punisher stare. The tension in the room is so thick, you can cut it with a chain saw.

"You said we were family, so I'm finna make it so you don't make no-mo family. I ain't goin' kill you but I'ma make you wish you was dead."

Bin chuckled and looked at his audience, bowed slightly, then turned back to Steven.

In his best Tony Montana impression, he said. "Say goodbye to your family jewels."

Steven wiggled his head fanatically "NO! NO! NO! Plezzz!" He yelled to the top of his voice, his face was creased with terror.

Bin slammed the door!

Chapter Thirteen

Innocent

Deadly Betrayal

I drove down to Gwinnett County in Georgia in my BMW, to the palatial mini-mansion M&M's, the exclusive whorehouse that Amanda and the girls operated out of. I needed to talk to Snoop, Jazzy Bell's son; his mama had answers to questions that I needed to know. I couldn't get to her, so my logic was, he would the next best option. I needed to pick his brain, but it wasn't just that. I liked the kid, he reminded me of my dead twin brother T.C. Snoop was in his pre-adolescence and in danger of becoming a thug or maybe even a drug dealer. I figured maybe I could save him.

After I picked him up, we drove in silence. I could tell he had a lot on his mind, so did I. I had killed a man in a bathroom stall, but the troubling thing was that it didn't bother me at all. I actually enjoyed it. It was my first step in the direction of finding the ghetto Bin Laden, even though I knew the police would come calling soon.

As I drove, a joint called "Murder to Excellence" by Kanye West and Jay Z was playing. I saw Snoop bobbing his head and wondered if his thoughts were on murder too.

I asked casually, "What you know about a nigga named Bin and the Naptime Gangstaz?"

At first he didn't answer. He just looked at me with his eyebrows raised, and replied, with a subtle shrug, "They're bad, real bad. A few weeks ago, they shot up a house looking for a dude, killed a two year old baby and his mamma." Snoop said, while looking out the window.

I could tell his thoughts were distant, like he really didn't want to talk.

I needed answers, so I delved further, "What about your mom, Jazzy Bell, does she know Bin?"

Snoop turned all the way around to face me. One of his locks fell over his forehead. He brushed it back with his hand and responded, "I dunno what's going on."

That said it all. In the hood, that was like pleading the fifth. He wasn't going to tell on his mama. I didn't dig further. We drove in silence as I tried to put together the pieces in my mind.

"Where can I find them? Where do they hang out at?" I asked as we turned into his project, an ecology, sort of like prison. A microcosm of a world within a world, where people wanted to get out, but a lot of them couldn't.

"Bin and them be at the Foxy Lady all the time, but you better have yo burner with you, and some help because they always roll deep".

I nodded my head. Snoop was the second person that had told me I could find Bin at the Foxy Lady; the other person was a dead man.

As soon as we turned the corner on his street into his projects, I heard what sounded like gunshots. The first person I spotted was a lookout, a causal looking youngster, about twelve years old. He had two dooky dreads in his head. He watched my car like a hawk.

Then he saw Snoop. Snoop threw up the deuces as we passed. The youngster continued his vigilant watch for the police and worse, the Jack Boys. Up the street, somebody had a convertible red Caddy sitting on 26 inch rims. The music was so loud, it made my windows shake. That's when I noticed all the people coming out the residence. It was a "Trap House" across the street.

"Which spot you staying at?" I asked, feeling slightly uncomfortable.

To my surprise, he pointed to the trap house on the corner. I saw a guy serving a crack head right in the front yard. Snoop saw it too. His body went rigid, stiff as a board as he hollered out my window.

"Tweet, what you doin' man?"

Before I could stop the car all the way, Snoop hopped out and ran over to confront the guy. There was an exchange of words, then I saw Snoop snatch the money out the guy's hand and punch him in the mouth. The next thing I know, about ten people came piling out the house. I see guns, three chicks are with them. One of the chicks was big as a whale. Then it dawned on me that she was pregnant, she had a scarf tied around her head. I learned later that she was Snoop's baby mama.

Damn! I reached into my pocket to pull out my nine.

Just as I was about to get out the car and get into the mix of the drama, people began to scatter. I looked in my rearview mirror and saw the police. Two white burly cops jumped out of their patrol car and began a foot chase. I eased the car in gear with the nine still in my hand. I placed the car in drive. That's when I noticed Snoop and his baby mama standing on the side of the residence. Snoop waved; I tooted my horn and kept it moving. But there was no doubt in my mind that I would be back. Snoop held the answers to questions I needed to know.

―――――――

As soon as I pulled on to Martin Luther King Drive, I just happened to look into my review mirror. I saw a white Cadillac SUV two cars behind me, I remembered seeing the vehicle from somewhere, but then I thought it was just my imagination. But just to be sure, I made a turn at the light, so did the SUV.

"Fuck!" I eased the knife out my pants.

For some reason, I felt more comfortable with a knife than a burner. I purposely made another turn, so did the fucking SUV. That started my heart to racing in my chest with an adrenaline rush. The butcher knife was on my lap. I suddenly had a brilliant idea. I needed to find a secluded area to pull over, some place out of the way, in hopes that the vehicle would continue to follow me and fall right in to my trap.

Then my phone rang.

"Hello!?" I answered agitated.

I didn't want to be interrupted. I wanted to trap my prey.

"Baby I'm in jail; I need for you to get me out."

It was Tamara from Fulton County Jail. I bugged the fuck out! Up ahead I had seen an alley. I meant to pull in there, in hopes my victim would follow me, but I missed the turn. The vehicle was still behind me.

"What the fuck you mean you're in jail!!" I yelled over the phone.

She expelled a deep sigh; I could hear all kinds of ruckus in the background.

"Two police got shot. I'm charged with attempted murder, extortion and possession of drugs."

"Wow! Wow! Wow! Attempt murder on cops, possession of drugs?" I exclaimed.

"I have a one million dollar bond for the extortion; they didn't give me a bond for the attempt murder on the police."

"Tam tell me you're lying. You can't be fuckin' serious. What happened?"

"I can't talk now. Just get in contact with the lawyer try'ta get me a bond. I love you—"

The phone went dead. I banged my hand on the car steering wheel in frustration. I looked down at the speedometer. I was doing eighty miles an hour in a thirty mile zone. I slowed down and checked for the white SUV, it was gone.

———————

As soon as I pulled up on my block, I saw the media vans parked in front of my house.

"Shit." I cursed under my breath. I had to squeeze in next to a reporter's car to park next to Ms. Harvey's Camry. She must have brought the children back to get clothes and things they needed.

As soon as I parked the car, the news media pounced on me. I could hardly get out the car. For some reason, I was angry.

"I.C. Miller your beloved grandmother was murdered; you're a suspect in her death. Can we get a statement?" An attractive black woman spoke. I give her an evil glare.

"Get the fuck off my property!" I ordered.

Another reporter cut in with a microphone in my face.

"Your wife is in jail for attempted murder on two law enforcement agents and an assortment of other charges. Children's services says their investigating you and your wife for child abuse." That stopped me in my tracks.

"Child abuse!" I exhorted. It was a skinny white reporter that said it.

I started to wring his fucking neck. Instead, I shoved him out my way. In doing so, the 9mm nearly fell out my waistband. The reporters saw it and created a path for me to walk through.

Cameras flashed, someone yelled, "What is the gun for?" I ignored them and kept walking.

As I placed my key in the door, I turned and looked over my shoulder. To my surprise, the reporters were all getting back into their vehicles.

As soon as I walked inside the house, Ms. Harvey was standing at the door. She gave me a grim expression like something was terribly wrong.

And it was.

I looked up at the ceiling when I heard some banging. I saw a Mexican fixing the big ass hole in the roof. Ms. Harvey's mahogany cheeks were flushed pale when she said. "You have company."

She gave a tacit nod of her head. I looked in the direction and saw a large white man sitting on the couch with a stern expression in obsidian eyes and double jaws. He had an expression that told me he was going to be trouble. When he stood, I realized he was really a she dressed as a man.

Both twins ran towards me. When I bent to pick them up, I felt all types of pain, as I held them like I was holding my heart. That's when I turned and saw none other than Kenisha Williams seated across the room, in my favorite chair. My heart skipped a beat; I could feel the hair stand up on the back of my neck.

Both babies were shaking in my arms. I looked over and my son Tre was standing on the other side of the room.

"Hi Daddy!" He said and walked over.

That's when I noticed the wet spot. Somebody, probably Ms. Harvey, had tried to clean up the blood.

"W...what's going on?" I managed to say, as I awkwardly bent down and kissed my son on his forehead. He placed his hand around my waist.

The big dyke answered like she had a chip on her shoulder, "My name is Ms. Crabapple; I'm from the Department of Family and Children Services. There has been a complaint filed against you and your wife."

"There must be a mistake because we the ones been filing complaints. Somebody came into my home and killed my grandma." I said with grit in my voice.

"Our concern is your background. Your checkered past as it relates to this incident, may have put the children's life in danger, also your wife's recent charges and your criminal past.

"Criminal past! I have no criminal past, nor a history. I nor have my wife placed our children's lives in danger."

She cut me off in mid-sentence and placed an angry finger in my face.

"Maybe we need to let the courts decide that." She said, walking up on me.

"Maybe you need to get the hell outta my house!" I shouted at her.

The Mexican stopped working on the roof. Poised with hammer in hand, he watched us. I could vaguely hear Ms. Harvey muttering bible verses. The entire time, I could feel Kenisha's scandalous ass watching me intently as I walked over and opened the door wide. The dyke made a face and huffed.

"I will be back with a court order and the police!"

"And I'll be waiting with my lawyer!"

With that said, she stalked out. I slammed the door.

I turned to Kenisha with eyes of fury.

"What are you doing here? What do you want?!" I asked acidly.

"I saw it all on the news, Tam's arrest too. I just came to help." She said with a plea in her voice.

I gave her a look like she must have been out her fucking mind. I have known her since third grade. She was the chick that I suspected had started Tamara tricking for dollars in the schoolyard playground way back then. Whenever Kenisha comes around, bad things happen; people get hurt, killed or worse, lots of people die.

The last time I saw her, she had successfully instigated a war between two rival drug kingpins, Blu Baptist and Pharaoh Green. In the end, they were both killed along with their crews and Kenisha made off with millions of dollars in cash and drugs.

She had also saved my life, that dark and stormy night. I had to give her credit for that, besides the fact that when I was thirteen she gave me an STD.

"Innocent, I just need to talk to you... please." She persuaded with a quaver in her voice.

"Hell naw'll! Get out!" I walked off.

———

As soon as I walked into my bedroom, I took out my phone and called my lawyer, Jordan. The old dude had gotten me off death row. I trusted him with my life.

There was no answer and my mind was all over the place. It was still hard not to be emotional about my grandmother. She was everything I loved. This nigga Bin, I know him from someplace, but where? I pondered this as I absentmindedly walked over to the computer. A habit I had formed since I had gotten out of prison.

Suddenly, I had an idea. I emailed my dude, Meatball. He was from Washington, DC. Me and him had fought wars against each other and shed each other's blood until we figured out we were playing right into the racist white supremacy's hands. So, out of the necessity, and to survive, we put our differences to the side.

I left a message on CorrLinks the federal prison email system for convicts asking Meatball to find out anything he could concerning a dude name Bin and the Naptime Gangstaz. I also asked had he heard anything from my homie, MilkMan. Milk just seemed to have disappeared from the bureau of prison system into clear air. I had not heard from him since the infamous Atlanta prison riot, where over seven hundred prisoners were killed by law enforcement. Ninety-nine percent of them were black men.

Next, for some crazy reason, I logged on to Facebook to check my inbox. I had been receiving crazy anonymous communications. I was starting to wonder if there was a connection.

And sure as shit, there was a message from the anonymous Godsent. It read, *You need to be careful, watch your back.* That was it. I logged off, even more confused than when I logged on. It felt like I had the world's fucking biggest riddle in my head, my brain hurt.

I got up to sit on the bed and that's when I saw them. The letters hanging from under Tamara's side of the mattress, the letters I had starting reading, but couldn't finish when my home was invaded. Out of curiosity, I pulled the letters and miscellaneous papers from under the mattress and began to scan them.

A letter with a name on it caught my eye, Travon Harris. I had hated him ever since I caught him and Tamara kissing on her front porch. What the hell was he doing writing her? He was playing professional football for the Chicago Bears with at least six baby mamas I had read about while I was in prison. I read the letter thoroughly, my legs nearly buckled when I got to the part where he stated that Tre was his son and that he wanted to do a DNA test on his reality show.

"Fuck ass nigga!" I muttered out loud as I slung the letter across the room.

Next, I began to rifle through the envelopes. I found more bills and bills. I decided to call my bank. After listening to classical music and several mechanical voice operators, I was finally put on the phone with a live person who eventually told me that over one hundred thousand dollars had been taken out of my account.

I was livid when I disconnected the call and hung my head, dispirited. With all else that was happening, this was too much to bear. Not only was there a strong likelihood that Tre might not be my son, Tamara had betrayed me in the worse way. On top of that, she had been stealing money, our money. Big Mama's wise words resonated in my head like a mantra, *Baby you can't make a house wife outta a hoe.*

Even after all that, I was still determined to get Tamara out of jail. Call me a sucka for love, but I loved her that much. Besides, there was a chance that there could be a big mix up. That's what my heart said. My mind was telling me different. I needed to have a DNA test for my son to see if he was my child. But first, I needed to find this nigga Bin in the worse way. Then suddenly I had an idea.

"Kenisha!" I blurted out.

She knew everyone and everything about this town, it was the nature of her hustle. I got up and ran out the door. Soon as I opened it, Ms. Harvey was standing there about to knock, I startled her.

"Is Kenisha gone?" I asked.

"She was just leaving when I walked back here."

I rushed past Ms. Harvey and out the front door.

Outside, I looked up the street and saw a chick that looked just like Kenisha, but she had a big ole bubble butt and a hell of a strut. I had to do a double-take. Sure as shit, I realized it was her walking. The thing was, Kenisha has never had any ass. Her butt was as flat as an ironing board. She was walking toward a candy apple red Jag.

I called her name, "KENISHA!"

I was totally surprised when the woman turned around and squinted at me in the ardent sun with her hand shielding her eyes.

"Whaat?!" she asked disgruntled, placing a hand on her curvaceous hip.

I walked towards her. The entire time, I was trying to study her disposition, careful of the dangers that lurked.

Kenisha was the kind of chick that put the poison in the game. No man was immune to her venom. I got close enough to see the beauty mark on her left cheek; it seemed to enhance her amber complexion. A light breeze toyed with the curly locks of her naturally long coiffured hair. Kenisha's attractive appearance came courtesy of her Brazilian heritage. She dazzled all, tricked most, and conned anyone in her vicinity if they had what she wanted.

"What do you want?" She huffed, throwing her hand back to shake an unruly lock of hair off her forehead. She was showing so much cleavage with her double Ds that I could see a partial nipple poking out her Versace blouse just above the diamond baguette necklace she wore.

"I need your help." I stated as I scanned the street looking for white SUVs and anything else that might look suspicious.

"Nigga is you fuckin' bipolar uh, some shit. Didn't you fuckin' tell me to leave a minute ago? You kicked me out your house and embarrassed the shit outta me."

"I'm sorry." I said sincerely as I scanned the streets.

She just looked at me with loathing eyes.

"I need your help."

She shifted her feet, folding her arms over her ample breasts and bunched up her lips, pushing them to the side of her face. For a fleeting second, I thought I saw a smirk appear on her face as she huffed.

"Humph, what kind of favor? Look like somebody beat you up pretty bad." She bristled and leaned forward, caressing one of the bruises on my face. I could smell the scent of her perfume.

"It's a nigga named Bin, they call him the Ghetto Bin Laden on the streets. I need to find him. He is the nigga that invaded my home and killed my grandma. It's a bunch of weird shit going on."

Just the mention of Bin's name and what he did to my grandmother choked me up.

Before I could finish my sentence, her mouth dropped wide open. Her entire facial expression changed, and then her arched eyebrows raised a quizzical line across her delicate forehead like she had another idea, one more conniving.

"Yeah, I think I know where you might be able to find him. But what's in it for me?" She said in a sultry voice, brimming with her treason.

I saw it lurking in her almond shaped green eyes. Before I knew it, I grabbed her by her throat and squeezed hard.

"You not listening to me bitch! A nigga ran up in my crib and killed my grandma. I need to find him or I'ma start killin' everything that move, starting wit yo fuck ass!" I choked her harder, and watched her gag. Her face turned bright red with veins protruding from her forehead like they were going to burst.

"Okay! Okay!" She grumbled, trying to wrestle my hands off her neck. "There is a club called Foxy Lady… Bin and his goons, the Naptime Gangstaz hang out there…. It's a cutthroat strip …joint…they'll kill…you…"

I released my grip. Kenisha was the third person that had told me I could find Bin at Foxy Lady. She stumbled away from me, looking at me with mystic eyes that were hard to read. My hand left an ugly red welt on her neck. Instantly, I regretted my actions. Like it or not, she was the only real source of information I had that could help me find Bin. I walked up on her close. Her eyes were blood red. Maybe it was from me cutting off the oxygen to her brain, maybe it was her seething anger. Maybe it was both.

"I'm sorry, I didn't mean to do that." I said half serious. She just looked at me as her hand massaged her throat. Then a slight smile tugged at her cheeks.

"Nigga you got my pussy wet as fuck, a bitch be lovin' dat wild shit. I couldn't help but think about dat big ole dick of yours." She smiled awkwardly. Her face was still flushed red.

I knew Kenisha was a freak, she liked men and women, but what she said really throw me for a loop. Also I knew she was a conniving ass bitch that couldn't be trusted, and that she was up to something else, but what? I was at a loss for words. She must have read my thoughts.

"After I hit that big lick knocking off both Haitian Blu and Pharaoh Green and rescuing you and them babies, I had so much dope I couldn't possibly move it all. Soon, word hit the streets that my team had that work. I was selling dope like crazy until Bin and his crew caught wind of it. He killed several people in my crew until I agreed to pay him protection fees and still, the nigga robbed me. Caught me slippin' and took all my shit."

"Robbed?" I quipped.

"Yeah, the nigga jacked me, still, after I was paying him protection fees. I even tried to give his no-dick ass some of this pussy, he weird as fuck." Kenisha frowned.

"You used to fuck with dude like that?" I scanned the streets.

"Well, kinda sorta. I mean a bitch gotta do what a bitch gotta do. I just wasn't into paying no damn protection fees. I mean look at me, a nigga be paying me just to eat my pussy." She said and posed, running her hands over her shapely curves like she thought she was a black Marilyn Monroe. She continued. "I stalled on one payment to him and his Naptime dudes. Them crazy ass niggaz ran up in each and every one of my dope houses and killed three people and took all the dope and money. This nigga be doing shit in broad daylight, it's almost like he got the police or a root man in his pocket. He took my girl hostage and had the nerve to ask for three hundred grand on top of the millions he had already taken." Kenisha huffed, using animated hands and body gestures. I remembered her being like that when she was nine years old.

"Did you pay it?"

"Fuck naw'll. I mean I was thinking about it, but when he sent me three of her fingers in an envelope, I recognized one of the rings I had bought her on one of the fingers. He sent it to show he wasn't bluffing about the money. I kind of figured she might have already been dead."

"Damn, was she?" I drawled.

"A dog found her a week later in a shallow grave. She had been buried alive, her body was mutilated, throat slashed, breast cut off, fingers too. The police said it looked like someone had also taken pleasure in torturing her with a lit cigarette or cigar."

For a moment, I marinated on what she said. My mind flashed back to when Bin invaded my home, the things he said. He knew me from somewhere. The feeling was mutual. I spoke out loud as if talking to myself.

"It's strange, I remember this nigga from somewhere, and I think it's from the joint. It's personal."

"I know where his stash house is in Marietta. He also has a wife and kid somewhere in Altanta, but I don't know where."

"Tell me where the spot is in Marietta?" I asked anxiously and watched a U-Hall truck pass. A dog barked in the distance.

"What's in it for me if I tell you where his stash is?" Kenisha asked seductively.

I frowned like I was going to snatch a knot in her ass again.

"I told you, this nigga gotta go! He gotta be dealt wit!" Anger had surfaced in my brain again.

Just as I was getting ready to grab her, she took a tentative step back and placed her hand inside her Gucci hand bag.

"A bitch be liking dat rough shit, but you ain't finna spaz out on me again like that unless you're my man."

There was no doubt in my mind that Kenisha was packin' steel in her purse.

"Kenisha, you're not listening to me! This nigga took something from me I can't ever get back."

She took her hand out of her purse and responded in barely a whisper; her voice was breathy with her own selfish passion.

"I understand your loss Innocent. Some of my fondest memories as a child were going to your grandma's house to buy candy from your Big Mama, the candy lady. But if I'ma help you, you gotta help me too." Her voice purred in that feminine twang a woman uses when their trying to be persuasive, even cunning.

It suddenly hit me. Just as I suspected, Kenisha was up to something from the very first moment she stepped her trifling ass in my house.

"Help you?! Help you how?" I said with an edge in my voice, my fists were balled tightly at my sides. At first, she just looked at me with goo-goo eyes that I'm sure where lidded with larceny.

"In several ways. What better way to catch a man, than to use a beautiful woman as bait? I can show you where he lives, maybe even bring you his head on a platter."

She stopped talking and smiled as she walked closer up on me and placed a deft finger on my chest. She leaned forward and whispered in my ear.

"I just want the dope and money out of the stash house. There are millions in cash there and so many kilos of dope, you need a van to tote all of it away."

"So you telling me you want me to go up in this nigga stash house, rob him and give you all the money and dope?" Kenisha didn't answer; she just looked at me, as she continued to gyrate her finger on my chest.

"I know for a fact, there's a coupla million in it for you."

She must have read the manic expression on my face, because she took her hand off my chest and placed it back in her purse.

"Nigga, at least I'm giving you something. I'm helping you, you help me. Besides, Tamara's in jail, that bitch ain't no good. I'm right here at your side, doing what a bitch s'posed 'ta do in a situation like this. I'm all you got and you know it!" She shouted at me like a chick that was used to getting her way with dudes. Then she stared at me like she was waiting for an answer.

The last thing I wanted was to run up in some nigga's spot for some drugs for a chick I know was a manipulating, conning bitch. With Kenisha, she was so scandalous she could be setting me up to walk into a trap for Bin.

"Lemme think on it," I said with my mind in a maze.

As crazy as it may sound, I was tempted.

"Yeah, you think on it, also think about giving me some of dat phat dick. You ever thought about a threesome, a little ménage a trois. That would take some of the stress off you. I have a girlfriend that works at Magic City. She's a bigger freak than me. You ever had your dick sucked while getting your ass hole licked?"

I just shook my head "no" at Kenisha. She thought I was thinking about the sex, I was thinking about putting her scandalous ass in the trunk of my car until she agreed to tell me where Bin's stash spot was. She just didn't have a clue. The only thing on my mind was murder and revenge. I know I had to utilize my other options before I could deal with Kenisha and her scheming ass.

I mouthed silently as if talking to myself, "Foxy Lady?"

She heard me and responded apprehensively, "Don't go in there. All them niggaz is official goons, certified killers. A nigga gets slumped in there nearly every other week and they all roll in cliques. They jack niggaz in there for a spot, even the bitches rob niggaz. Lemme help you." She pouted and stomped her foot.

"I'll call you in a day or two if this does not work out."

"Boy you crazy as fuck, if you gone go into Foxy Lady looking for Bin."

I walked off. I was a man on a mission.

I trudged back into the house. Tre was standing in the living room, looking up at the hole in the ceiling as the Mexican worked. The twins played in the next room. At first, he didn't see me. I found myself staring at him, his skin tone, his features, even his hair. For the first time in my life, I wondered disconcertedly, if Tre was my biological child.

I noticed something I had never noticed before, not only did Tre resemble Travon, he had the same wide nose and they were also the same complexion. He caught me staring and ran over to me. I hugged him and said a silent prayer as an emotion came over me that I had never experienced before.

"Tre, I'm going to give you a DNA test when I come back." I said to my child, not really certain if I would make it back.

He just looked at me with eyes that melted my heart.

"Daddy what's a DNA?"

I was completely lost for words. I stammered, stumbling over my words, "It's a, huh, hmmm, uhh, something to show just how much I love you."

"I love you too Daddy."

With that, I had to turn my head and swallow the dry lump in my throat.

GOD, PLEASE LET HIM BE MY CHILD. AND WHAT IF HE ISN'T?

My thoughts churned, causing more emotions to spawn.

I squatted down to his eye level and talked to him like he was a man.

"I'm about to go away. I'm going to have to do something, take care of some business. I want you to be a big boy while I'm gone and take care of your brother and sister, until I come back."

He didn't answer; instead he dropped his head and fidgeted with his shirt.

"What's wrong?"

"Big Mama gone. My mama gone. Now you finna leave me." He began to cry. I ruffled his hair and tried to play if off with a chuckle and a smile.

"I'm not going to leave you. In fact, I'm going to get you that baseball glove you asked for, and we're going to the park and play catch."

He brightened up and looked at me with starry eyes. "When Daddy?"

"Real soon. I promise."

I was guilt ridden, I couldn't help it. I reached down and gave my son a hug.

Chapter Fourteen

A Bucket of Blood

As I drove down Piedmont Street, headed to Foxy Lady, a hole in the wall strip club, I glanced up at the sky. The night was eerie, a full moon embellished the earth luminously, with a sinister smirk. About half a block away from the club, my cellphone chimed. I answered it. It was Ms. Harvey, I could hear the babies crying in the background. She sounded distraught.

"Hello?"

"Innocent, the police was just here, they tore up the house. They had a search warrant and a warrant for your arrest. They want you to turn yourself in. I am certain they're going to come with Family and Children services as well. That dreaded woman that looks like a man was with them."

"Damnit!!" I huffed.

They must have got my fingerprints off the guns.

"I don't know why Tamara didn't just give them the damn guns in the first place."

"What, what did you say?" Ms. Heavy asked.

She didn't have a clue as to what I was talking about.

"Huh, nothing. Listen, take the children back to your house."

"I don't want to get into any trouble, besides I have to work in the morning."

"I'll be there to get them."

"Don't do anything stupid!" She admonished sternly.

"I won't." I said as I turned the corner.

Up the street, I saw the club. It was in the hub of the city. I saw a few dudes parking lot pimping and a lot of tricked out cars with their systems pumping loud rap music. The cackle of a woman's laughter rang in my ears, as if taunting me. I suddenly had to screech on my brakes as three scantily dressed chicks walked in front of my car. One of them was tall and slender. She had purple hair with a skirt so short, I could see her ass cheeks when she sashayed by. Her girlfriends were just as provocative in their attire with matching handbags and lots of hairweave. The shorter plump one waved at me and blew a kiss as they walked in front of my car.

I happened to find a parking place on the street down from the club. For a moment, I just sat there in the idling car with my heart beating in my chest. I knew what I was about to do was suicidal, but it wasn't my mind that was leading me, it was my heart. I was out for blood and was willing to walk into the lion's den to get it.

The night was alive and vibrant as I watched people come in and out the club. My palms were sweaty as I reached for the nine in my waistband and placed it under my front seat. I was dressed casually in my Polo shirt and True Religion jeans. I had on my brother's dope, iced out BHM chain he took from Haitian Blu. Big Mama had given it to me along with a Presidential Rolex that had so many glistening diamonds, it sparkled like a chandelier on my wrist.

As soon as I got out the car, my conscience told me to turn back. I was out of my lane, out of my league, Big Mama once told me that if you follow your first instincts, people will think you're a genius. That night I continued walking. The air was humid. I could smell the scent of frying food and blaring music coming from inside the club. As soon as I walked through the door, I caught a whiff of funk, weed and cheap perfume that hit me in the face as loud music blasted. Neon lights flashed, I had to adjust my eyes. All the while, that voice in the back of my head kept telling me to turn around.

I saw a big booty chick wearing nothing but a nipple ring and stilettos heels with a few slut tattoos. She was gyrating her wide hips to the music with a drink in her hand as she talked to the bouncer. Her long black weave hung down her back. The bouncer was huge, ashy blue- black with a bald head. He looked like he worked out every day of his life. He stood at least 6ft 8 three hundred pounds of muscle and looked evil enough to bite a snake's head off. He had an ugly dent on the side of his head like a transmission or something had fallen on his head.

The stripper standing with him looked at me and stopped what she was doing with her drink poised in hand. She looked at me like I was candy as she licked her strawberry glossed lips with a salivating tongue. She arched her brow in concentration.

Up close, she had a pretty face with a pecan complexion, but her breasts sagged. I saw stretch marks on her stomach and what looked like a deep gunshot wound on her hip. I paid the twenty dollar door fee and was surprised when the bouncer placed a band on my wrist.

The entire time, the stripper continued to watch me. As soon as I stepped through the metal detector it screamed like a rape victim. The bouncer was on me with a quickness. It suddenly dawned on me that I had the butcher knife on me.

Fuck! I had forgotten all about it. In prison, I'd rather get caught with it, than without it. My problem was, I wasn't in prison anymore.

"HEY! YOU! Go back through." the bouncer barked.

That's when I saw the gold grill in his mouth shimmer like dull pennies. Just then, a clique of chicks walked in. They were wearing practically nothing too. Lots of makeup and, fake risqué colored hair, mini-skirts and costume jewelry. They were loud and boisterous.

I pulled up my shirt and showed the bouncer the horror of what had besieged me. My official introduction into beast mode. The hacked, horrific, brutal scars that ran like train tracks all over my brawny chest and six pack abs. Death defying wounds I had suffered, courtesy of racist police beatings and bullets, knife fights in prison and several shank attacks where I fought for my life.

"Yo dawg, I got metal pins n' my chest and a bullet in my leg." I said to the bouncer with my shirt still raised. The chicks and the bouncer all stopped talking and looked at me aghast, like I was a walking horror show. They drawled in chorus at the same time.

"DAYUM!!"

"Want me to walk back through?" I asked, feeling like all eyes were on me.

Before I could get the words out, he rushed up on me, a bear of a man. I wasn't intimidated by his size. I had knocked dudes his size out cold before.

"Turn around, let me frisk you," he said.

At first, I started to buck, but it was something about the tone of his voice. Besides, too many people were watching. I complied, I hadn't even made it into the club and was about to get thrown out.

To my relief, he just glazed his hands over my body, not really touching me.

"Okay." He said with a nod.

I took off walking like I know my way around the joint. The place was jam packed. People galore, too many people, I was instantly uncomfortable. I pretended to be interested in the second rate strippers dancing on polls. As I headed towards a table near the bar, I passed a den of thirsty looking cutthroats sitting at the table. They watched me like a hawk, a few of them mean-mugged me. I mean-mugged them back as I swagged on by.

I took a seat at a small table next to two hood rats and saw my reflection in the bar mirror. One of the chicks sitting at the next table was a redbone. She was very attractive, wearing a skin tight body suit that left little to the imagination.

She took one look at me and called, "Heyy wit your fine ass!"

Her and her girlfriend laughed. The female with her was chubby with a pleasant cherubic face. But even in the dim light, I could see that she had a bad case of acne. I seized the moment and went into my spiel. I leaned forward, and tried to smile like I hadn't come there to kill a man, maybe several men.

"Wuz up shawty, dig, I'm looking for an old friend, his name is Bin. I want to surprise him, have you seen him?" I had to yell above the music to the redbone.

She smiled a beautiful smile with perfect teeth and dimples. That's when I noticed she had hazel eyes that flickered in the light as she responded back.

"Naw'll I don't know him Boo, but what you in to tonight."

"Just partin' waitin' on my lady." I said to throw her off. She frowned like she smelled something stank.

"Oh, okay." She retorted and turned and whispered something to her girlfriend, together they laughed and continued their conversation.

Before I knew it, the stripper that was at the door when I first came in, strolled up to me. She walked with a slight limp, but still poised.

"Hey sexy you want a drank with your sexy self."

"Drank?" I repeated. "I thought you were a dancer."

She giggled, "I tend the bar as a waitress and dance too. Why you want a lap dance?" She eased close up on me. The redbone was watching intently.

"Naw'll I'm good."

"What's your name? You look familiar." She asks in my ear, intentionally brushing her breast against me.

"My name is Innocent. What's yours?"

"Goodhead." She yelled in my ear.

"Goodhead?" I repeated. I couldn't help but smile. Then added humorously, "Okay, I'm not going to even ask you how you got that name."

She laughed, "You don't have to, I can show you." She said and stuck her tongue out.

It was as long as my middle finger. People passed by us up close. A Drake song came on and the strippers went wild. Behind me, someone threw money up and damn near started a stampede.

It looked like it took everything in her power not to join in the ruckus behind me. I decided to run my game.

"Ms. Goodhead, maybe I can buy a drank in a minute with a nice phat tip, and if you're not doing nothing, we can bounce outta here, but I need a favor."

"What you want baby?" she asked anxiously, easing closer to me. She grinded her pussy against my leg.

"I'm tryna find an old friend. I want to surprise him. I'll break you off a coupla bills."

"Okay." She nodded her head at the sound of money.

"I'm lookin' for Bin. Short dude with a beard, rolls with the Naptime Gangstaz."

She curled her neck away from me and almost stumbled into a patron as she stepped back. Her entire facial expression changed.

"You're a friend of Bin and you want to surprise him?" The way she repeated it, instantly put me on guard.

"Yeah," I smiled awkwardly and went into my finesse game and reached into my pocket. I pulled out a stack of money, all hundreds. I passed her a bill. She looked at it, wiggled her ass and walked back up on me.

"Okay, I think I might know him. If he comes in I'll let you know so you can surprise him." She did the little wiggle thing with her ass again and said. "Let me go serve some customers, I'll be back. What you want to drink?"

"Patron."

"Okay," she beamed and strolled off. I tried to keep my eye on her, but the place was too crowded. I lost her.

As I focused my attention on the club and people watching, I also did my reconnaissance. I checked for doors, exits, escape routes, anything that could be to my advantage in the event I needed to move fast.

That's when I looked up and saw her coming to me, undulating and curvy, a lot of voluptuous woman in motion. She had sensuous wide hips, small round perky breasts, a taut waistline with a navel ring and a tattoo partially covered around her panty line. As she neared in the dim flashing lights, it suddenly occurred to me that she was a white girl with long blond hair and a body thick as some of the finest black girls I know. She wore pink Prada jeans with a low cut satin matching female wife beater shirt. I could see her nipples, hard as ripe strawberries, outlined in her shirt as she walked straight to my table and sassed with witticism.

"Dawg, you must see something you like, looking at me like that." She placed her hands on her hips. Neon lights strobed her face as people passed. I thought I saw a hint of a smile crease her thin lips as I searched my mind for a quick reply and came up short. I didn't even realize I had been staring.

"Shit, you had to be looking at me to know I was looking at you." I shot back lamely.

She burst out in laughter. I couldn't help but smile. I looked at the table across from us and saw the sexy redbone giving me the evil eye.

"My name is Georgia May; my friends call me Game for short." She extended a well-manicured hand.

As we talked, every black dude that passed looked at her round ass. She acted as if she was accustomed to the attention.

"I.C.," I said trying not to look at her curves. I wasn't there for pleasure. I had come to inflict a lot of pain.

"You look familiar, even with the bruise on your face." She said, easing closer and invading my space. I could smell the sweet scent of her Burberry perfume.

"Oh, really?" It still fascinated me when chicks said that. I was still careful to check my surroundings.

"You have dimples," she teased.

"Only when I smile."

"Do I make you smile?"

"Maybe at the right place and time you could," I said bobbing my head from side to side trying to look behind her, checking out faces and people.

I needed to see Bin first before he saw me, if he was here. For some reason, I had an uncanny feeling that somebody was watching me. The white girl got annoyed.

"Heyy, you looking for somebody or something?" She said, placing her hand on my arm.

"Yeah, I mean, no, huh, sorta, you know a dude name Bin?"

She gave me an incredulous scowl like I had just told her I was gay. Then suddenly, the waitress, Goodhead returned.

She pushed up on Game, "Bitch what you doin' talking to my man, hoe you better kick rocks."

Game didn't back down, "Yo, man? Humph, well bitch you betta put a tag or a leash or s'umptin on his dog ass. Cause if he keep sniffing around me, I'ma take his ass home and give me something to eat."

The redbone sitting at the next table erupted in laughter with her friend as I looked on in shock. The last thing I needed was to call some unneeded attention to myself. I was almost relieved when Game cut her eyes at me with pure disdain, sucked her teeth and strutted off.

"What the hell did you do that for!?" I asked the woman known as Goodhead.

She passed me my drink.

"Dat trifling ass bitch ain't no good, she just a gold digger. She got a baby by Rasheed that play for the New York Knicks. She keep his ass in court asking for mo-money. Besides, I'm tryna to help you find dude, you want me to help you right?"

I nodded my head, took a long sip of my drink and responded reassuringly, "Yea wuz up?" She just smiled.

"I'll be right back." She threw up a finger and walked off.

Chapter Fifteen

The Treachery of a Bitch

Unbeknownst to Innocent, on the other side of the packed club, the stripper known as Goodhead had rushed over to the table with the cutthroat goons that had mean-mugged Innocent when he first came in the club. They were six thugs deep, seated at the table. The ring leader's name was Buggy. He was medium build, dressed in powder blue Coogi shirt and pants.

"Okay, nigga where my money at?" Goodhead yelled above the music, not realizing Game was seated at the next table with a few of her girlfriends. She just happened to hear Goodhead's conversation.

"You sure you put the mickey in his drank and it's going to work?" Buggy asked as he stood looking over at Innocent sitting at his table. The rest of his crew anxiously peered over too.

Goodhead retorted, "Hell yeah, that's why he keeps shaking his head. That shit strong enough to knock a horse down. In fifteen minutes, he'll either be dead or knocked the fuck out. Now gimme my money, Buggy." She held out her hand, as people squeezed by.

He reached into his pocket and passed her some bills. Three hundred dollars. She retrieved the money and held it up to the light.

"Bitch don't go too far, it's mo where dat came from. After I hit this lick, I want some of dat smokin' ass head and a shot of dat ass."

"I ain't goin' nowhere, I'ma be here. Dat nigga got a pocket full of money." She said and walked off.

Game's mouth dropped wide open as she eased her chair back to continue eavesdropping on Buggy and his goons plotting on Innocent.

Buggy had a plan, a clever plan to get paid twice. He looked over at his dawg Taga, he was only sixteen and wild as fuck. He was big for his age. Buggy let him hang out with them because he would do anything to prove himself and be accepted by Buggy and his crew of cutthroats.

"Yo, Taga, you walk over to dude and bump into him, start a fight. We gone roll over behind you and beat his ass and strip him of his money and jewelry at the same time."

All the thirsty goons agreed in unison. As young Taga got up from the table to kick the off the brawl, Buggy stalled him with a hand. He had one more trick up his sleeve. He pulled out his cellphone. As it rang, he watched Innocent…

"YO! Bin dis Buggy. I'm at the Foxy Lady, chilling with my niggas. A nigga walked in named Innocent. He been flossing, passing out money asking about you—."

"INNOCENT?!" Bin exhorted over the phone. "Hold dat nigga there. I'll give you a stack. Me and my team are on our way. I don't care what you have to do to him, but hold that nigga there. Give me a minute."

CLICK!

The phone went dead as Buggy stared across the club at the unsuspecting Innocent seated at the table, shaking his head like he was getting a bad headache. Whatever the fuck Goodhead had put in his drink was taking effect. All Buggy could think about was five bars of "lean," a phat blunt, a couple of pills and the waitress Goodhead sucking his dick.

Buggy knew he had to move on Innocent before them Naptime niggaz arrived with that crazy ass maniac Bin. As he stood, a fine ass white girl brushed against him as she rushed by.

Chapter Sixteen

Death on Wheels

Innocent

What the fuck is going on?!?! I was having trouble breathing, my version was blurred. It felt like all my senses were shutting down as the room began to spin. I began to sweat profusely as I sat dazed and disoriented. Suddenly, I felt someone bump into me and grab my arm. It was the white chick from earlier. She exhorted urgently.

"Hurry! Come with me, that ugly bitch, the waitress put a drug in your drink. She set you up to be robbed. Some dude is gonna pick a fight with you, kick your ass and take your money and jewelry."

"Muthafucka!" I huffed as I struggled to walk.

Hyperventilating, I nearly keeled over as I dragged my feet. We bumped into people, staggering as the white girl led me. I heard someone call my name.

"Yo-Innocent!! Hold up." It was my would be attackers coming up behind me.

My legs were rubbery. Game was damn nearly carrying me as I dragged my feet.

"That's them behind us. You gotta hurry up. Walk faster!" Game screeched as I stumbled along. I remembered that I had the butcher knife tucked in the small of my back.

As we moved past the metal detector, I heard the bouncer chuckle. "Damn dat nigga got wasted dat fast?"

"Naw'll a bitch put a drug in his drank." Game retorted angrily. It would have done no good to alert the bouncer to what was going on. He was just as corrupt as the goons that pursued me.

As we stepped out the club, the nocturnal cool breeze felt good on my damp skin. It felt like my body was shutting down, it even felt like my internal organs were malfunctioning as I wheezed, trying to breathe.

"Where is your car parked?" Game asked as she held on to me. I pointed with a limp hand.

"Up... ahead..."

We moved forward. We were damn near running as I stumbled along. I saw what looked like my BMW twenty yards away. My vision was getting worse.

"Is this it, the BMW?"

"Yeah." I reached into my pocket for the keys.

"Hurry! Hurry!" Game said, while looking back over her shoulder.

I passed her my car keys and leaned against the car, panting and struggling to breathe.

"Oh, shit! Here they come!" Game said, panic stricken.

I looked up. In the middle of the street, walking towards me, I could vaguely see the silhouette of them coming as Game wrestled to get my key into the door. I thought about my burner underneath the seat, but they were too close. Besides, I was in no position to bend and search. Instead, I moved on blind instincts and determination; like ice water in my veins. I reached for the knife in the small of my back. I pulled it out just as she got the car door open. She turned and looked at me with the big ass butcher knife and gasped in shock.

I braced myself, placing my back against the car; prepared to fight to the death.

Prepared to die.

There was a 9mm stashed under my seat, I struggled to breathe as I spoke.

"Get the ... gun from under... my seat."

"Gun?!" Game exclaimed and looked at me with the knife in my hand.

"Yeah... pass it...to me."

Just as she reached into the car, a young dude ran up on me as his partner slowly walked up behind him, waiting for whatever they had planned, to pop off.

"Nigga you bumped into me in the club, didn't even say fuckin' excuse me!" He said, inching close.

I saw the treachery lurking in his eyes. Game was taking too long to retrieve the gun. My primal instincts were kicking in, even though a lot of my other senses were numb. My senses to survive were still there. Then, young dude reached back to try to steal on me. I saw the punch coming, and slightly moved my head. The blow grazed my chin, just as Game pulled the nine out the car. Too late. I slammed the knife in his chest and grabbed him, holding him tight in a death embrace as I turned the knife, twisting it deep in his gut. I felt his warm blood saturate my hand. Heard him scream, not like a man, but like a child.

I shoved him off me. His friends ran to help him, that's when bright lights hit me in my face. An automobile was speeding towards us, gleaming ominously with its mighty engine roaring. Tires screaming, burning rubber, the sound was like hell's fury. I knew it was Bin and his henchmen the Naptime Gangstaz. The speeding automobile headed directly towards us.

The white girl screamed, dropped the gun and took off running.

I couldn't move. They had me trapped from both sides of the street as I struggled not to black out. The only good thing about death, I figured, as I stood with a bloody butcher knife in my hand and the speeding SUV, coming towards me, was that it would come soon!

Tires screeching, motor roaring, lights beaming, the automobile headed straight for me. I was blinded by its bright headlights. I closed my eyes. I remember feeling a breeze, then lots of tempestuous wind blowing against my skin. I heard a loud thump, human carnage. A woman screamed her horror in the night.

I opened my eyes and was surprised to see the white Cadillac SUV pass by me with such a force that the velocity of the wind nearly pulled me into the street as it ran over the guy I had just stabbed. At full speed, the huge SUV plowed head on into my attackers. The sound was incredible as bodies were tossed in the air along with the screams of anguish and terror as the phantom vehicle wreaked havoc on the unsuspecting.

Two of the goons were already dead. One of them lay in the street with his leg badly mangled, contorted, and twisted in the opposite direction with the bone sticking out. However, the leader was still standing. The vehicle had just barely missed him because he had jumped out the way.

He stood in the middle of the street firing a Mac 10 at the back of the SUV. Suddenly, the vehicle skidded to a stop, went into reverse and sped backwards as he fired on it. Just as the vehicle got close, he tried to jump out the way and slipped. There was a loud crunch, and then a scream as the vehicle hit him and the guy already lying in the street with his leg broken. The loud crunch of bone and flesh was maddening. I could hear bloodcurdling screams of agony as the vehicle trapped him underneath and sped off, dragging his body. In its wake, several bodies littered the streets.

The woman was still screaming. I turned around to look; it was Game screaming at me to get into the car.

That was the last thing I remember.

To be continued

Innocent's Revenge Pt. II

Chapter One

She's Got Game

I was submerged as the prison guards held me down, dumping my head in the icy cold water. Warden Scott watched and laughed a dry cackle. More icy cold water hit me in my face as I kicked and thrashed. I opened my eyes to face my indomitable foe.

It was the white girl, Game.

She stood over me with a bucket in her trembling hands, a scowl of desperation on her face. She was dressed only in pink panties and a matching bra. I raised my trembling hand. My teeth began to chatter. My tongue felt like it was stuck to the roof of my mouth.

I spoke lethargically "Coo...cold... water..."

Too late, she dumped another bucket of ice water on me and I began to violently shiver. My body went into convulsions with my eyes rolling to the back of my head. She panicked and dropped the bucket, jumping up and down.

"My God! You're alive! You're alive!"

"Co...cold." I chattered.

"Oh, shit you're going into hypothermia. Let me help you outta there."

She reached into the tub and grabbed me. I tried to hold on to her, but my arms were stiff as boards. We struggled, splashing water out of the bathtub, until finally, I was able to latch my arms around her neck. Teetering, I managed to rise up with her help, like she was pulling me out of quick sand and I was pulling her in.

I was completely nude. She nearly carried me as I padded across the bathroom floor, dripping water, slipping and sliding. We made it to her bedroom. I collapsed on the bed. I was getting worse. My body was cold to the bone. I began to blank in and out of consciousness. I didn't know if it was still from the drug poison I had suffered or her trying to freeze me to death with the fuckin' ice bath.

I watched in a mental fog. Like an illusion, she raced around the bedroom, gathering blankets. She delicately placed the blankets on top of me, then cursed emphatically.

"Damnit! Don't you fucking die on me!!"

With my eyes closed and damn near comatose, my entire body was an icicle. Then, I was overcome with a warm ethereal sensation all over my body. The white girl known as Game had gotten in bed under the covers with me and was urgently massaging my body, trying to get my blood circulation back.

"Please wake up. Don't go back to sleep on me again." She crooned pensively.

And as bad as I wanted to open my eyes, as bad as I wanted to wake up, for some reason I couldn't.

"Please wake up!?" she had begun to cry hysterically.

Fatigue riddled and tired on the brink delirium, for the past twenty four hours, she had frantically been trying to resuscitate me to no avail. As her hands worked on my body, I felt a hard slap across my face.

"You gotta wake up baby, don't di—."

It was at that moment, that I stopped shivering. I opened my eyes. She had her legs wrapped around me; her hand was drawn back as she prepared to slap me again. We were huddled like a human cocoon. I could feel the warmth of her vagina. Her feminine heat was like a miniature furnace pressed against my thigh. I remember thinking that God was perfect when he created man and womb-man. Body heat really does work.

Moments later, maybe it was hours, I lay with my eyes open as ambidextrous hands massaged my body. My circulation was getting better, I was semi-conscious. The inertia of drugs and my duel with the freezing cold was wearing off. Game's cooing words continued to pull me out of my slumber as I dreamed with my eyes wide open. The phantom white SUV stopped before me, and my grandmother got out of the car. I laughed and reached out to hold her, then I realized the white SUV was really a casket. I cringed, and tried to leap from my dream. I felt arms around me, holding me tight.

"No! No! No!" I tossed and turned.

"Shhhh, you're having a bad nightmare. Please be still. Don't go back into shock again. You scared me... I can't take it."

I couldn't speak. I listened and relaxed. I felt her soothing body ease further on top of me. I felt her heartbeat pounding fremitus, in perfect sequence with my own. She had awakened something dormant and primitive inside of me. I felt my dick getting hard, rising between her legs, wedged across her pussy, stretched across her butt cheeks. I heard her gasp.

"Good Lord, damn you're huge!"

I could feel her ass wiggle as she tried to ease off my stiff erection. The scent of her body was like an aphrodisiac. I was allured, my body was on autopilot. I palmed her ass and squeezed, spreading her cheeks apart. She wiggled some more and splayed her hands across my bare chest. I could feel her silky pubic hairs on my stomach as she spoke in a breathy timber.

"Are you sure you want to do this?"

My only reply was to grind my dick against her pussy and butt cheeks. She was wet and succulent. The fevered heat from her body continued to entice me, arousing my manhood to the point that I was hard as a brick, thick as a log. Forcefully, I grabbed her slim waist, pulling her back down on top of me.

She groaned, "I'm tight, real tight, not like your average girl." Her words fell on deaf ears.

I pulled her legs apart and groped with my dick around her hot spot until I found the entrance. I nestled my dick inside of her moist womanhood. She was tight, tighter than any woman I had ever experienced. With just the head in, I moved slowly. She began to squirm and moan seductively, her fingernails dug into my chest. I know she was going to skin my dick up, but I didn't care. I was out of my mind in the mental spree where a man's mind goes when he just wants to fuck with no inhibition, no restraint, and no worries.

It was as if I had no control over my actions. As my body got stronger with each stroke, she raised to sit on top of the apex of my dick in order to temper my stroke and to control the depths of my dick. I glanced down as the blankets fell away from our bodies. It looked like she was easing atop a poll, mounting my stiff masculinity as she carefully positioned her body to better take me in slow. I grabbed her waist, seized command and rammed my dick half way inside, causing her to scream and yell like she was being tortured. I rabbit punch her pussy with at least a hundred short strokes, causing her neck to snap back like she was riding a rodeo horse, all the while, listening to her wails, cries, and plaintive pleas of molesting pain.

Slamming my dick in and out her tight pussy was pleasure for me and pain for her. My dick wasn't even all the way in. In certain strokes, it bent painfully and felt like I was splitting her pussy in half as she bucked and moaned, trying to balance herself on my dick, while at the same time, trying to stop me from entering her all the way.

"Shh, shh, shhiet. I... told you ... I was tiiiiight." She said with a grimace and moaned, complaining with peevish lips like my dick was a culprit she had given a guilty verdict, and pain was part of the sentence.

I rolled over on top of her, my strength was still weak. I spread her legs wide and delved all the way inside, pinning her to the mattress. She screamed and began to resist me. She scratched me across my back, drawing blood. Fingernails raked across my body, all the way down to my butt. For some unknown reason, her thrashing and screams almost worried me. I thought about another rape case, I needed to slow down, go slow, but I couldn't. Her pussy was just that good. I deep stroked her in and out. Long greedy strokes, insatiate wanton suckling on her breasts as they bounced. I ravaged her body until the headboard banged against the wall.

"Yoooou hurting... me."

I fucked her with unquenchable thirst. I couldn't help myself from digging in and out her guts. I didn't know where the energy was coming from, maybe it was the drugs; a dope dick. Maybe it was all the pent up anxiety in my twenty-three year old body. Maybe I was losing my mind.

I enjoyed the painful scowl on her face, the smacking slippery wet sound of flesh on flesh being abused and misused. My body on top of hers, I was in deep, indelicate, carnal; fucking her brains out as she continued to scream and scratch my body. Then she did the strangest thing. As she began to shake and tremor, her neck jerked forward with a scowl as her mouth opened wide, her forehead was crinkled with veins. Her complexion turned red.

"OOOOHH, Go...Go... Goddamnit-mother-fuckerrrr... I'm cumingggg!" She yelled and placed her hand between us onto her clit and feverishly began masturbating herself, while groaning and moaning.

Instantly, my dick was saturated with her juices and somehow, someway, her sex, her tight pussy was revitalizing me, invigorating me as I dug deeper, faster, and thrust harder. I held her body captive as she cried and cummed a river on my dick. I was on the fringe of an orgasm and fucked her like she was the cure to all my problems. I gave her my dope dick. The extra strength version rough-housed the pussy as she began to resist again.

I neglected the sound of her pleas .Then I came, my body shook, I forced her legs further apart and molested her pussy. Bestiality was my depraved personality. I needed to devour her, consume her, every inch of her body, as I came in a stream of milky white. Taking my dick out, I spewed all over her stomach and chest, bathing her in my semen as we both breathed like two boxers that had just went fifteen rounds. I turned her over on her stomach.

"Wha... w...w are you doing ...You ain't tired yet?" She gripped my wrist and tried to sound calm, but I could hear the panicked voice.

Her words fell on deaf ears and I admired the roundness of her thick phat ass; its shape, its curves, its huge plumpness and what I had in mind next for her. There was no way I was going to be denied, she was about to be my conquest. I spit on my hands and slapped her butt hard. I loved the way her ass jiggled. I spread her butt cheeks wide, her asshole winked at me as I wiped my saliva across her anus. She shuddered and looked back at me.

"Wha... what are you doing?" She asked with her lips slightly puckered.

"I'm finna fuck you in your ass."

"Huh, uhh, no you aint! You too big, you'll split me in half," Then she demurred, and tried to hit me with the bait. "I only do that for my man." She said, and smoothed her hair away from her face and then glanced down at my dick.

Her ass was still ripe and waiting, as I fiendishly stroked my dick while rubbing it against her inner thigh and butt cheek. She licked her lips seductively and moaned, then tooted her body up as if inviting me into her Garden of Eden.

"Where did you suddenly get all this energy from?" she muttered and reached back and stroked my dick as if she was preparing me, or maybe herself.

I was anxious to puncture her pink asshole. To my delight, she grabbed a pillow and placed it under her belly. I pushed the head of my dick between her butt cheeks and aimed, she grabbed the sheets tight like she was going to tear them apart. As I eased the head in, she reached back and spread her ass. Her anus was not as tight as her vagina. With the first thrust, the head and several inches went in.

"Yes, yes, I want you to give it to me! Make me your lady!" She commanded me on and began to massage her clit again. Game was a bigger freak than I thought. She eased back onto my throbbing dick. Just when I was prepared to ram her, there was an intrusive knock at the door!

I stopped.

We listened.

Waited...

Her hair was pasted to her forehead with perspiration as she looked back at me and gave me a scowl.

"Oh, shit, that's somebody at the front door! Get up! Get up!" She pushed my joint out her ass and leapt from the bed as my dick dangled.

I rolled off of her with a feeling of apprehension and dread.

Trouble had followed me to her door.

———————

I frantically looked around for my clothes and my burner. I didn't see either of them. I needed a weapon. I needed to get up and get going. I stood on wobbly legs and instantly got a head rush, like the after effects had me woozy. I could hear voices coming up the hall towards the room I was in, as I stood listening, looking around for my clothes, my gun, and a weapon.

The door burst open. I grabbed the lamp off the table to use for a weapon to protect myself and prepared to fight.

To my utter surprise, it was none other than Kenisha decked out in a loud ass peacock yellow miniskirt Marc Jacob outfit with matching purse, shoes, and the whole nine yards. She looked at me, naked with the lamp poised in my hand prepared to strike and bugged out as Game stood behind her looking very much agitated.

"What da fuck you doin' here?!" I asked, aggravated.

I sat the lamp down, not bothering to cover up. Eyes glazed with something I couldn't discern Kenisha, stepped forward.

"Naw'll nigga what you doin' here naked in this bitch house?"

"Bitch??" Game retorted and bumped into Kenisha as she entered the room.

"You got me fucked up, who you calling a bitch?" Game was in Kenisha's face.

Kenisha hissed, "Hoe you heard what!" She kicked off her heels and began to take off her earrings.

I walked over nude, and stood between them to defuse the problem. The last thing I needed was a catfight. I slightly shoved Kenisha. They continued to fume, staring daggers at each other.

"How n' the fuck did you get here?" I asked pissed at Kenisha. Everywhere she went, trouble was sure to follow.

Game tossed a long lock of hair away from her forehead. "I called her." She said, and took a step back.

Both their demeanors suddenly changed, like the quiet after a femininity storm. I shot Game the evil eye. She sighed deeply like she knew she had fucked up.

"After the shooting, I managed to get you in the car and drove you here. I had to get my neighbors to help me get you in the bathtub; I told them you were drunk. You wouldn't wake up, you were sweating so badly." She frowned with sympathy, and then added. "I didn't want to call the police because of all the bodies—"

"Bodies?" Kenisha asked, while putting her shoes back on.

I gave Game a warning glare to watch her mouth. She cut her eyes at Kenisha, then gave me a subtle shrug as if to say *my bad.*

"Anyway, I went through your phone, and found her number. She and some other chick in jail had been trying to call you. I called her yesterday. She said she was your sister." Game glowered at Kenisha.

I ran my fingers through my locks. It dawned on me that I was completely nude, when I noticed Kenisha leering at my joint with a lustful grin as it swung back and forth. I picked up a blanket off the floor.

"Yesterday! How long have I been here?" I raised my voice incredulously.

"For two days." Game said timidly.

"Two days!"

"Yep, and you missed your grandmother's funeral." Kenisha spat.

"Ohh, nooo." I groaned taking a seat on the bed.

"It's a good thing you weren't there because the po-po and everybody else has been looking for you, including Ms. Harvey with the children. The police are looking for you to question you about a body that was found in a hospital bathroom and the guns found at your house."

I didn't answer, just hung my head, crestfallen. They say God will only give you what you can bear; well my cup was running over with what I could bear.

I needed to pick Kenisha's brain. I looked up at Game and asked, "Can I speak with her a second? Also, get my gun and clothes for me."

Game just stared at me with her eyes narrowed into tiny slits of contempt. Kenisha stole a glance at her ass as she slammed the door.

Innocent's Revenge Pt. II

Coming Soon!!!

Acknowledgments

First I would like to thank God for blessing me with the ability to write and the compassion to be disciplined and think outside the literary box that confines some authors. There is wisdom in words that can empower others to think.

I would also like to thank my mama, a single Black parent for doing the best she could to raise me, her only child. There isn't a day that goes by, that I don't think of her and reminisce about the wonderful times we shared.

"Dear Mom, I miss you so much and it still hurts. May your soul rest in peace and your spirit continue to comfort me".

I want to thank the entire Sullivan family, too many to name, besides I always get in trouble by forgetting someone. So this way I don't get cursed out. Lol, I love y'all even the ones that didn't come visit me and now you got your hand held out.

To my best friend and confidant, Taya R. Baker. Thank you for being the cornerstone of my life. There is something about our friendship that mystifies people, even myself. You have been with me through thick and thin. When I couldn't walk you carried me, when I was wrong you corrected me. You showed me a facet of myself that I learned later was humility and dignity. A mirror image of yourself that is a reflection of me whenever I look into your eyes. LOVE YOU TAYA B!!!!!!!!

To my assistant at Sullivan Productions, Ms. Tien Homes. I know I never tell you this, but I am so very proud of you and I can never thank you enough for the hard work and dedication you have shown me. You actually believe in my dream as much as I do. Thank you.

To my editor, Ms. Tina Nance and her company, PERFECT PROSE EDITING. Your service is great. It is both an honor and privilege to work with you, a true professional and perfectionist. Don't forget about our bet. All I will say is that it has something to do with this book and some changes. We'll see...

Okay, I'll keep the best for last. Here I am a brotha with a shoe string budget and God sends me this sista. Come to find out she is the Queen of underground networking and promoting books, she took me under her wing and promoted the hell out of my books. I was just coming home, and it's a difficult transition, but she took my hand and led me. Yes, I'm talking about none other than Ms. Renee Camille Lamb. Thank you Queen!

I have to thank my brotha David Weaver for reaching out to me in a time in my life I was thinking about giving up writing. You really inspired me. He has the Bankroll series of books. Also, the "Power Family and the upcoming Bawss. He is a national best-selling author. Be sure to cop his books. He is the new shinning prince of the urban lit right now. Also, Blake Karrington with his Country Boy series. He is an animal with the pen. We have a book out together, "24 Karats - A Player's Saga". Be sure to get it, it's hot!

Okay, I'm saving the best for last. None of this would be possible if it wasn't for my fans, YOU!! Thank you so much for supporting me from way back in the days of LIFE, my debut novel. I promise you I will not disappoint you with this series, nor will I keep you waiting for part II of Innocent's Revenge. In fact, if you're reading this, it might already be in my editor's hands. What I would like is for you to post a review on Amazon.

Unfortunately, there are a lot of people that have not heard of, nor read a Leo Sullivan novel. One last thing, just to stop the confusion, this is the order of the series :(1.) INNOCENT (2.) INNOCENT FOREVER (3.) INNOCENT'S REVENGE (4) INNOCENT'S REVENGE PART II.

Also, my other book titles are, IN THIS LIFE and the sequel, LIFE WITHOUT HOPE. A GANGSTA'S BITCH ONE AND A GANGSTA'S BITCH TWO. A Gangsta's Bitch was formerly titled Dangerous. Since I am releasing the title on my company's distribution, I change the name.

Leo Sullivan can be contacted at osiris_scribe@yahoo.com , or you can hit him up on Facebook: Author Leo Sullivan

A Gangster's Bitch

(Formerly titled *Dangerous*)

O·N·E

It was five o'clock in the morning and Gina had just built up enough courage to tell Jack that she was tired. Her feet hurt from walking all night in stilettos. She wanted nothing else but to go home, take a long, hot shower and get into her comfortable bed. She looked into his handsome face, but his eyes were trained on the entrance of the hotel. Etched on his face was an expression of deep concentration, unblinking, unfailing.

"There! There!" He spotted his target. "There the nigga go right there," Jack said, exercising extreme calm, the kind an experienced hunter uses when stalking prey.

Gina's body perked up and she became alert and focused as she slid her eyes off of Jack, and over to Damon Dice, one of the richest niggas in New York City. Instantly, she felt a rush of high-octane adrenaline. She was about to become the kind of weapon a man uses when he'd rather have court on the streets. Court would soon be in session, with Jack being both judge and jury.

"Listen Gina," Jack spoke, never taking his eyes off of Damon. "You gotta get this nigga to walk you close to the car so I can get his testifying ass in the trunk." His tone was hushed and his forehead knotted.

For the past three days they had been tailing Damon Dice and his entourage. Earlier that night they had been in a club called The Tunnel in Manhattan. It was the spot where all the ballers, shot callers and entertainers were known to mingle. That night, the place was jam-packed. The music was pumping bass so hard that Gina could feel its pulsating rhythm in her chest. Somehow, it seemed to hype her up as all the colorful lights strobed throughout the club. She strained her eyes in search of her target. Finally she spotted him and the big-ass platinum chain around his neck.

Scantily dressed in a chic tight miniskirt that showed off all of her goodies, and accentuated her plump round ass, she slowly sashayed toward him, sensuously moving her hips from side to side. She wasn't wearing a bra and her see-through silk blouse gave little to the imagination as her gorgeous breasts rose upward in salute to her youth. Boldly, Gina strutted into the VIP section of the club as if she belonged there, walking right up to Damon Dice and his crew. All eyes were on her. Show time! All their mouths dropped like old folks with lockjaw.

Get the nigga to follow you out da club Gina heard Jack's words in her mind as she neared Damon, never taking her eyes off him.

She arched her back, thrusting her mouth-watering nipples forward, parallel to Damon's eyes. He sat in his seat staring at her, mouth agape, drink in hand. As she approached, she held him spellbound. All the members of his crew were also entranced. Her sweet perfume marinated in their nostrils as she bent down, showing them some peek-a-boo cleavage.

Coyly, she whispered in Damon's ear, her lips brushing against his earlobe, "Nigga, I'll suck that dick so good your balls will get jealous." Damon choked on his drink, accidentally spitting on his boy sitting next to him, who erupted in laughter.

Damn, this chick is bold, he thought as he watched Gina.

"I got the world's best pussy." He could have sworn he saw one of her nipples wink at him as he took in all of her audacious, shapely curves. That was around the time he got an erection.

They struck up a conversation and the drinks began to flow. She cozied up to him, flirting and touching; doing all the things that Jack had told her to do. She played her part well.

Stealthily, Gina would reach her hand under the table and play with his dick, stroking him as she poured a heavy dose of her feminine charm all over him. Finally, she had cast her spell. She could see it in his eyes. He was filled with lust and enchanted by her beauty. If she wanted to, she could have fucked him right there on the dance floor.

Ever so gently, she took his hand, the fox leading the chicken, and moved past his bodyguards and crew of henchmen. She led him toward the dance floor, with him palming her ass like two basketballs. Drunk, he followed as if he were a lost child. As they passed through the crowd, they headed for the exit.

Slyly, Gina smiled as she thought about Jack waiting outside. All of a sudden, five yards from the door, all hell broke loose. A salvo of gunshots rang out, causing pandemonium. Like a scared rabbit, Damon Dice didn't even try to protect her. He just took off running back to the safety of his bodyguards.

"Punk-ass nigga," Gina cursed as she ducked down and headed for the exit door.

T·W·O

Damon Dice

Damon staggered out of the Galaxy Hotel, intoxicated by a cocktail of exotic drugs. He wore so much heavy jewelry that when he walked he made loud metallic clinking sounds.

Inebriated, he wobbled over to the wall and grabbed hold of it as if he were trying to stop the building from falling. The front of his pants was soiled with a large piss stain that ran the length of his left pant leg. That night, he was faced with one of the biggest dilemmas of the day – should he take his dick out and piss right there in front of the hotel or vomit first? With his world spinning, his bodily functions didn't give him a chance to decide.

With his dick in his hand, he began to vomit and urinate uncontrollably. It truly was a sight to behold.

Afterward, with his mouth ringed with vomit, he staggered away while trying to place his joint back into his pants. He looked up, and through bleary eyes, he saw Gina floating toward him. He tried his best to stand up straight, but the damn building kept leaning to the side.

Damn, she fine as a muthafucka, he thought as she sauntered up close. He tried to wipe his mouth with his shirt sleeve and smile. Even in the dim light, he could still make out the symmetry of her body. He staggered slightly in a failed attempt to gain his equilibrium.

"Heyyy fella!" Gina caroled seductively in a breathy voice as she walked up to him, enrapturing him with the wiles of her charm.

"Damn … you the broad … I mean … ahh … uhh," Damon stammered as he recalled seeing her.

His mouth was still partially ringed with vomit. Everything was still spinning, but starting to slow down. He let go of the wall, his legs wobbling unsteadily like a child just learning to walk.

Gina came closer. He reached out and fondled one of her lovely breasts. She rewarded him with a giggle as jubilant as a young schoolgirl on her first date. She furtively glanced over her shoulder at Jack hunched low in the car watching her every move.

"Shorty, you wanna come inside the telly? A nigga got everything you need. You like to smoke? I got … I got …" Drunk, Damon lost his train of thought as he scratched his head. "I got what you need," Damon said, causing Gina to tentatively take a step back.

Goddamn! His breath smell just like horse shit, she thought as she noticed a puddle of vomit on the ground in front of him. It took everything in her power not to frown as he once again caressed her breasts. Talk about being an actress—she deserved an Oscar.

"I would love to come inside," she drawled. "You still want me to suck that dick?" She licked her lips and reached down to rub him.

As she did that, she felt a wet spot. *Nasty muthafucka,* she thought to herself as she removed her hand and placed it on her shirt, slyly wiping her hand.

"Big daddy, why don't you walk me to my car first, to lock it up ... tight," she cajoled, puckering her luscious lips, showing him one of her sex faces.

"Wha ... wha ... where ya parked at, shorty?" Damon asked.

She giggled innocently, taking his hand and walking him toward Jack in the parked car. He staggered a few steps and suddenly stopped in his tracks. His eyes popped open as if he'd seen a ghost. He stared at something in the distance. Whatever it was spooked him, causing him to sober up quickly.

"Naw shorty. I just saw something across the street. A light went on in that van."

He squinted his eyes as if trying to focus in his inebriated fog. Damon pulled away from her hand and started to backpedal out of her grasp.

Not again, Gina thought as she remembered the scene back at the club and how mad Jack was with her for letting him get away.

Think fast! Think fast! Trick-ass nigga getting away! Her mind churned. She reached into her purse and pulled out an elegant gold-plated .357 Derringer pistol. It was the size of a Bic lighter, but powerful enough to drop an elephant.

"Take another step, bitch-ass nigga, and I'ma blow your whole fuckin' back out. Now try me!" she said coldly, between clinched teeth.

Her face was a mask of deadly intent. For some reason, in her mind, everything moved in slow, surreal motion. A lavender sky was starting to peek over the pitch-black horizon as dawn, like a dir ty sheet on the canvas of the night, exposed the good, the bad and the ugly. In the distance, birds were starting to chirp, summoning morning.

"Pah-pah-leese don't shoot me!" Damon begged.

They were standing only inches apart. A lone car passed, and its luminous headlights traced their bodies, stalled in the night. The air suddenly turned cool with the imminent threat of death. Sweat gleamed on Damon's forehead as he stood panic-stricken, overcome with fear. Gina could tell he was thinking about bolting. There was no doubt whatsoever in her mind—if Damon tried to get away, she would kill him.

The lobby doors opened, and out walked Damon's bodyguard. The man was huge. He stood about six feet, seven inches, three hundred and something pounds. He had broad shoulders like a mountain. The man's name was Prophet. He was an ex-con and a well-known killer. As soon as Prophet got out the joint, Damon Dice gave him a job as head of DieHard Security. Next to Prophet stood G-Solo, who was slightly built, with a baby face and long eyelashes. He resembled the rapper Chingy. Both men were strapped with guns.

"Yo, son! What the fuck is going on out here?" Prophet asked suspiciously as he took a step closer. His deep, throaty baritone voice seemed to resonate with the timbre of a man that commanded authority.

Playfully, Gina laughed and hugged Damon as she placed the barrel of the gun against his rib cage and whispered in his ear as Prophet approached.

"Tell them you'll be inside in a second."

"I'ma ... I'ma ... I'ma be inside in a second," the frightened man said, raising his voice.

"Nigga, you know you got on too much ice," Prophet warned as he stepped closer. He was only a few feet from Gina now.

"Come on man, let's go."

"You fitna be shittin' in a plastic bag, rollin' around in a wheelchair," Gina whispered in Damon's ear, feeling Prophet's presence was too damn close. She pushed the gun harder against his ribs.

"Man! I told 'cha, I'm fuckin' coming! Leave me the fuck alone!" Damon yelled at his bodyguard, causing him to exchange looks with G-Solo.

They both shrugged their shoulders as if to say, "fuck him, let him have his way with the bitch" as they walked away. Gina could feel Damon's arms shaking like leaves on a tree.

"Pah-pah-pahleese don't kill me," Damon pleaded.

"Shut up, nigga!" Gina said as she peeked over in Jack's direction, huddled in the car.

Just then, a weary crackhead prostitute walked up. She was dressed in raggedy clothes – a pair of blue jeans that looked like they had not been washed in days, sneakers and a once-white halter top that was now gray. Her eyes continued to dart suspiciously back and forth across the street as she smacked her lips as if she had just bitten into a sour lemon. She jerked her long neck, snaking it from side to side hyperactively with her hand poised on her body as she patted her foot on the concrete. On a crackhead's impulse, her eyes began to search the ground as if this was the sacred ground where she had lost her rock the other night. Her foot did a casual sweep of the pavement as she made a face, twisting her lips as she said matter-of-factly, "Girlfriend, I think that's the po-po across the street parked in that van." Hearing that caused Damon's body to flinch uncontrollably.

"Shit!" Gina muttered as she glanced over at the white van.

Why didn't I recognize it earlier? she thought.

"I'ma scream if you don't let me go," Damon whimpered.

Something about hearing the word "police" had emboldened him. "Nigga, you stunt if you wanna, and I'ma leave your punk ass slumped right here with a hole in your chest!" Gina hissed as she cocked the gun and pressed it harder against his ribs.

Damon was standing on the balls of his feet as if that would ease the explosion if the gun went off, shattering his rib cage and blowing his whole back out.

The prostitute continued to look back and forth in all directions, including the ground, akin to a junkie's perpetual paranoia.

Once again, Gina glanced over at the car with Jack in it and then looked at the undercover police van.

"Shit!"

"Unit six to Captain Brooks …"

"Go ahead, this is Captain Brooks," an authoritative voice returned over the sporadic crackling of the police radio.

"Lieutenant Stanley Goldstein is trying to reach you on your cell phone."

Brooks turned on his cell and it rang instantly. The Lieutenant spoke urgently. "The suspect and his entourage have just turned off Pennsylvania Avenue onto Linden and Stanley. They're at the Galaxy Hotel."

"You're in fuckin' Brooklyn now?" Captain Brooks shrieked over the phone, thinking about the friction it would cause with the 75th Precinct. They already had a bad rivalry, and this would only make things worse.

"I want you and the rest of the unit to stay clear of the suspect until I get there and give the order to take his black ass down," the Captain barked over the phone.

"Captain?"

"What?" Brooks answered brusquely.

"Sir, there appears to be a white Cadillac with a black female driving. There is also another individual in the car that we can't seem to make out. They have been trailing the suspect all night long. The car is now illegally parked in front of the hotel. How shall we proceed?"

"Leave the car alone. We don't want to risk tipping off the 75th that we're on their turf about to make a major bust. They're probably harmless groupies. Tell your men to hang tight. I'm on my way." Brooks hung up the phone and made a U-turn in the middle of the street.

As he drove, his mind went over every detail as it related to how he was going to make the bust. Damon Dice was actually out of Brooks' jurisdiction, but since his department had tailed him from Manhattan to Brooklyn in violation of possession of drugs, the arrest was going to be perfectly legal. Now all Brooks had to do was plant the dope.

The good thing about what he was doing was that the Mayor himself was behind the special task force to arrest as many rappers as they could, and so far so good. His department had been having a field day. The only thing that kept Damon Dice on the streets for so long was the fact that he was a police informant and had been giving Brooks information for a long time. That was until he turned music mogul.

Damon Dice had switched hats from hustler to entrepreneur in the blink of an eye. He now felt he was invincible and refused to provide Brooks with any helpful information. Brooks hated that he didn't bust Damon earlier. Now he was selling hit records just like Suge Knight and J. Prince.

This fueled Brooks even more as his nondescript Ford sliced through the night. What really pissed him off was to see a black man making so much damn money, legally. They were becoming a threat. Hell, the rapper 40, one of the hottest in the industr y, had just bought a mansion with forty rooms, a bowling alley and a movie theater. Another was partial owner of a basketball team. It was becoming a trend. *How do they do it?* he pondered.

His knuckles were white as he tightly held onto the steering wheel as the car reached speeds of over a hundred miles per hour. He was consumed with anticipation of the bust. He felt the adrenaline of a policeman's head rush – the set-up, the chase, the capture and then the arrest. Just the thought of it gave him an erection. He would teach the fucker who he was playing with. Besides, Brooks wanted to please the Mayor. He was already told to treat all rappers as potential drug dealers until proven differently. Now all he had to do was follow the first law of police work—if there isn't a crime, invent one.

Captain Brooks made the excursion from Manhattan to Brooklyn in seventeen minutes flat. Lights out, he cruised past the White Castle restaurant where a few prostitutes loitered.

Unbeknownst to him, somewhere, somehow in the hub of this naked city, the streets were watching, waiting, listening. Brooks eased his car behind another unmarked car. As he exited, a dog barked in the distance. A crescent moon, embellished with stars, hung from the night sky like a lucid scratch on the underbelly of the black canvas of the night.

A weary prostitute ambled by. The woman took one look at the supposed undercover cop and decided he damn sure was not a trick. She took off walking fast, looking over her shoulder as if to make sure the cop made no attempt to tackle her.

The night air felt crisp and cool against Brooks' pale skin as he walked toward the surveillance van. He realized that he was starting to sweat under his cotton shirt, causing it to stick to his skin.

The foul odor of rotten garbage mixed with New York air pollution only seemed to enhance the moment. Eyes alert, he could feel his senses tingling as he felt for the ounce of crack he had in his pocket. He intended to plant the dope on Damon Dice. That would get his ass to talking.

Lieutenant Goldstein opened the van door. Brooks grunted as he squatted, struggling to get in. The forty or so pounds he had picked up over the last few years were starting to take their toll on him. There were four other undercover officers in the cramped van.

"Captain, I just received word from the 75th Precinct. They want to know what we're doing on their turf. They're asking us to back off and let them handle the arrest."

"Handle my ass! I'm in command here. My authority comes all the way from the Mayor's office," Brooks screeched. He thought about the dope in his pocket intended for Damon Dice.

"Tell whomever it is that I said to fuck him and the horse he rode in on!"

"Holy shit!" one of the undercover officers lamented as he looked through the night vision binoculars. Brooks snatched the binoculars and peered out the window.

As he bent down he accidentally hit a light switch causing the inside of the van to light up.

And as usual, the streets were watching.

Made in the USA
San Bernardino, CA
09 October 2013